HOME FIRES BURNING

HOME FIRES BURNING

To Barbara Dyke
a new cruise friend!
who was so much fun!
Enjoy! Love,
Vonda Crocker

Vonda Crocker

Library of Congress Control Number: 2012912155
ISBN: Hardcover   978-1-4771-3942-4
                     Softcover   978-1-4771-3941-7

To order additional copies of this book, contact:
Xlibris Corporation
1-888-795-4274
www.Xlibris.com
Orders@Xlibris.com

Home Fires Burning is dedicated to all Army spouses, past, present, and future.

Contents

FOREWORD

SOME YEARS AGO the chair of the Fort Lewis, Washington, Women's Conference invited me to be the keynote speaker hopefully to give the army spouses, too often left alone by men at war, a lift in spirits. The topic I chose was "What Makes an Army Rock." The premise was that most of us begin our military spouse adventure as loose dirt with little knowledge of what is in store. My dirt was looser than some as I had no military contact other than a navy brother five years my senior. We step out to meet the world because we love our military partner. Most military wives, who stay the course, become strong, flexible, knowledgeable, compassionate, and solid as a rock as they keep the home fires burning.

The trials, stress, pressures, loneliness, and joys of that journey make an impressive military rock. In my case an army rock. This book is written to share the journey of one army spouse from dirt to rock.

The journey in snapshots is told to the best of my recollection, and apologies are given here if my impressions offend anyone as I have tried to honestly tell my story from my perspective of events and people.

1 | Fort Riley, Kansas
"Welcome to the Army Life"

THE STORY OF my girlhood in Arkansas and the fateful meeting of the love of my life, George, is another book for another time.

In 1966 after a military wedding in Little Rock, Arkansas, followed by a honeymoon in Florida, the newlywed Crockers hooked up the U-Haul with all our earthly possessions. Our new blue VW Beetle, with air-conditioning mind you, valiantly pulled us out of Arkansas. George's new red Corvette was but a beautiful memory, and Daddy kept my much-loved first car, a MG-B Roadster, as we couldn't afford payments on either one. It was a huge vehicle come down for us both, but true love does demand sacrifices.

I had been out of Arkansas four times: Texas, Oklahoma, Georgia, and a 4-H Congress trip by train to Chicago. They were the extent of my travels. As we drove away from the heart of family and all I had known and loved, it was as if a scrapbook of my growing-up years was being left behind. This new adventure, however, was so exciting that my heart was filled with love and hope for a grand future together.

George has a penchant for kidding with such a serious face; he is believed before common sense takes over. He had me believing all kinds of horrors. As we drove across Kansas heading to his first duty station Fort Riley, Kansas, he told me about the cowbirds we saw flying in the fields. He warned me that I would have to wear a hat or sunglasses outside because they would peck your eyes out. Okay, so I was a college graduate, but he was so serious it took me a few minutes to realize I'd been had. After all these years, he can still get me.

Late that day we drove through the small town of Junction City, Kansas, and into Fort Riley. George checked us into the guesthouse for newly assigned personnel. It was a World War II wooden barracks building. Two rooms were connected by a bath that both occupants shared by locking the opposing door. It was August, and it must have been 110 in the shade. A fan had been installed above the door at the end of the hallway, but with all the doors closed for privacy, only the hallway had a breath of air. The windows had been nailed shut so the room temperature seemed to be 200.

We were so tired from the long day on the road; we wet towels and laid them on the two single army cots. Steam literally rose from the beds, but sleeping on wet towels was preferable to being broiled alive on a cot. Growing up with brothers had made me resilient to many things, but if this was army life, it was going to be a long haul.

The next day we got the good news that there was no housing available for captains and below. As a second lieutenant, George was at the bottom of that list. A tornado had hit the area months before destroying many hotels and apartments. To acerbate the problem, the Ninth Infantry Division, to which George was assigned, was gearing up to full strength for deployment to Vietnam. That meant we were two of hundreds looking for a place to live.

We checked out horrors like the basement apartment with mold growing up the walls to way-over-our-budget lovely big apartments. Finally, George ran into a Captain Sosnowski who told him of an apartment complex he and his wife, Barbara, had found in Manhattan, Kansas, near Kansas State University campus. We went immediately to check it out and quickly signed the lease. It had two bedrooms, one bath, unfurnished with no appliances for $100 per month at 1851 Todd Road Apartment C2. George made $325 a month.

We went to Caw Valley Furniture store and found a black "pleather" couch set with reversible cushions that would double as a guest bed. It had a corner table with rather thin legs which fit over the intersecting couch ends. We felt it would last a few years at least. Tres chic!

The red rug we chose was so cheap every time we swept it, having no vacuum, fluffs of red fiber floated out the door.

I covered two cardboard boxes with burlap, cut and stained plywood squares for the top, and we had end tables. The TV was borrowed from Howie Kirk, one of George's West Point classmates. It was perched on the standard A1M1 concrete block and board bookcase. Our bookcase, however, was a cut above as one side of the concrete blocks had a ceramic glaze. We rented a refrigerator and stove and found a used metal and Formica kitchen table with six orange chairs.

The bedroom was furnished with a bed frame, no headboard, mattress set, and a dresser all from Montgomery Ward. I made curtains from sheets.

The walls were so thin, when our neighbor arrived home, his combat boots sounded like they were coming up our stairs. The same couple would take a stereo out on trial, enjoy it a few days, and take it back as unacceptable. Then they would go to another store and repeat the trial. Each of their free trial systems bass would vibrate the wall between our apartments.

Barbara Sosnowski, the helpful captain's wife, and Bert Kintigh, another neighbor whose husband was already in Vietnam, and I developed a friendship. Barbara thought our apartment looked so much bigger than hers. They had many wonderful antiques from Europe; so of course, my meager furnishings took up far less area, giving the illusion of space.

The Ninth Division was busy preparing for the deployment to Vietnam. The men spent long hours training. One night I had fixed a special meal expecting George home at around six thirty, early for once. Their captain had them in a meeting where he was attempting to put a pistol together after cleaning it. According to all accounts, all the men were leaning forward most eager to do it for him as he seemed to be unable to reassemble it. After nine thirty George finally arrived home, frustrated. We sat down to the most awful meal imaginable. Sour cream and shrimp do not do well in a keep-warm oven for three hours. We gave it to our dog, Piker, who refused to eat it. George said, "I thought you were a home economics major!" I assured him I was but had specialized in dress design.

With the Vietnam War in full swing, some of the courses for new second lieutenants were waived. George did, however, go to ranger school. Ranger school consists of three phases: Fort Benning, mountain, and Florida. The West Point classmates at Fort Riley went together in October. I was pregnant and very grateful to Barbara and Bert for their friendship. Both their husbands were in Vietnam by this time, so at night we would watch a chick flick on TV. Inevitably we would be reduced to tears by the end of the movie. Barbara had a handgun she carried to and from the meeting apartment, and we just knew she was going to shoot herself in the foot one dark night. We developed a system where the two who traveled to the third person's apartment would call the hostess upon arriving home, let it ring once, and hang up. All was well when that signal was given.

Daddy had just won election as justice on the Arkansas Supreme Court. He drove my little MGB to Kansas for me and spent a couple of nights with us on that lovely flip cushion pleather couch. I really hated to see him go when the all-too-short visit ended.

Because we couldn't afford the $89 car payments, we sold the MG-B to a local nurse. She was totally inexperienced driving a stick shift. I was in tears as she jerked the little car off into the night.

George's company commander may have been incompetent, but his battalion and brigade commanders were the opposite. His battalion commander was Lieutenant Colonel Blackie Bolduc. He and his wife, Mary, had nine children; and she was the most fabulous role model a new army wife could have had. She would drive their van to visit each of us. Unfortunately, she inevitably would find me sitting on the living room floor sewing on my portable Singer sewing machine that was perched on a hassock. Fabric, pins, thread, and scraps would be all over that red carpet. She never seemed to mind the mess. She always came with a plant, cookies, or some other treat and a lot of care and concern.

She read French for fun, never wore hats because she didn't like them, and truly did her own thing. We all wore hats and gloves because you were "supposed to," so we adored her. She was our own rebel heroine.

We went to an Officer Wives' Club luncheon once where, for some reason, I was the token second lieutenant's wife to sit at a table with the battalion and brigade commanders' wives. When pregnant, I rarely got sick but passed out instead. During the main course, I vaguely remember falling forward into my plate awakening on the couch with the commanders' wives patting my hands and wiping mashed potatoes off my face. Humiliation is not a strong-enough word for the feeling that swept through me. For some reason, that was the last time at Fort Riley I sat at the command table.

I took two courses at Kansas State University for graduate credit since we were only two blocks from the campus. Looking for something to do, I also tried a ceramics course at the on post craft shop. That Christmas everyone received ceramic crèche sets. The courses and the class were great ways to meet other people and keep busy.

Through the university, I heard that my daddy's old friend, Senator William J. Fulbright, was to speak on campus, so I made plans to go. During his speech he stated that since no one was there from Arkansas he could safely say his next statement. I don't remember what it was, but I do remember going up to him afterward and reminding him that Arkansas and Kansas weren't that far apart. He thanked me for the reminder and sent Daddy his best.

The captain who had trouble putting his pistol together invited three lieutenants to dinner in his home one evening. George was the only one married, so we went as a couple. Trying to do everything just right, we four loitered on the sidewalk so we could all arrive at the exact invitation time. At the appointed time, we walked to the door and rang the bell. The captain opened the door with a confused look on his face but invited us in. We all sat cozily on the couch two feet from his son who was watching TV. The son had vision and hearing problems, we assumed, because he sat a foot from the set and it was so loud we had trouble talking over it. I looked around and noticed there was no sign of dinner, and the bare table didn't look promising either.

The captain brought out a bag of potato chips, warm beer for the men, and a coke for me. After about thirty minutes of stilted conversation, his pregnant wife slowly made her way down the stairs followed by her mother. They were both attired in robes and house shoes which flopped on the stairs with every step. After retrieving drinks for themselves, they trudged back upstairs. We were totally ignored. That was our cue.

The etiquette book stated that the woman makes the first move to depart an event, so I said, "It's been lovely, but we really must be going." We all jumped to our feet, thanking him for the drinks and chips and hurried outside.

On the sidewalk again, we grinned at each other. Starving, but broke, we pooled our funds and went to a local pizza parlor where we shared a pizza and a pitcher of beer as we rehashed our evening. The captain obviously forgot he had issued the invitation nor had he consulted his wife. She probably still thinks we just rudely showed up.

When George first returned from ranger school, he had lost weight and the bottoms of his feet had calluses at least a half-inch thick. We trimmed them with a sharp knife. They had been so sleep deprived he was still trying to catch up days later.

Going into what we thought was labor, we rushed to the hospital on post, but the hospital at Fort Riley sent me home. That night there was no question it was labor, so George rushed us toward the hospital again. The small town between Manhattan and Ft. Riley was known as a speed trap, but labor is a great reason for speeding especially when it is your first. We were barreling along but still not fast enough for me when we heard, then saw, the siren and flashing lights. George pulled over and explained our rush. The police officer came around to my side and after one look escorted us to the town limits. After several hours of labor with no baby in sight, George went back to work with the admonition to make sure and call him when the baby was born. In those days, fathers were relegated to the waiting room, so it wasn't as if he could hold my hand. As a Type A first-time dad, sitting and waiting was not something he did well.

Twenty-four hours after our arrival, Cheryl Lynne Crocker was born. The delivery had been long and arduous, as are many deliveries, so her head had coned during the birth process. George was amazed that she would be normal shortly. We also were told my blood type was AB negative, so a shot was necessary immediately after birth to prevent my antibodies forming. She was a gorgeous baby who slept a lot and seemed to have a sweet disposition. First-time moms believe many old wives' tales, and

I was not immune. I had heard that stress affects nursing, so I decided that George leaving for Vietnam was about as stressful as one could get, so I decided not to nurse her. Of all times, that would have been the best thing to do. There was no one in those days to counsel new moms with any helpful information.

The nursing staff was efficient but totally lacking in sympathy. We were told to get up on day one and make our beds. We were jokingly criticized for little things, in my case it was the Vogue pattern robe I had made. First-time moms must truly lack a sense of humor because they had most of us in tears at least once a day. Thankfully, those days are gone. One mom was discovered missing at bed check. They found her in the bathroom jumping off a chair, trying to encourage her fourth child to get on with the program.

Twelve days later, the love of my life walked out the door to spend the next year in harm's way in a country on the other side of the world.

The nightly visits between the girls continued but usually at my apartment because Cheryl was so little. Also continuing were the TV movies and the nightly phone calls to signal a safe return.

I wrote to George every day telling him all the little things that occurred. Each letter had a number by the return because he was so isolated with the Riverine Force that he would receive several at one time. He had to follow our daughter's first year through letters and pictures.

Shortly after he left, in the confusion of getting everything ready for his departure, we were overdrawn at the bank. My heart was in my stomach at the possible horrible repercussions for George. Not married a year and already messed up! The bank was in Pennsylvania, a state I had never been in but was a favorite of West Point cadets. At that time the bank had a military section, so I called with my heart in my throat. They were wonderful and assured me all was well. In fact, they added, if I needed to write a check before the end of the month, go ahead and it would be covered with no penalty. It is now called PNC, and I still remember how relieved I was.

One thing military wives do is to try not to add worry to the serviceman in harm's way.

After a few months, we decided to meet in Hawaii for rest and recuperation, better known as R & R. This was discussed through letters and those rare phone calls that were frustratingly interspersed with over and outs. The thrill of hearing his voice was often enough to blank out all thought, so I learned to write things down. On his end there was often a line of soldiers awaiting their turn to call a loved one, so most conversations were devoid of all but whispered endearments.

During these months, news was never missed, hoping and praying for a glimpse of him. Shots of GIs on mini rest and recuperation (R & R) on Vietnam beaches made me pray I wouldn't see him squiring around with some cute Vietnamese or Donut Dolly.

The plane fare and money for that trip was totally out of our budget. Of the $325 he made per month, $100 went for rent, $35 for stove rental, $25 for refrigerator rental and the rest divided between utilities, food, car insurance, and necessities. However, there was no way that meeting wasn't going to take place.

I went to a local bank, talked to the loan officer, who, by some miracle, lent me $500 without collateral for the trip. It was years before George even asked how I got that money. For five months afterward, I paid the bank $100 per month, skimping everywhere to make up the difference.

A few days before the trip to Hawaii, I packed up the VW and drove to Arkansas. Cheryl was snug in her collapsible bed in the backseat, sleeping most of the way across Kansas and Oklahoma.

Somewhere in Kansas, a rather frightening event occurred. I noticed a car with a single male driver that appeared to be following me. If I sped up, so did he. This continued mile after mile. As I was trying to decide what to do next, a huge semi rolled beside me in the next lane. As I sped up, he whipped in behind me. Another semi pulled alongside trapping the man behind us all. We rode that way until the next rest area where we all exited, leaving the tailgater headed southeast. The relief was overwhelming. The truckers got a grateful wave as they both roared back onto the interstate. Cheryl was hungry and wet, so we made good use of the break and were soon safely on our way.

The plan was to leave Cheryl Lynne with George's mother who was a housemother for the Arkansas Tech University athletic dorm. My mother was teaching home economics at Ridge Road Junior High in North Little

Rock, so she couldn't take care of a baby without taking a week's vacation. Leaving Cheryl with many kisses, I drove to Little Rock to leave my car and have Daddy take me to the plane.

With great excitement, I boarded the plane in Little Rock for the big reunion.

The layover in Los Angeles was a real eye-opener. Arkansas and Kansas weren't teeming with hippies, but Los Angeles was! Only southern upbringing kept my mouth closed as one apparition after another crossed my vision.

The flight from Los Angeles to Honolulu had an exceptional crew. They knew many of their lone women passengers were meeting husbands serving in Vietnam, so they brought us plastic glasses of champagne from first class. There were many acts of kindness interspersed with the hyped antiwar movement.

When we landed in Hawaii, several of us had gotten acquainted, so we shared a taxi. My luggage had been misplaced, so one of the girls offered to lend me an outfit until mine could be located. Hotel reservations had been made with no idea of the accommodations available. The taxi was to wait while I checked in, then I would go with my new friend to borrow that offered outfit after she checked into her hotel.

The taxi pulled up to a seedy-looking establishment crammed between a row of equally squalled facades. With great trepidation, I asked to see the room. We climbed some rickety stairs lined with walls covered in peeling paint to enter a tiny room with twin beds on the floor. My heart fell to my toes. Seizing on the twin beds, I told the manager how sorry I was to cause him extra trouble, but there was no way we could accept twin beds. Thankfully, he didn't have a double available.

Literally running down the stairs, I hopped in the taxi to go with my new friend to her hotel, the Ilikai, wondering what in the world I was going to do.

The Ilikai was on the beach beside the yacht harbor. Amazingly the hotel had reserved the entire top floor, the Aloha suites, for R & R couples. Even more amazingly, they had a room available at a discounted price that matched the price of the hotel from which I had just fled.

The balcony view from the room was the one on *Hawaii Five-o* where

Jack Lord stood in the introduction with Diamond Head in the background. They asked if that would be acceptable. Squashing hysterical giggles, I assured them it was perfect. After doing a victory jig in the gorgeous bedroom, I prepared to meet George.

George came in on a bus from the airport with others on R & R, all of them grinning. They were delivered to Fort DeRussy where they were met by a surging throng of delirious wives and girlfriends. We, shorter girls, were jumping to find our fellas.

George at six feet one inch was looking for five feet two inches me and walked right by. My hand snatched his arm before we lost each other in the masses.

There are not words to describe the incredible high of knowing you have made it through weeks and months of fear to safety of a body to body hug. We had found each other and didn't want to let go.

For a week we did touristy things, drank many mai tais at the Fort DeRussy Bar and Grill, and tried lots of local restaurants. We walked for miles it seemed, swam in the ocean, and of course spent a lot of time in bed.

One night we went to a Hawaiian show featuring someone we didn't know. He was really good, so we decided he would probably make it big someday. His theme song was "Tiny Bubbles." Only later did we discover, he had already made it big, and everyone had heard of Don Ho but us.

When that week ended, it broke my heart to see him get back on the plane. It was as if a part of me got on with him. As in all wars, you wonder if that is the last time you will hold and kiss him. There are so many things you forgot to say. We all watched through copious tears until the plane was but a speck.

Back on home turf in Arkansas, I drove to Russellville to retrieve our daughter. During that week, the football boys, who adored Mom Crocker, had spent countless hours trying to spoil our child. A box of change for the boys' use was kept near Cheryl's crib. The boys would sneak into Mom Crocker's room where Cheryl slept and rattle the box of coins as loudly as possible. The boys would emerge carrying a now-wide-awake baby. They loved to play with her to the detriment of her sleep needs. The great schedule she had been on was a distant memory.

2 | Vietnam and Russellville, Arkansas
"Alone on Home Turf"

GEORGE AND I had decided that to save money, I would move back to Arkansas to live in his mother's house, as she lived in the dorm.

My younger brother, Lyn, drove back to Kansas with me. I called the transportation office at Fort Riley to arrange for the furniture to be put in storage with a few exceptions like the baby bed, linens, and clothing. We packed up the VW with Cheryl again in the backseat, drove to Arkansas, and settled in for the rest of his tour.

Often Cheryl and I would drive to Little Rock to spend time with Mother and Daddy. Mother had a Victorian couch with high arms and back that she would turn to the wall for Cheryl's bed. It was perfect for us as it was in the guest bedroom with me.

In August George's mother asked if we'd like to go with her to Panama to visit her sister, Madelyne Curtiss (Aunt Mimi), whose husband, Colonel Curt Curtiss, was stationed there in an intelligence capacity. She would pay our way, and we would stay several weeks.

I was so excited and agreed to go immediately.

We flew on TACA Airlines from New Orleans. We had driven to New Orleans to catch the flight, staying overnight with a high school classmate, Shannon Brown Meistral. Her husband, Mike, was in medical school.

Little Cheryl was off on another adventure at only six months old.

We stopped in almost every country between the United States and Panama. One airstrip on which we landed was literally on top of a mountain. Armed guards stood around a chain link fence enclosing the field. The chain link fence was the only thing between the end of the runway and a nosedive off the mountain.

Another stop had everyone deplane to fix the plane's air conditioner. Filing back on to the plane, everyone was literally dripping with not perspiration but sweat. The terminal had one sad ceiling fan that only moved the hot air, so the now cool plane was a relief.

We finally arrived and spent a month with great relatives touring much of the beautiful country of Panama. The Canal Zone itself was gorgeous but a strong contrast to the poverty seen everywhere else.

We had shopped quite a bit because everything was so inexpensive. We toured the free zone, which was open to everyone at that time, to get even better bargains. We took the train across the isthmus to Colon and back. Local lore stated a giant boa would check out the passengers, picking the juiciest each trip, so we were to stay away from the windows.

One beautiful day Aunt Madelyne took us shelling. We walked across a spit of land to a small island, watching the time carefully so not to be stranded there as the tide came in. We returned to the car with our bags of specimens to find the car minus its battery. Locals had stolen the battery, leaving Aunt Madelyne muttering "Serves them right! It was on its last leg. Probably won't last a day!" Cell phones hadn't been invented yet, so without means of communication, we waited. We hoped Uncle Curt would notice we hadn't returned by suppertime and come to the rescue. He was babysitting Cheryl, so we assumed he would be anxious for our return.

After a few hours, we heard voices and movement in the jungle. A line of United States soldiers came into view, eliciting a huge collective sigh of relief from us all. They were on a field training, so they called for a jeep to take us home. One of our rescuers was a West Point classmate of George's.

When we arrived back at the Curtisses' quarters, Uncle Curt and my baby daughter were enjoying a mai tai. Cheryl was giggling and trying to sit up but falling over. I absolutely couldn't believe it! My precious baby girl drunk before her first birthday! Poor Uncle Curt was chastised by all of us, and I vowed to never leave her with him again.

First-time moms are notorious for overprotecting their babies, but I tended to go overboard on that trip. Aunt Madelyne had a dachshund who knew the minute a meal was over; he could sit at the table in her lap to get leftovers. That didn't bother me, but when the dog was placed in the baby stroller for a ride, I very obviously scrubbed every inch following with a Lysol spray before Cheryl was allowed to ride in it again. One morning, the feral cat Cousin Judy had spent months taming was found strolling down the center of the dining table. I yelled at it, and Mother Crocker grabbed it, opened the back door, and slung it outside. It no doubt used one of its lives landing on its feet. For the remainder of our visit, the cat hid in the dirty clothes basket in a closet. Judy couldn't imagine why it was suddenly so shy.

George's mother, the consummate shopper, had bought a *lot* of things. We packed our suitcases, sitting on them to close. To help us through security, Adele had some tricks up her sleeve. We had purchased several Panama hats. Adele had three, so we each wore two with Cheryl's small plastic toys between the two crowns. When we went through customs, the cases were opened but immediately slammed shut. She had cleverly layered Kotex on top of all her clothes. I tried that a few years later, but the agent had a grand time riffling through all my "stuff."

The rest of the year went slowly. I substitute taught elementary school in Dardanelle across the Arkansas River from Russellville to earn a bit of extra money. Cheryl seemed to enjoy the day care one block away.

Every few days, I would go to the Laundromat to wash clothes and diapers. I'd bring them back to hang on the backyard clothesline. The Laundromat took a chunk out of our meager budget.

Adele bought us a washer for our combined anniversary, birthdays, and Christmas present just before George got home. I was thrilled!

Cheryl and I went to the local Presbyterian Church every Sunday we were in town, but every beautiful weekend we drove to the lake house my parents were slowly building on a bluff overlooking Greer's Ferry Lake. Daddy had blasted into the cliff so the house was half underground in the front. He had dug a septic tank and drilled a well. We made a makeshift shower by wrapping a piece of fencing around a tree, covering it with beach towels, and draping a hose over it. The toilet was flushed with a bucket of water.

One of the weekends we were there, Betty Hendricks, a lifelong friend whose husband was also in Vietnam, came up for a weekend. We sent our fellas pictures of us behind the towels in our makeshift shower.

It was beautiful up there and peaceful.

When George finally came home, there was no fanfare, balloons, flag waving, or parades; but there was a little family, giddy with joy at his safe homecoming.

3 | Fort Benning, Georgia
"Airborne School and Roaches"

GEORGE HAD ORDERS for the 82nd Airborne Division with mandatory airborne school at Fort Benning, Georgia. We drove through the south toward Georgia en route stopping in Selma, Alabama, to call an old friend from high school, Phyllis Parsons, whose husband was in pilot training. We had a brief phone conversation promising to get together.

We arrived at Fort Benning and began the apartment hunt. We quickly found and moved into an apartment in the huge infamous Camellia Apartment Complex. It was anything but clean, so I sprayed Lysol on every surface. Cheryl's crib took up one tiny room, and ours wasn't much bigger. No amount of Roaches-B-Gone affected the giant roach infestation, but we valiantly fought the fight.

If I needed the car, I would take George to airborne training before daylight and try to remember the maze of one-way streets to return to the apartment. Every morning the radio announcer would talk about one of their sponsors, Nehi. He would spell it out, "N-E-H-I, Nehi contents ten flu ozes." We still say that every so often.

A few days after we arrived, we were watching the evening news on our little TV set. The news anchor spoke of a tragic accident at the air force flight school in Selma, Alabama. In horror we listened as the name of the dead pilot was confirmed. It was the husband of my friend we had just spoken to en route to Georgia.

Airborne school was short but very physical, so George would come home exhausted. He loved jumping out of airplanes which was a good thing since he would be doing just that most of his career.

One morning, roads were changed from two way to one way, forcing me to drive around lost for almost an hour. My panic rose in increments as Cheryl was asleep in her crib at the apartment with the girls next door listening for her. Finally, the correct road was found; I raced in the door to find Cheryl fast asleep just as I had left her. That was too scary to repeat even with the next-door girls assuring me she was fine. Thereafter, she got bundled into the car before dawn.

George finished airborne school successfully, and we survived the great roach infestation so we were ready for the next assignment.

Driving to Fort Bragg, our next assignment, we had secured a trunk of our belongings to the Volkswagen top. The trunk of our little car left little room for three people's "stuff."

We were cruising along a two-lane highway in the middle of farm country when a large semi roared past. We heard a loud noise, and as I turned to look, George was looking in the rearview mirror cussing. We watched in horror as the trunk, having been ripped from the car roof, was merrily bouncing down the highway.

George pulled over and backed up. The lid had snapped open somewhere during the third or fourth bounce spewing clothes, toiletries, and the rest of our belongings in a wide swath. We ran around in the middle of the road, grabbing items before another car came. George's mandatory calling cards were littering a cow pasture, my bras were hanging on barbwire, and the hot curlers had bounced along leaving a trail of hot rods in the ditch. Clothes and items seemed to be everywhere.

Another car came along, stopped, and helped pick up items. I tried to get to our underwear first. We crammed most of the items back in the trunk, which miraculously still latched, retied it to the roof, and continued keeping an eagle eye behind us. The calling cards we left for the cows.

4 | Fort Bragg, North Carolina
"The First Hooah"

FORT BRAGG, NORTH Carolina, is the home of the airborne. Men jumping out of airplanes is the max of machoism, so the "esprit de corps." there is unbelievable. Airborne is a form of conversation. One battalion commander could carry on an entire conversation with that one word using a thousand inflections.

Our arrival to Fort Bragg was, of course, coming from Georgia. As we drove into Fayetteville, a huge billboard loomed next to the highway. It featured a hooded Ku Klux Klan man on a rearing horse with the words "Join and support your local Klan. Help fight communism and integration." It was chilling, and we both wondered how black soldiers and their families felt arriving with that welcome.

We stayed in temporary quarters a night or two as George checked in for duty. The wait for housing was several weeks, so we rented an apartment at 1400 Briar Cliff Road, Apartment 1 in Fayetteville. George had a Triumph Motorcycle he rode to work daily. We ended up staying there for two months until we were finally assigned quarters.

We were thrilled to get a separate house instead of a multifamily unit. The little house at 100 Knot Circle had a large eat-in kitchen and two bedrooms with one bath. The living room was in the front of the house so those curtains made from sheets came out again.

It was a corner lot, so we felt blessed.

Our next-door neighbor was an OB-GYN doctor. To the chagrin of the army families on the circle, the air force officer across the street was receiving extra pay for living in substandard housing. Despite all our differences, the neighbors and unit became a close-knit group. The men serving in the 82nd Airborne Division could not leave the phone while on two-hour recall. The 82nd had a standing no notice immediate contingency deployment mission. To meet this requirement the division designated a division ready force or DRF-1 that was placed on a two-hour assembly recall. So we spent many weekends on the back steps using an extremely long extension cord connecting us to the possible call from headquarters. Countless gallons of rum were consumed making margaritas and daiquiris.

At the end of the month, the wives would meet in the backyard to pool our resources. We fed our families using the leftovers we combined from all our pantries. Hot dogs were a big item. Most of us used gas credit cards and even those were shared. The OB-GYN doctor next door had an old 356B Porsche normal coupe, and he swore he would starve before giving it up so our food closet was his saving grace.

George was the Battalion S-2 until he made captain in June of 1968. He was slated to then take B Company.

April 4, 1968, was a sad day in the nation with the assassination of Dr. Martin Luther King Jr. Riots broke out in our nation's capital requiring the 82nd Airborne's deployment to quell the disturbance. Riot companies were dispersed throughout the city. George was in Spingarin High School, sleeping on a cot in the gym with Headquarters Company. Others were in a Buick dealership, a tire dealership, and the police precinct.

That was also the day our friends, Mark and Jo Ponzillo, were married. Jo's wedding night was spent alone as Mark boarded the plane to Washington DC. Welcome to army life!

When George made captain, he took command of B Company I-325 Airborne Infantry Regiment from David Supenski. With the promotion came a small pay raise so we decided to trade in the Volkswagen beetle for a snazzy Pontiac Firebird.

To go to and from work, George bought an old beat-up Volkswagen for $100. The passenger floor was rusted out; we covered the shredded seats with cheap stretch covers, and he was good to go. It was perfect to drive the mile or so to work. The starter was broken, so George started it in the mornings by coasting downhill. In the evening, troops in the company would push start him in the Bastogne Street "B" lane. When we left, George spray painted it with camouflage paint and sold it to a neighbor for $100.

Colonel Sandy Cortner was the battalion commander. He led the weekly Friday night gathering at the Airborne Annex.

On one of the first nights we attended, he insisted I try a special drink. It was a sloe gin fizz and sounded really good! After bringing me three of them, I was fine thinking they were just like fruit punch! When we got home, I fell flat on my face. It was like being hit with a ton of bricks. That was my last sloe gin fizz.

On a field training exercise, George had come by the house for about five minutes to get something for the unit. That night, the women had a function where I casually mentioned his brief visit.

The executive officer of the battalion was a man named Gene Fluke. He was thought to be rather anal retentive, so when his wife casually shared that George had dropped by his house, he went ballistic. I learned not to share even the most mundane things with the group at large.

During this time, Fayetteville was, not so affectionately called, "Fayetnam." The town was wild especially on pay days. Shootings, stabbings, and wild gatherings were common. The Barn was the only restaurant in town with tablecloths so was patronized only on really special occasions.

Rapes and muggings were very common, even on post.

The houses in our court and the apartments behind us backed on to a grassy area several blocks long. Our house was at the top of the grassy strip.

One morning, we were awakened at about 5:30 a.m. by the sound of garbage can lids being lifted and replaced. When George investigated, we were told the military police were checking for evidence. Our neighbor two doors down was raped after her husband left for a predawn jump. We didn't hear her screams over the window air conditioner in our room. We were stunned!

Two doors down the other direction, a wife had been receiving breathy threats from a man who threatened to come over. Her husband was gone, so the neighborhood men gathered, had her set up a meeting when he next called, and lay in wait. The perpetrator quietly entered her home, and she called for him to come upstairs. He began disrobing on his way up. The neighborhood men sprang into action, tackling him in his BVDs. To the dismay of all, the clothing strewn on the stairs was a military police uniform. If your husband was away, you could put your name on a list for the MPs to check on you periodically. She had done that. We all felt he went way beyond the expected attention.

At the monthly coffees, the wives' discussion always came around to self-protection. We discussed how to shoot an intruder so he would fall in the doorway thus making it a legal clean shot for self-protection.

One of our coffee group members was babysitting a friend's children and dogs one night. A man tried to break into her back door. We all had multiple locks on the doors, even sleeping with loaded pistols under our pillows when alone. I had George's grandmother's Colt 380 automatic under my pillow when he wasn't home.

The dogs she was keeping, and her own, slept through the rattling and banging at her back door. As this little Italian spitfire lay there terrified, listening to the noise at her door, she began getting mad. Finally she was furious! She leapt from her bed, stormed into the kitchen cussing and yelling. The criminal was so startled, he turned and fled. She found the door on an angle and almost off its hinges.

A description of one of the rapist was circulated on post by the military police. Unfortunately, a very nice, innocent young man who delivered flowers for a local florist looked a bit like the description. He lost his job because no one would open their door to him.

The Dr. Jeffery McDonald Green Beret family murders happened down the street as well. We were all horrified at the event but also by the criminally bungled investigation. Years later, I would teach with one of the investigators; and he was, as we say in Arkansas, dumb as dirt.

I decided to apply for a teaching job for extra money but had to first take the National Teachers Exam to receive a North Carolina teaching certificate. The time for the day-long test arrived as did several of George's West Point classmates.

Drained from the all-day testing, I arrived to find one of our favorite people, Bob Albright, and several other classmates getting the party rolling. I had fixed some fast snacks and the heavier hors d'oeuvres for later. The beer was flowing, Cheryl was miraculously sleeping, and a fun time seemed to be had by all.

One of the guys had too much to drink and was throwing up in the toilet. He was followed by another, and that was when the plumbing stopped up with no help till Monday. All the guys eventually passed out in the living room either from alcohol or exhaustion, so I covered them up, finding pillows and leaving them all to sleep it off. The next morning after breakfast, they all rolled off into the morning light. The post engineers arrived Monday, digging a huge trench across our front yard to fix our plumbing problem.

For a semester, I got a job teaching biology at Hope Mills High School. It would be my first time teaching boys. The only other full-time teaching job had been in a Catholic girls' school teaching high school home economics. It was an eye-opener. I did have a degree in science but somehow had never had biology. Zoology and bacteriology would have been a snap. I studied more than the students to stay ahead of them.

The extra money was well worth the long daily drive. Now freeways connect Fayetteville and Hope Mills, but then it was all back roads.

During Christmastime, we were offered a set of field-grade quarters. You can't imagine how thrilled we were at this great gift.

We borrowed Dave Hendricks and his 1955 Ford pickup truck to move us the few blocks to 3 Avellino Drive. Dave, another Arkansan, had married Betty Boyson who had lived next door to me when I was four. Betty had visited me at the lake house while our guys were in Vietnam. It took three loads with the last being our fully decorated Christmas tree standing up in the bed of the truck with George holding it for dear life and Dave trying to avoid swerving too much.

We off-loaded it, plugged it in, and voila, Christmas!

Before we could settle into our spacious, to us, new quarters, we had to clear the Knott Circle quarters. They had to be cleaned, and I do mean cleaned.

This was another fun aspect of army life. Being raised by a home economics major, Mother who's middle name was frugal (a result of living through the depression), it seemed such a waste to pay someone else to clean your house, when really we were talking elbow grease here! So disdain for my weaker army sisters, I rolled up my sleeves and started to scour. The army list of "to do" things seemed to get longer daily. The windows had to be cleaned inside and out, every surface sparkling, top of doorways and windows dusted, the refrigerator shining, and above all the stove, spotless. I finished all of it wearing my cuts and bruises like metals. Everything shone on the stove as I had used SOS and a screw driver to clean every speck of baked-on grease.

I challenged anyone in the family to put a fingerprint on anything . . . after all, the horror stories of white-glove inspections was a hot topic at unit coffees.

When the inspector showed up to clear us, I'll be darn if he didn't pull out a pair of white gloves, sneer at me, and start going through the house swiping those pure white gloves on everything! It was true! White-glove inspection *meant* white-glove inspection. However, I felt confident that the old elbow grease and a week of slave labor were worth every bruise. When he got to the stove, he raised the hinged top while I thanked God I had earlier discovered the top comes up on some stoves. He slid that still-white glove over the wire and to my horror, and his, came away grease smudged. "How did I miss that?" I asked, trying not to panic. He smirked at me and said I had one hour to correct the stove before he returned for a final inspection.

In total irritation, with SOS in hand, I scrubbed. The grease on the wires had been there for years, so the wire coating was soft and gooey which was the reason it wasn't spotless. Unplugging the stove and muttering under my breath, I scrubbed and scrubbed, even polishing when possible. When he returned, the wires sparkled in the sunlight with not a speck of grease but no protective coating either. So there! I felt vindicated when he growled, "Looks good, you pass!" It felt even better to think he would have to replace the entire stove or at least the wiring.

We put the orange chairs and Formica table on the side walk for the trashman to pick up. A couple walking a huge Great Dane knocked on the door, asking if they could have it. Of course! It was lovely to know it had a new home.

The Three Avelino Drive duplex had three bedrooms, a bath and a half, as well as, to our estimation, tons of storage.

Cheryl went in one bedroom, we took the bedroom with the luxurious half bath, and the third bedroom housed George's weight set. One closet had nothing in it but the vacuum. We were really living in high clover. Cheryl went to child care during the week while I taught school. I was about three months pregnant when she came home with German measles. A call to Mother determined that no one could remember if I had ever had the measles. Measles and pregnant women do not go together. My doctor took a tine test to see if I contracted the disease, but it had to be done three times so many weeks apart. Serious birth defects can occur if you contract measles while pregnant, but we had decided we would go ahead with the pregnancy no matter what the test showed. It would be better to know in advance if a problem existed, so we were doing the test.

George received orders to Carlisle Barracks, Pennsylvania, to be the commandant's, General William J. McCaffrey's, senior aide. The curtains I had made for the living room still had pins in the hem which was just as well since the next place may have longer or shorter windows.

There were two remaining tine tests to be done. Each was to be sent to Carlisle Barracks hopefully to be compared there. As is often stated, "Hope is not a course of action."

We drove to Arkansas for a few days' leave, stopping at the Little Rock Air Force Base clinic to have the second test done. By the time we reached Carlisle, neither of the first two tests had arrived. They were eventually determined to be lost.

A terrific feature of the Pontiac Firebird was the backseat that folded down to form a platform. On the road, Cheryl would insist she had to potty, so I would dig her little white plastic miniature toilet out of the floor board. She would sit on her throne reading a book, unconcerned that numerous motorists were swerving all over the road as they stared.

We drove into Pennsylvania to start our next tour.

An adventurous spirit certainly helps when you move an entire family from one new place to another every year or so.

5 | Carlisle Barracks, Pennsylvania
"The Mill Experience"

OUR NEW HOME was on the second floor of a two-hundred-year-old mill converted into five apartments: two on the third floor, two on the second, and a large one on the ground floor. The walls were thirty-nine inches thick, the wiring was the original from the 1926 conversion, and the kitchen outfitted before washers and dryers.

Every evening, you could hear someone running down the back fire escape to the basement to replace an old cigar-shaped fuse. Occasionally that someone was one of us.

The mill had been a working one on the LeTort Creek since 1768 and still had a working mill wheel. A porch had been built in the back of each apartment with the fire escape stairs between. Over the years the porches had sunk somewhat into the damp ground thus the porch was on a definite angle. My sewing machine was on the porch, so when I sewed everything on the machine cabinet bounced and slid off onto the floor.

One 220 volt outlet had been installed on the wall between the kitchen and the dining room. We put our washing machine in the space allotted and the dryer above it in the window with a long extension cord to the plug. One had to climb on a stool to open the dryer to add or remove items.

We installed a window air conditioner in the dining room window with the same extension cord solution. If the dryer was on, the air conditioner had to be unplugged and vice versa. Because the windows were so deep, the dryer and air conditioner fit perfectly.

Occasionally at night, we would hear a bird frantically flapping in the walls. Somehow they would get in and couldn't find their way out. It was very distressing to hear. Fortunately, I hadn't seen any horror movies about birds.

Reportedly beneath the mill was an entrance to a cave in the Civil War era underground railroad. It had been boarded up for safety, so we couldn't explore, which was very disappointing.

Our neighbors upstairs were delightful—Karen Shoupe had one small son, Tommy, and a baby girl, Jackie. She was of Italian descent, a great cook, and a ton of fun.

Carlisle Barracks is home of the army's war college. Most of the residents there are lieutenant colonels and colonels selected for the one-year course. It is one of the schools for which officers aspire to be selected. As a captain's wife, we younger wives were a real minority. Therefore, there wasn't an OB clinic on post. My OB doctor was off post and quite elderly.

On that note, at a formal dinner party given by the McCaffeys, we were invited because we were new. Remember how I fainted when pregnant, well that night the feeling came over me, so I sat down before I fell. In those days, one did not sit down in the presence of senior ladies unless they sat. Being mortified but with little recourse, it seemed better to sit than to fall face forward into the onion dip. Been there, done that.

A brave, kind lady, whose name I cannot recall, sat down next to me. After learning of my difficulty, she stayed regaling me with stories of her children and made it appear that I had joined her on the couch. That was one of those kindnesses that was still tucked warmly in my memory. It is also the reason why at every function after that, I looked for the ones standing alone.

The town of Carlisle, Pennsylvania, is a charming spot in the middle of a farming country, yet a short drive from the capital, Harrisburg. The historic town is lined with interesting shops, cafes, and very old structures. The local cemetery is filled with tombstones remembering the Civil War dead as well as those of more recent demise. The feeling of battles fought and stories untold hung in the air. Townspeople were very friendly, I think, because the cherubic face haloed with blond ringlets was exuding charm in the stroller I pushed.

The Carlisle Indian Industrial School, where Jim Thorpe became famous, was part of the original post. Its graveyard was on the back side of the post, and it's a walk through history to visit it.

We were close to Amish country, so we took a couple of trips and found the entire area fascinating. To find the sign posts to Blue Ball and Intercourse was a shock. Sometimes, it seemed ludicrous that the stoic city leaders would have selected such names.

George's mother drove up to visit, so of course, we made several trips to every shopping venue within one hundred miles. One day, I took her to downtown Carlisle, where we stopped in the local Goodwill store. They had a lot of neat things, but the antique high chair was my favorite. It had metal wheels, collapsed to a child-size chair, and sported a spindle back and side trim. It was $24! We talked about it all the way back. That afternoon, Adele went shopping alone while Cheryl and I caught our second wind with a nap. She called me to say she saw another similar chair, and they wanted $150. "Call that other place right now, and tell them we'll take it," she demanded. So of course, I did. The saleslady having had only one pregnant woman in that day, remembered me. She agreed to hold it for me but said the couple trying to decide about it would be disappointed! Close call! We picked it up agreeing to pay $12 each, and I still have it today. The saleslady, who was eighty plus, told us its history. It had been hers as a baby and in her family before that. One leg split in a move, and even after repair we hesitated putting a squirming baby in it. Today it holds our granddaughter's dolls because they don't squirm.

It was at Carlisle where I learned a valuable lesson. Never serve a dish from a recipe you have never before tried. We invited some neighbors over for dessert one evening. I had spent two days making a sabayon. The sponge cake had been appropriately soaked in rum and the whipping cream topping whipped. We all sat in the living room with dessert plates on laps, coffee cups nearby. Everyone took a bite. The expressions around the room went from shock to horror. I put a bite in my mouth. It was the most awful thing I had ever tasted.

I swallowed mine with difficulty, went around collecting plates, offering apologies and paper napkins to dispose of first bites. Fortunately we had ice cream, so we had bowls of that instead. In my recipe book, that recipe is now covered with "Yucks!" "Horrid!" and a skull with cross bones. No doubt, our guests still remember that evening and not because of our charm and graciousness.

After five wonderful months in Pennsylvania, General McCaffery received orders to the Pentagon where he could not take aides, so we were again at the mercy of Army Headquarters Personnel Assignment Branch. In those years, as in these, the expectation of another war tour forever loomed on the horizon. Wives' views of the possibility are often the opposite of their military counterparts. Most military men deplore war but are trained to protect their homeland no matter what. The wives and families left behind are warriors in their own right. We fight to keep the home fires burning, everyone safe, and everything functioning. We heap love on our children, yet discipline for two. Never do our children hear, "Wait till your daddy gets home!" That could be a year or never. The façade shows strength, courage, and determination. The reality, in private, is weak knees, bending in supplication to a higher power, a deep seated fear kept battled down, and a mental effort to appear purposeful, calm, and collected.

We also decorate government quarters or apartments every year or so, making or buying curtains for windows that *never* fit the next new home. If you paint walls, they have to be painted back when you leave.

The furniture that is perfect for one home may be a challenge to arrange in the next.

With relief, I received the news we were again headed for Fort Benning, Georgia, this time for the Infantry Officer's Advanced Course and not immediately back to Vietnam.

We got ready for the move, and this time the stove sparkled the first time it was cleaned.

6 | Fort Benning, Georgia, Again
"A Year for Family"

FOR ME, GEORGE attending the Infantry Officer Advanced Course (IOAC) meant at least a year delay before Vietnam loomed again. Maybe it would be over by then!

We arrived in the heat of the Georgia summer, only this time pulling a trailer with a brand-new Triumph motorcycle glinting in the sun.

We were to await quarters at temporary housing in the Sand Hills area. It had a playground, so Cheryl was thrilled. This was our third permanent change of station (PCS) (poor choice of terms) during my pregnancy.

A small mishap occurred as we off-loaded the Triumph from the trailer. The lift gate released from the "up" position, banging into the front fender and toppling the bike to the Georgia sand. No great harm to the bike occurred. It only sustained a few scratches, but it scared us terribly.

When George signed in, we called to schedule an appointment at the OB-GYN clinic at Martin Army Hospital. My appointment was for 9:00 a.m. a few days later.

On the appointed day, George dropped me off with instructions to call when ready to be picked up. He and Cheryl would have a great time together.

I checked in with a large woman who barely glanced up from her paperwork, then found a seat in the incredibly crowded waiting room.

Women in various stages of pregnancy were being ushered in and out like cattle at an auction. Ten o'clock came and went as did eleven. By then two of us remained—a shy young Mexican girl and me. I asked the same very snappy receptionist how long she thought it might be. She said, "I have no idea. The doctors have gone to lunch. Why are you here? Are you pregnant?"

By this time, I had gone to the bathroom four times, leaving my name with whoever was next to me, in case I was called and was close to tears in frustration. Don't ask why I said it but something snapped. Standing there with my stomach leading the way, I said, "No, ma'am, I'm not pregnant. I have a huge tumor, and that's why I'm here on OB day." She snapped back, "Well, did you show me your ID when you came in?" I told her no, she didn't ask to see it. She glared at me and snapped, "Can't you read? It says right here on that little sign show your ID cards. You will have to make another appointment." Putting my arm around the now sobbing young mother-to-be, who also obviously "couldn't read," I did as my daddy taught me. I smiled through tight, clenched teeth and said, "Thank you so much. You have been most helpful." I pivoted and dragging my still sobbing sister in need out the door, I went straight to the phone to call my hero who arrived in record time, grim faced, blue eyes steely. My new friend stuck like glue. George went through the proper hospital channels ultimately assured we would be seen the minute the first doctor returned from lunch. We both were seen, and all was well.

George, Cheryl, and I then marched to the "complaint department" to file an official complaint. They appeared surprised as the rude receptionist in question had never gotten a complaint. I assured them it was a miracle because she really needed to be on the psych ward, not dealing with emotionally fragile, pregnant women who had probably all left in tears, never thinking of filing a complaint, but only getting as far away as possible. She is probably still there!

George was early for the IOAC course and got picked up for the pathfinder course. That meant he had to be out in the field several nights a week.

One of these times, I received a call from the moving company based in Phoenix City, Alabama, across the river from Columbus, Georgia. They were notifying me they would be at our newly assigned quarters with all our worldly goods the next morning, the same day I was to sign for those quarters.

When you sign for quarters, there is a routine where you and a representative of housing go through to check that everything works and mark down any discrepancies. I told the moving company caller it was too short notice as we hadn't even signed for the quarters. He told me if he didn't deliver the next day it would cost hundreds of dollars to deliver it later. Between a rock and a hard place was where my pregnant body was caught. I told them to come on.

The next morning, two-and-a-half-year-old Cheryl and I waited for the movers and the housing representative. The housing officer got there first to give us the keys and check out our new home. The quarters were the Capehart-style duplex with a small front porch and a large backyard. The only thing missing was a refrigerator. When asked when it would arrive, he said he didn't know but would try to get it there that afternoon.

The moving van pulled up while he was there. Four or five men piled out and started unloading our "stuff." Cheryl during all of this chaos was crying, wanting a drink of water. We had not one glass anywhere, so I tried the hand-to-mouth technique to little avail. Meanwhile, the movers were bringing in box after box faster than I could check them off the inventory. I scurried from room to room trying to keep up with boxes, telling movers where to put them. After two hours, it seemed there were twelve movers, all asking questions at once.

When the man from housing dropped into this chaos to tell me a refrigerator would be delivered in two days, I lost it. I sat down among the boxes sobbing that my husband was in the field, the movers came a day early, my daughter was thirsty and starving with nothing unpacked to soothe her hunger or thirst. Sniff. Sob. Sniff. He fled. An hour later, a brand-new refrigerator was delivered, and I thought *maybe* we would survive the day.

When the band of movers left after supposedly "unpacking," I went from room to room to inspect the damage. Every room was piled high with "stuff" on every surface. Beds were reassembled but were covered with piles of clothing, bedding, toiletries, and other items that had previously been neatly packed in boxes.

Usually when movers come in to pack military families, one checks often on the packing, making sure every box and item are numbered and on the inventory.

At the other end, the inventory is checked off as each box or item enters the door. If things are unpacked, they are checked for breakage. All items broken or missing are listed so a claim against the moving company can be made. Beds are put back together. I rarely asked them to unpack everything but always had the glassware and dishes unpacked to check for breakage.

Being the only one on site and trying to comfort an increasingly cranky two-year-old didn't allow for much supervision.

In our room the movers had literally untaped boxes, turned them upside down, and dumped the contents on the bed. The bed resembled Mount Everest capped with underwear and socks. Some days seem loaded with more than you can take, and this was one of them. We are promised we will not be given more than we can handle, so I had to assume my vine was being trimmed or my clay vessel fired to make it stronger. I tried to be thankful.

When we left Carlisle Barracks, a Civil War rifle that had belonged to George's grandfather Ellis was packed in a locked antique chifforobe with serial numbers on the inventory sheet. When the chifforobe was opened in Georgia, the rifle was missing.

As Cheryl napped I plowed through the mountain of dumped items on our bed. George's grandmother Ellis (Nana) had given me the Colt 380 automatic pistol which her husband had given her as a wedding gift in the 1900s. It was a prized possession that had been in my lingerie drawer. The gun had spent many nights under my pillow at Fort Bragg and had given me great comfort. It was missing! All the perfume bottles had been opened, tested and left open, the jewelry box of cheaper jewelry I shipped had been examined and everything had been pawed through, so by now my anger was reaching the frothing at the mouth stage.

When George returned from the field, he walked into a five feet two inch maelstrom of frustration and indignant anger. The only bright spot was the *new* refrigerator! As we slowly made a semblance of order to the unpacked, dumped chaos, several things were found missing or broken.

Not only did we file a claim but filed a complaint with transportation about the missing guns. Because they crossed state lines (legally) the FBI was brought in. The moving company headquarters in California called us for a taped phone interview.

A week later, late at night, when the doorbell rang, we opened the door to a bleary-eyed truck driver from the moving company who stood there with our rifle in hand. He said it had been found in the corner of the local moving company manager's office where it had been placed for safe keeping. *Sure it was*, we thought. Judging by his obvious fatigue and bloodshot eyes, he had been dispatched to a distant point to retrieve the rifle and return it. The pistol never showed up, and I'm still saddened at its loss.

About a month later, the moving company manager committed suicide, so we assumed our shipment was not the only one that ended up in parts unknown! Hanging on to that thought, we unleashed the burgeoning feeling of guilt that our complaint might have contributed to his demise.

Tara Leigh was born October 13, 1969, after only twelve or so hours of labor and only two weeks late. It was a far easier birth than the forty-eight hours with Cheryl Lynne. Mother had taken time off teaching in North Little Rock and flown in to help. Tara was a very good baby just like her big sister had been. Cheryl wasn't sure about her at first but soon adjusted. It was great having Mom to cook and clean while I took care of Tara and Cheryl. She left us frozen casseroles that were very appreciated for days after her return home. Shortly after she left, Jo and Mark Ponzillo, our friends from Fort Bragg, came by and brought a spaghetti dinner. Mark exudes energy with a bigger-than-life personality, and sweet Jo is his perfect foil. I still smile thinking of her stories of, Georgia peach that she was, meeting Mark's New York Italian family for the first time.

Mark came into the kitchen with a flourish brandishing a big knife, pepperoni, and a sauce that had cooked all day. He threw in the chopped pepperoni and served it with crusty French bread and a salad. Delicious! It is still my favorite way to have spaghetti. Since I was nursing my newborn,

Tara had a rather uncomfortable night—I think it was gas, as the smell of pepperoni permeated her crib.

George had gotten us "new parents" gifts of two bicycles. We did get to ride a bit with a child seat on the back of his.

It was about this time the classmates of West Point Class of 1966, who were together for this year, discovered golf. Weekends of being golf widows after years of being left to handle home and kids quickly became old.

Kaye Chitty, the wife of Charlie, had a fabulous idea—we would also learn to play, so we could spend lots of leisure time with our true loves. Betty Hendricks, Kaye Chitty, Maureen Dubia, and I would often form a foursome. We hacked around the first few times out and took several lessons to correct really bad technique. Soon we were partnering with our spouses, taking little ones to child care, and forming close friendships that would last a lifetime.

Besides the golf, my macho husband found the Dr. Kenneth H. Cooper's aerobics book *Run for Your Life.* Consequently the book became his basis of adult good physical conditioning. He was so ardent in his desire to get us healthy that he shamed me into running with him after the girls were asleep. We only went two blocks so weren't too far from the babies. The first few times two blocks was about my limit—some of us can use the excuse "I just had a baby" for years! Soon, the two blocks turned into four, and before the year was over, we had to take turns running. One stayed with the girls while the other ran. To this day I hate to run but love the way it feels afterward. George on the other hand loves to run and does so through wind, heat, rain, and pain.

The people who shared the duplex with us were Jean and Tom Fickle. They had a son about the age of our Cheryl. Once when the children were playing in their side of the duplex, they disappeared for a brief while. When you deal with two- to three-year-old toddlers, this is *not* a comforting event. When Jean went to search for them, they were discovered giggling in a closet playing medical personnel whose line was "Show me yours, and I'll show you mine!" She was so horrified she could hardly tell us of the event and apologized for weeks! It was *not* that earth-shattering, but we did realize it was time for a very open discussion of body parts and why closets were *not* the place to observe these differences.

My poodle was still with us and still very much a one-woman dog and spoiled. George hated him as he had been a present from an old boyfriend given to me before we even met. We were going out to a movie one evening, leaving Piker tied on the front porch when Cheryl ran up to tell him bye. He had just decided to have dinner, so when faced with a child racing in his direction, it no doubt appeared she too was hungry. He crouched, bared his teeth, and growled, snapping at the little hand extended to him. A roar from the big daddy behind the wheel, who was so incensed that the hated dog should even think of growling at his baby, was the dog's ultimate undoing. I had to agree that the dog had to go. We sold him to my younger brother, Lyn, for $1. Pike ended up living with my parents, who fell in love with him, and he became the only dog ever allowed inside their home.

Our year of real family life was to be a distant memory because the orders for our next assignment came, and my worst fears were realized. It was back to Vietnam for our guy. The time before, we had spent six months in Mother Crocker's home with many ups and downs. So the decision was more difficult this time. Where do we go? Mother and Daddy were still building on the lake house, and George's mother was still a housemother, only this time in a girl's dorm. George was an only child, so her experience with college girls was negligible. She had great rapport with the football boys because she had raised one, but the girls were a different matter. She agreed to our staying in her house, again, probably to get the grandbabies nearby.

Again we stored most of our furniture, only taking what we would need to supplement Adele's fully-furnished house. Sorting through a houseful of furniture, deciding what to store for a year, labeling everything, and sorting into rooms was a chore. With every move, we learned new tricks of the trade so to speak. I took pictures of each room full of sorted items, and as it turned out, that was a fortuitous precaution.

This time around, I was not so flustered with the move, but the sorting was truly a game of chance. Our stored items were packed in the usual boxes of various sizes, labeled, and hauled away in a moving van ready to be stored in a huge warehouse in Columbus, Georgia.

The rest of our "stuff," we couldn't survive a year without, was packed up and hauled to Russellville, Arkansas. We spent two weeks at the lake skiing, visiting old friends, and of course, loving each other at every opportunity. We spent long nights of sleeping wound together, wondering if these would be the last and the hollowness inside at that thought. The hardest part of sending a loved one off to war is the speed at which the days pass before his departure. The closer departure comes, the faster the days fly. The need to touch grows constant, plans are discussed for communication, codes devised in case of capture, instructions for car maintenance, and the list goes on. The worst item, of course, what to do if he is killed. The chill to the heart is a physical thing during that discussion. Because death is certainly a possibility in war, it is *not* the time to say, "I don't want to talk about it because you will be fine." Sticking your head in the sand does two things: first, it leaves both spouses feeling unprepared and should the worst occur, the survivor really doesn't know the wishes of her warrior. Second, it is a cowardly act that leaves the warrior feeling additional stress, knowing you couldn't discuss such a serious and important matter.

Fear is in the heart of both spouses, who try not to communicate that fear to children. We planned to use tape machines this time to send tapes back and forth so the girls could hear their daddy's voice and he all of ours. He also taped stories the girls could listen to at bedtime.

The awful day arrived way too soon. We drove him to the airport in Little Rock, seventy-three miles away and tried to put on the brave face he wanted us to have, but the tears came in gushes as he disappeared down the hallway, turning often to wave and blow kisses. The onlookers rarely made eye contact, either out of respect or because of personal opinions about the conflict. One young woman did make eye contact and amazingly it was the glowing face of my first cousin, Trecia Chedister. Her husband, Rob, was just returning. It would be years before we saw each other again, but that was such a precious gift at a difficult time.

7 | Vietnam and Russellville, Arkansas
"The Long Wait, Again"

THE DAYS TURNED into weeks and the weeks into months as our life took on a semblance of normalcy. I rarely missed the news, always hoping to catch a glimpse of him but knew I would not. He was assigned as the senior advisor to a crack RVN Ranger Bn about as far south as you could go. Mail rarely got to him, so again, I numbered the daily letters, sending pictures of the girls, and haunted the mailbox for any response. His letters were read repeatedly and diligently inspected for any hint as to his well-being.

At the beginning of that year, the dean of Arkansas Tech University asked if I would be the cheerleader sponsor and coach for the Tech team. It would entail evaluating one practice a week, driving the school van, taking the team to football games, and generally keeping them out of trouble. Adele agreed to keep the grandchildren in the dorm apartment when I had to drive to away games. As someone who grew up being involved, it was a natural transition wherever we were. Russellville was no exception. Because of my experience as head cheerleader at the University of Arkansas, it was something I really enjoyed doing, so I agreed. The small salary was also appreciated.

The team was a dynamic group of young men and women who worked hard to be the best they could be. We only had about four games far enough away to make us late returning. The girls would spend the night with Adele as would I when we returned late.

Unbeknownst to me, Adele told Cheryl who was so obviously her favorite, that I was out with "friends," and she had to keep the girls so they wouldn't be left alone. Why she would keep putting such poisonous thoughts in a little girl's mind I have never understood. Cheryl was an adult before we knew of the unbelievable stories she was told as a little one. I can only think Adele had an illness of some sort to make her act so maliciously. At first I thought the girls must have misunderstood her when they would say things. As the year grew on, I realized Adele had a side kept hidden from most. She was a talented, fun person, but it didn't take more than that year to make me realize I could never confide in her about anything, and the less said and the less time we were there, the better for us all.

One weekend I had invited her to come for dinner and had spent the week's food allowance on ingredients for a big meal, thinking we could have leftovers for a week. The ham came out beautifully as did the other dishes. The girls were excited to set the table for company and added their own special touches. The time for her arrival came and went. We waited thirty minutes and then called to check, worried she may be ill or had car trouble. She answered and said she had decided not to come as another housemother had invited her to a movie. What do you say to that? Again I used Daddy's advice, so I gritted my teeth, smiled, and said, "Oh that's okay. Have a great time!"

We did not invite her again. I got the message the first time.

For Easter, she gave me two big stuffed rabbits and told me to put them in the girls' Easter baskets from the Easter Bunny. I did so, and they loved them. A week later, we had driven to Green Forest, Arkansas, and picked up my grandfather, Fred Hoback, for a few days' visit. George's aunt Mimi and uncle Curt, the ones we visited in Panama, had retired from the army and were living in Arkansas. They had a party barge they wanted to share with us. Grandpa was delighted at a chance to fish in Lake Dardanelle. He had taught me to cane fish when I was a very little girl, so for him to show my girls the same was to be a real memory. However, the memory we brought home was not of cane fishing. Aunt Mimi was Adele's big sister, so there was a certain amount of jealously there on

Adele's part. As we neared the middle of the lake, thoroughly enjoying the beautiful day, a thunderstorm moved quickly into the area being lead by a horrific wind. The party barge began to buck and sway with the high waves. George's Special Ops uncle Curt, with great effort, got us near the shore where we could tie to trees in the water and ride out the storm. We were all sitting there thankful to be in an upright boat and casually visiting when out of the blue Adele turned to the girls and asked how they liked the rabbits she had given them.

Thinking she had perhaps forgotten what she told me and my mind racing I said, "Oh, the Easter Bunny brought them beautiful rabbits they love." The girls agreed, gushing about the rabbits. Adele's eyes tightened as she looked at me and said, "That's nice but what about the two I gave you to give the girls?" This was no lapse of memory! Doing the smile with clenched-teeth thing again, I told her I couldn't imagine, but she must have hidden them so well they couldn't be found." On her anti-Vonda list she mentally marked another minus ten, and I mentally gave her a plus ten for meanness.

A different sort of fear occurred one late afternoon. A young man supposedly selling educational resource books knocked on the door. I kept the storm door locked asking to see his ID. It was a picture of someone else, so I said I wasn't interested. As I started closing the door he asked if he could speak to my husband. I told him no, he was napping. He did leave, and I watched him from the window as he walked to the end of the block not stopping at any other house. When you are alone with children to protect, the suspicious gene kicks in with a vengeance. I called the neighbor across street who was a retired army major who listened intently to my story and immediately thereafter his car pulled out of his drive.

He picked the young man up a block away, told him to get in, and drove him toward the police station. He passed a patrol car, so he stopped and explained. There was a Blue Lake law in Arkansas prohibiting door-to-door solicitation. They escorted the young man to the city limits and told him to go home, wherever that was. It turned out he was with a group of people trying to sell books that weren't even published and were only trying the middle house in each block. Before I heard the entire story, the night was spent with the loaded shotgun under my bed (safety on of course) and one ear always on every creak and crack of the settling house.

That summer we began spending weekdays at the lake house with Mother and Daddy. We would drive to Russellville on the weekends to do laundry as the lake house didn't have a washer or dryer yet. We went to church in Russellville, the girls to Sunday school, but left for the lake right afterward.

I had a long visit with our minister discussing the obvious mean spiritedness of Adele, flipped with charming fun the next day. It was so sad not to be able to love her as I would have liked. I simply didn't trust her one bit. Her friends would make strange statements that told me she would say anything to be perceived as a long-suffering mother-in-law. All of those I ignored, but found I loved Adele for one reason: she was the mother of the man I loved.

As the years went by, I did my best to overwhelm her with kindness and cater to her needs and desires. She was hard-pressed to make it appear anything but that.

My mother and her sisters had hypoglycemia. It is a condition that is the opposite of diabetes. Too much sugar in the blood makes one sleepy, and if it really spikes, it can cause a coma. The sweet tooth I had battled all my life, after I became old enough to care, was causing me to often desire naps. Knowing it was an inherited condition, I spent a day at the Little Rock Air Force Base clinic having a blood test done. I had had nothing to eat for a day before and then drank sugar water for the test. The girls spent that day at the Post Nursery. After spending a boring day of testing, I picked up the girls and headed to Mother and Daddy's. The child care caregiver told me Cheryl was not feeling well and had complained of stomach pains. On the ride back to Mother's, she continued to say it hurt, but she couldn't think of anything she had had to eat that Tara had not had!

By the time we arrived at Mother's North Little Rock house, Cheryl also had a fever. Mother came out to greet us and observed Cheryl's discomfort. She took Tara, and I returned to the base to see a doctor in the emergency room. As Mother, carrying Tara, hurried into the house through the garage she slipped, fell, and hurt her hip. Getting to her feet, she painfully got to her bedroom with Tara, where they spent the evening on the bed together.

The doctor in the emergency room did a blood test, and as he poked around on Cheryl's stomach told me he rarely saw children. The pediatrician was home enjoying a binge as he had just received orders for Vietnam. That did not sit well!

He had poked Cheryl so often the pain could not be pinpointed as she hurt all over her stomach. After four hours, they determined it *might* be appendicitis but didn't have an operating room. They called the Children's Hospital in Little Rock, and they also did not do emergency surgery. St. Vincent's was my next choice, and thankfully they assured us they would await our arrival! I called Mother, who called Daddy to meet us at the hospital. I drove like a bat out of hell through North Little Rock across the Arkansas River bridge separating North Little Rock and Little Rock and headed for the west side of the city and St. Vincent Hospital. About four miles from the hospital, the car began to shutter and shake. Not now! Not now! Having no idea what it was, but worried it would die a mile from the hospital, I whipped into an open gas station laying on the horn. An operator rushed out, popping the hood as I babbled a convoluted story of our dilemmas. He evidently understood "five-year-old," "emergency room," and "hurry" because he did hurry. He said it was the alternator. "Can I make it to St. Vincent?" I asked. He assured me, "You can but don't take it any farther." With that, I put the pedal to the metal and peeled out of the drive. Careening into the emergency room drive a few minutes later, the emergency medical technicians, nurses, and doctor were waiting with a gurney. The doctor took one look at her and stated, "Appendicitis!"

I paced the waiting area, knowing Daddy was en route from the Supreme Court Building.

Thirty minutes later, the doctor came in to tell me they had removed her appendix just in time. It was leaking and about to burst. Daddy arrived as they wheeled her into recovery.

I put two chairs together and slept in her room. As with most small children, she needed tons of hugs and assurances but would heal quickly. Meanwhile Mother was told to stay in bed another day as the crack in her hip needed to be kept immobile. It was a clean break so did heal quickly, and she was back on it within two days. Tara had played quietly in Mother's bed, reading books and napping. It was a miracle!

I discovered a week later, after bringing Cheryl home, that the very same day Cheryl had surgery George had been medivaced in an unconscious state with a very high fever suffering from what turned out to be typhus. He was delirious and unconscious for three days until the fever broke. God doesn't give you more than you can handle, so sometimes he just doesn't let you know about all of it at once.

The car was towed, alternator replaced, and back in service by the time I took Cheryl home. Daddies are the *best*!

Shortly after the bout with typhus, the Vietnamese Rangers and my husband were pinned down on a mountainside. The Vietnamese troops would lose face if George were killed, so I prayed daily and nightly for all their safety knowing the rangers would rather shield him with their bodies than have him killed in their midst. Not only were they pinned down but the battalion had the Viet Cong pinned down on the opposite mountain side.

A bullet caught George in the back of his head, and the first I knew of it was a picture he sent me of a white bandage encircling his head. The bullet had glanced off his skull, not penetrating the brain. Looking back, I wondered if we could have survived even one more traumatic event.

Just before the midpoint of his tour, he called to say he was being sent home for a two-week leave in a new program. In addition to losing weight on the ranger's diet of fish and rice, plus the bout with typhus, he now had a serious infestation of worms in his digestive tract. When he got off the plane, he looked like a skeleton of his former self. I had sent him care packages of "rice-go-withs" like chili, salsa, and any kind of canned food to supplement his meager diet.

During the two weeks at home he had contacted a local doctor about the worms which were quickly dispatched with plain old penicillin. He resumed eating like a starving man, which he was! Those two weeks were like an oasis for us. Tara got to know her Daddy and Cheryl reunited with him. They again had the real thing in place of a picture and voice tapes. For us it was another of the multiple honeymoons army life affords you. Saying goodbye again was another blow to the heart, and that empty spot he left in our lives was more bearable because we planned for the next R & R in Hawaii in May.

As he deplaned in Vietnam, General McCaffrey, deputy commanding general of U.S. Army Vietnam, asked him to again be his senior aide. Not only was the answer a no-brainer, but you just don't say no thanks to a general. George admired General McCaffrey so much he would have been honored to accept the request, no matter where it was. His life seemed to go from rags to riches as he left rice balls for the generals' mess, sleeping in trees to an air-conditioned trailer, and constant vigilance for the enemy to traveling all over the area as General McCaffrey visited troops.

As he was adjusting to his new role, I was going on a crash diet to look my best in Hawaii. I drank gallons of tea out of a quart mason jar, of course, had cereal with skim milk for breakfast, a small salad for lunch, and most nights we had a hamburger party without bread, tomato, and green beans. They were very balanced meals but no frills. By the time R & R came around, I had lost the weight and was ready for the trip to Hawaii.

This time, Tara who was only two, stayed with George's mother and Cheryl with my mother who was finishing up a school year. Being older, Cheryl could go to school with Mother and keep busy in the Home Economics Department.

Cheryl and Tara were both blonde-headed cuties. While Cheryl was with Mother, Mother left her with Daddy for a few minutes one night to run an errand. Cheryl obviously got scared in her little bed in Mother and Daddy's room and went to find her Papaw. He was in his home office, reading appeals when, as he tells it, he looked up to see Cheryl's angelic face framed in tousled long blonde ringlets in a little pink nightgown with her toes peeking underneath. She told him she was checking on him, thinking he might be scared.

Being a very wise man, Daddy sat her on his lap and told her stories and let her chew the gum she found in his desk until Mother returned. He recounted that evening hundreds of times over the years as it touched his heart. Since George's dad had died during his cow year at West Point, mine became the Solomon we all went to for advice. Daddy was the perfect one to be a stand in male influence for my children while their daddy was at war. His calm wisdom and dry humor was the bedrock of the Jones clan.

The date to leave for Hawaii finally arrived, this time with wiser preplanning.

My navy brother, Voland, was stationed in Hawaii; so I planned to stay with them one night, meet George the next day, and go to Kauai for two days. We planned to return to Oahu for the final days of his R & R.

The meeting was much like the first, practically swooning in anticipation only this time in my own clothes. The things you want to do and say are censored by decorum, so with self-control slipping more by the minute, we managed to get to Kauai without creating a scene or getting arrested for inappropriate display of affection.

The first dinner in Kauai was an eye-opener. After months of hamburger patties and green beans, the thought of a steak and lobster took my breath away. George on the other hand was tired of the nightly surf and turf in the generals' mess. My vision did become a reality the first night, but after that we tried local specialties.

We toured the island, even renting a motor cycle one day. It was gorgeous. Our friends, Rick and Patti Shinseki, were from the island, and Patti's Dad had developed the famous passion fruit pie we heard about all over the island. We even looked at land thinking how wonderful to own a piece of paradise.

We returned to Oahu and squeezed every second of togetherness out of the remaining days. Voland invited us to dinner in the Officer's Wardroom on his ship, but we declined which we have forever regretted.

When we first dated, I found myself touching him even with fingertips just to feel his nearness. It was a habit that certainly was in evidence that week and even today, riding in a car the hand reaches out just to touch.

There is something about a separation for war that is different from other less menacing separations. Everything intensifies including fear, trust in God, prayers, life, deep yearning in the heart for the one absent. The nightly letters continued, and the calendar countdown was always so many days and a wake up.

The secret survival techniques I used was to immerse myself in something. Crafts, teaching, learning something new, reading, whatever presented itself was what I did. The girls and their activities and the weekly trips to the lake house were a big part of every week. Every wife handles separation differently, but my technique was to keep busy.

As we left Russellville after church with the car packed, the routine was to stop halfway at McDonald's. The girls ate Happy Meals in the car as the second half of the drive was on a two-lane road. Every Sunday, without fail, they both had to potty at the same place Cheryl had always had to stop before. We pass by now and look for the totally dead spot by the road.

The lake house was still being built by Mother and Daddy. The same washtub was put in the yard to heat water by the sun. The girls took turns being first in the bath water.

The couple next door were weekenders who had girls the same age as ours. The four girls wore a path between the properties, spending countless hours serving tea with sand sugar, swinging on a tire swing, and eating tomatoes straight from the vine in Mother's huge garden. Now our children's children play together proving that even military families can have continuity.

On one rainy day, Mother called the girls into the kitchen, and they spent the entire afternoon making and decorating Barbie hats out of styrofoam cups put in the microwave. When nuked, they melted just enough to fit Barbie's head. Each one turned out differently, and the girls had a blast decorating them with colors, glue, and trims from Mother's sewing box.

Finally, the long year was over, and the family reunited again. A few more scars, both physical and mental were chalked up.

I was beginning to form definite ideas about priorities. Number one was God, and after Him came George, then the children, the immediate extended family, and then the army extended family. The last two could be flip-flopped depending on the occasion but never the first three. So often, I saw women who forgot they married their husbands and loved him before the children came along. Some had trouble with the admonition to leave thy mother and father and cleave to thy spouse. I loved my parents and brothers dearly, but they were third on the consideration list. The other big was trust. Men who spend most of their career away from their family must be able to trust you will be faithful. If not, the focus is not on surviving day to day, but on you back home.

After thirty-four years of army life, George is just now hearing of some of the events that occurred while he was away. They can't fix problems when they are far away and why worry them about things you have already taken care of. Stepping up to the plate and taking those problems on one by one is what makes an army wife survive. After all, why would you share those things that only cause worry? It might make you appear a martyr, a helpless female, or one who is totally indecisive. The only things I pretend to be helpless about are outdoor grilling and opening wine.

8 | Erlangen, Germany
"The European Experience"

OUR NEXT ASSIGNMENT caused extreme excitement in our home and extended family. George was to be assigned to Second Battalion Forty-sixth Infantry in Erlangen, Germany. I was thrilled at the prospect of living in Europe. George had been there as a West Point Cadet but dare I say that experience and moving with a wife and kids could hardly be compared.

I scrambled for winter clothes for the girls, making many of them. *Cheryl's traveling outfit was perfect,* I thought. I made her a long sleeve navy dress with a matching cape to wear over tights. She thought she looked very grown up. Unfortunately, the darling outfit wasn't wool; it should have been as she ended up being very cold.

We drove to Georgia where it was 110 degrees in the shade, then on to New Jersey where we shipped the car at Bayonne, New Jersey, shuttling to a guesthouse to spend the night, then flew into Frankfurt. The many hours on the long flight had our usually well-behaved daughters fidgeting and fussy. They each had a premade box of "keep busy" items. Coloring books and new crayolas, blunt scissors, a pad of paper, straws to build things, a deck of cards to build with, an Etch-a-Sketch, socks to make puppets, and other survival gear. Most of it worked fairly well as we doled it out as interest waned in the current activity. As the evening wore on, they were obviously ready for sleep. We made a pallet at our feet where they both went immediately asleep, knowing protective parents sat directly above them.

We arrived at the Frankfurt Airport where we were met by Lieutenant Larry Lessie who drove us the few hours to Erlangen.

The town of Erlangen was home to Siemens Headquarters and the University of Erlangen. It was a charming town in North Bavaria where most of the military housing was outside the fenced post. The temporary quarters assigned to us were up four flights of stairs in what obviously had been maids' quarters in times long past. The top floor consisted of an entrance into a long, narrow living room off which there were two baths. One housed the toilets and sinks and the other sinks and a huge tub. The bathrooms opened into the living room. The kitchen and dining room were next opposite each other at the beginning of a very long hallway. The rest of the way down that hallway were ten bedrooms: five on one side and five on the other. We discovered bunk beds in one room, so the girls got that one, and we took the one across from them furnished with a bed and dresser. One of the bedrooms obviously was a storage room for excess mattresses. We asked if they might be used and were given a go-ahead. The four of us tugged and pulled, padding the floor wall to wall with mattresses. The girls loved it as it was a jumping, tumbling, somersaulting room. Some of them were three deep, making a great jump off height.

The ceiling slanted, it was an attic after all, so George kept bumping his head every time he stood from the couch.

We once had a visitor who arrived unexpectedly, trapping me in the bathroom having a leisurely bath. As he and George visited, I tried not to splash, quietly finishing my bath and sitting there as the water got colder and colder. Leaving was *not* an option as a towel just wasn't enough coverage. George kept trying to work him toward the door, but he was not inclined to take a hint. George kept repeating, "We don't want to keep you." Finally he departed, and I was rescued sporting a blue pruned body but extremely clean.

We had arrived in October, so that Christmas we still lived in temporary quarters. A fellow soldier lent us an old Volkswagen, so we did have transportation. Not knowing that overseas, if you see something for Christmas in October, you'd better get it because things go incredibly fast, since a limited number of everything was shipped; I had not prepared. I had picked up a few things for the girls, planning to go with George to do the major shopping. One day turned into a week, and before we knew it, it was Christmas Eve. We put up a Charlie Brown tree with a few decorations, and I waited for George to get home to rush to the PX to get the main gifts. He was in a helicopter reconnoitering with Colonel Schenck, who hadn't a clue he was holding up Christmas, so they didn't return until 7:00 p.m., long after the PX closed. A modern cell phone would have saved the day.

We did the best we could in keeping traditions we had established, such as reading the Christmas Story in the Book of Luke and setting out cookies and milk for Santa. The meager gifts were divided equally on opposite sides of the tree.

The next morning at the crack of dawn, Cheryl came running into our room shouting that Santa had come. She began listing her gifts which included everything from under both sides of the tree but one item. She stated, "And Tara got a pully." I had made a pillowcase for a new pillow, and that had been on Tara's side. We had a bit of difficulty explaining that part of the list was obviously for a younger girl.

The laundry room was in the basement where several washer and dryers were lined against two of the four walls with an adjoining room filled with rows of clotheslines. We were assigned wash days, and the machines and lines were always full. The trek up and down four flights of stairs was great exercise for me, but a climb up and down Mount Everest for the short legs of the little girls.

In February, we moved into the permanent quarters at 162 Schenck Strasse, a few apartment buildings up the street. It was an older building which housed enlisted personnel with officers being slowly housed there instead. We were the first officer family, so there was no doubt a lot of speculation about us. Sergeant Major and Master Sergeant Lennon lived on the first floor. They had no children. On day one, as Cheryl was helping Barbie leap from the second-story window to the small white-fenced front yard, Tara was screeching with delight as Barbie did a head dive in the shrubbery. The Lennons' window swung open, and a very terse reminder was given to the girls that others lived in the area. Barbie was taken back upstairs where her wild leaps were forever put on hold. The girls were marched downstairs to apologize and in the effort became a soft spot in Mary Lennon's heart.

During the Barbie adventure, George and I were upstairs checking into quarters. The first thing we noticed was the big stains on the area rug. The hesitant explanation was that the previous occupants' baby was potty trained by moving the potty chair from room to room. Great! We asked them to remove the rug as it was only room size. When we checked the kitchen, the stove burner units had been spray painted silver to cover grease and who knows what else. Remembering the Fort Bragg white-glove inspection, I caulked it up to the German cleaning team equivalent of stripped wires.

The front door opened off the second floor landing into a living room. A waist-high divider separated the living room from the dining room, a small kitchen off that, and behind a frosted glass door in the living room was a short hallway off of which lay three bedrooms and a bath.

For this move, we brought very little in the way of decoration, thinking it would give us more poundage to bring back things we found in Europe. Every move had weight limits depending on rank and where one was stationed.

The first thing we purchased was a Rya rug in 1970's modern high-pile design. George painted the same design on a big piece of plywood that became our focal point in the living room. The mixture of quartermaster furniture was very interesting. Mary Lennon told me how to switch furniture to get things to match. By the time the next people moved, we had a few things to match and eventually, we had all living room chairs to match and upgraded some of our older pieces. Obviously much of what we ended up with had probably originally been in our apartment.

The girls had Swedish bunk beds with storage drawers underneath that we purchased at the PX. The Winnie the Pooh bed spreads and curtains we ordered from Sears added some color to their room. I used one of the mattress cartons to fashion a large tree with spreading limbs. It was painted a tree brown with green leaves and attached to the wall with the limbs attached to the ceiling at different points. A bird sat on one limb and stuffed Pooh sat in the crook of the trunk and limb. The girls loved it.

We set up a working budget since everything was cash. A folder was divided into categories like food, gas, presents, entertainment, clothes, etc. Every month, we put x amount of dollars in each envelope, and that was it. A certain sum was put in the credit union for a car when we left. Often money was moved from folder to folder to make ends meet.

Germany was probably the most interesting assignment considering the personalities and characters in the units. George was the battalion operation officer for a year and a half, then company commander of C Company First Battalion Fortieth Infantry. By then, the Second Battalion designation had been changed to First Battalion with the unit colors arriving from Vietnam as part of the drawdown and redesignation of units.

The First Battalion commander was only there two months, so we didn't know him well. The second one was Rodger Schenck and his wife, Misayo. Misayo's sister, called Auntie by us all, lived with them. The Schencks were a warm, giving couple who would call us all and say, "Come over on Saturday. The pantry is full of hot dogs and hamburger buns. We'll grill out. Bring the girls." There never seemed to be too many people at their quarters; the hospitality was so warm. Auntie did much of the cooking and sewing, even making gifts for our children. The brigade commander at the time was a very intelligent and eloquent man who had a problem controlling his alcohol consumption. The stories about his escapades flew around our little Peyton Place like wild fire. His wife pulled him from the Officers' Club on more than one occasion, and he was so hung over at his change of command he could hardly stand thus his trooping the line was cancelled.

In those days, it took a hardy bunch to stay in the army. It was filled with men who had strange ideas and unhealthy habits, to put it mildly. Some of the wives displayed a side I had not even read about in my protected formative years.

Rumors ran rampant, and one never did anything the entire post didn't know about the next day.

One drunk, passed-out lieutenant's wife was found in a bedroom with two troops. Another lieutenant's wife had a list of conquests often conquered in unique environments such as on the O' Club back room pool table. Another wife sported incredibly tight leather pants that were held together on the sides of each leg with leather thongs, allowing a good three inches of flesh to show from waist to ankle. She did have the body for them but not the decorum.

One wife was so clean-minded she wasn't seen until noon because all morning she was on her hands and knees scrubbing floors under all appliances and furniture.

When the men were in the field, several wives could be found hanging out in the O' Club bar and NOT to have a friendly drink with the girls.

After the tippling brigade commander left, a new one came in. He was most interesting and his wife very "old army." Misayo picked up an enlisted girl walking to the commissary from off post, took her to the commissary, waited, and took her home. It was a lovely gift of time and caring. She was called on the carpet by the colonel's wife and reprimanded for picking up an enlisted wife! Amazing! We've come a long way, baby.

The next battalion commander had an unusual name and a more unusual wife. George was deep into his third company command when she called one night to strongly suggest I attend a company commander's wives' class to be held in Birchesgarten. I assured her I should be delighted if the trip was paid for because even though it was his third company never have I thought I had all the answers. The trip was out of the question if we had to foot the bill as our finances were literally planned to the penny. Her inference was obviously that I needed *lots* of help since the other company commander wives weren't offered the opportunity. The class never developed beyond the planning stages.

At one of the monthly wives' coffee, she entered the room late, looked around, headed straight for me, and asked me to move since the chair I occupied fit her perfectly. I assured her it would be my pleasure because I could sit in the chair two down just like it! I know we can sometimes dislike another for no apparent reason, but several of us truly felt singled out. Some of the girls with their husbands were called on the carpet in front of the commanding officer's desk on a Sunday to be reprimanded for something the commanding officer's wife herself had done, not the reprimanded crew. Her husband either had believed everything she said or found it easier to respond to her accusations than investigate her allegations. We learned years later that she was mentally ill which answered many of our questions.

It must be said that from each of these women I learned a great deal, how to and how *not* to do things.

The opportunity to live in another country, not just visit, is priceless. Many people liked to come visit, which we encouraged.

Mother and Daddy came for a week which was just a week after their house in North Little Rock was struck by lightning and burned. The only clothes not damaged were the ones packed for the trip to see us. Daddy would still be in Germany reading everything in old castles, old towns, cathedrals, and museums if we hadn't dragged him from place to place. My Baptist mother had her first wine! German local wine often tastes like fresh squeezed grapes, so she was hooked. I took them to Paris and had a blast watching them enjoy the city. The taxi ride, accomplished mostly on two wheels and horn blaring, was another highlight.

We truly enjoyed showing them around! The last night they were there, I prepared a special meal including fresh whole green beans wrapped in bacon. They had been prepared earlier then frozen so they had to be separated. As the knife was doing the separating, it slipped and cut my finger very badly. We wrapped it in a towel and drove the short distance to the emergency room. The doctor on duty was the one no one wanted to see because he was in Germany for only two reasons, skiing and sightseeing. He put my hand in a bowl of ice water and left for twenty minutes to take a phone call. When he came back, he was amazed there was more blood than water in the bowl, so he decided a few stitches might be in order.

The scar and lack of feeling from several nerves is with me still. I do not remember him with kindness. When Mother and Daddy left, I felt bereft. Their visit had been a constant joy.

Another company commander's wife, Ilsa Chamberlain, and I planned a trip to Italy. If we waited for our husbands, we would doubtless see little of Europe. George's mother and sixteen-year-old female cousin, Jeffery Ellis, came for a month visit; so the timing for an Italian adventure seemed right. Ilsa's car was wrecked shortly before our departure date, so she borrowed a lieutenant's yellow VW bug for the journey. Ilsa and her husband, Turk, were first generation German Americans; so her fluent German was a real plus. We loaded up the Firebird with Mother Crocker, Jeffrey, Tara, Cheryl, and me plus luggage for all. Caravanning behind Ilsa with her two children in the yellow bug, we left Erlangen in our dust.

Our route took us through the Brenner Pass where we stopped for a coffee break. With my limited German, learned in a two-week German course, I asked for a coffee with cream. What I got was a demitasse cup of semiliquid coffee paste with a hint of milk. It was wonderfully full of flavor, but I have never been so wide awake.

The amazing thing about Europe is how close countries are together. One can depart one morning and be in another country that afternoon.

We arrived in Vicenza and immediately got totally lost. We obviously looked lost because a carload of GIs pulled up to ask if we needed help. *Absolutely*! Today we might have hesitated.

Not only did they lead us to our hotel but made sure we weren't overcharged and gave us some great advice about the local area. Angels of mercy come in all forms. We could not have been more grateful!

We soon realized we were in a hotel over a boccie ball alley—akin to our bowling alley. The one bathroom at the end of the hallway was one big room. When you took a shower, if you weren't careful, the toilet paper got soaked. There was no shower curtain or room division of any kind.

As drivers, Isla and I we were very tired, but everyone else was rearing to go. We compromised by going downstairs to eat and calling it a night. Even the boccie balls slamming into walls didn't keep us up.

The next day, we found the train station and loaded up for a short trip to Venice. All four children loved the train ride!

Ilsa and I had read the guide books' advice on seeing Venice on the cheap. We decided to take the fast boats called Vaporettos to the shopping area. One area between two bridges was reported the area for bargaining, but George's mother was determined to shop elsewhere. We let her lead, do her shopping, then we retraced our steps to the bargain area. We found many great items at reasonable prices, which left Mother Crocker fuming she had been "taken" at her selected shopping area. We could not have agreed more, but judicially didn't say so.

To be in Venice and not take a gondola ride would not have occurred to us, so we all piled into one for the romantic ride of which we had all read. The gondolier suggested no one touch the water as it was filthy. We saw many interesting things floating in it so were not even remotely tempted to trail a finger. Unfortunately, my memory of Venice's romantic gondola ride is with my mother-in-law. Not so romantic.

We arranged for Mother Crocker and Jeffrey to go to Paris for a few days, then later to Spain, as they were so close. They had a fabulous time but came back with a terrific story of checking into a hotel in Spain. The manager asked Mother Crocker to step into his office. She was lectured about the hotel's fine reputation, the decorum expected of all guest, and that certain behaviors were simply *not* permitted! Totally at sea, Mother Crocker asked, "What are you talking about? Those are the very reasons we chose this hotel." The manager sputtered something about a woman of her age trying to have a young man stay with her.

Mother Crocker, smothering a laugh, asked him to wait a moment. She went to get Jeffrey who was so obviously a girl, no words needed to be said to accept. "Sir, this is Jeffrey." For the rest of their stay, they had excellent service.

We took them to the usual places we took all our guests, castle tours, Rothenberg, Nuremberg for Nuremberger Brat, and on and on.

They returned to the United States, and we went on with our usual routine.

My younger brother, Lyn, came by himself for a visit. We had so much fun sharing Germany with him. During a stroll through Nuremberg, he saw a violin in a shop and mentioned how he would love to have one.

Of us three children, Lyn got all the musical talent rolled into one person. When I sang in the church choir as a youth, the director asked me to just lip-synch the songs, which I did with vigor. Lyn's talent was admired by us all. He played the piano, guitar, and flute, wrote songs and sang but was best known for his harmonica prowess. He has been sponsored by Hohner Harmonica for years.

For his birthday that year, we bought the violin he had so admired and sent it to him. He played it in public two weeks later!

One evening I took him to a local gasthaus in Erlangen. We were sitting in a booth made of a giant wine keg cut in half, enjoying the great German beer when a group of University of Erlangen students shoved into our booth, trapping us against the back wall. This was common practice in

Europe, the sharing of tables, so we weren't offended in any way but smiled at them and continued our discussion. My German was not at all fluent, but I picked up enough to know we were being discussed in a less-than-flattering light. When our beer was finished, I summoned all my German and smiling tauntly asked them in German if we could please be excused. They quit talking and quickly slid out of the booth to let us pass. I seriously doubt it bothered them at all that we might have understood their conversation, but I felt better.

After World War II all Germans had to take English, so all of them of a certain age certainly knew some English. I tried very hard to use German when dealing with Germans, as it was their country, and it only seemed right to use the local language, much like I expect foreign visitors to try to use English in our country. In most exchanges, the local person would quickly change to English as my German with a southern accent was probably horrid. The effort to try to use German was appreciated, however.

Lyn returned to the States, and we really missed him. Living in a foreign country enhances the pleasure of spending time with family.

My older brother, Navy Captain James Voland Jones, known to family as Voland but to everyone else as Jim, his wife, Penny, and children, Jay and Laura, came through Erlangen on their way from India back to the States. Voland had been stationed in India for a year, attending the Indian War College.

They arrived on a train at the height of the European energy crisis. On Sundays no motor vehicles but taxis were allowed on the streets. The streets were deserted which was fabulous for walking around but not for retrieving visiting relatives. A taxi was called for them, and they managed to get to our quarters.

I had selected new chenille bedspreads for the guest bedroom. Penny laid her black coat on it only to realize too late that chenille sheds. I was mortified, and Penny had been traveling for days with two small children, so she had a meltdown. She no doubt doesn't still have the coat but wherever it is, it probably still has lint on it! It was that bad!

We took them to a gasthaus for dinner, dragged them to Cheryl's music recital at school and, as we did everyone, took them to the incredible walled city of Rothenburg ob de Tauber. We dressed the cousins in the girls' ski clothes as it was very cold in Germany compared to India.

We had eaten breakfast but hadn't thought about lunch as we had eaten late. Our plan was to stop at a café in the old city for a pastry and drink early afternoon then dinner at the gasthaus.

Everyone seemed to be starving about two, so we stopped at a café. The muffins were extremely expensive and totally out of our budget, but we got one for everyone but us, then continued with the tour. Looking back, it would have been kinder if we had done a quick car tour of the Erlangen area, but we wanted to share as much of Germany as possible in the short time allowed. What we managed to do was exhaust an already-exhausted family. It is to be hoped that my brother and sister-in-law have forgiven us long ago. We did love their visit and seeing our adorable nephew and niece was certainly an added bonus as it would be several more years before seeing them again.

Workers in Germany would arrive at job sites on post with tools and cases of beer. Before noon, half of the beer would be gone, and not one of the beers would have been chilled. We were amazed.

The beer man would deliver beer by the case to your quarters which was a most helpful service when anyone had a party.

The wine, as Mother discovered, was wonderful. The essence of the grape captured so well, Mother thought it was like grape juice. Yes, it was, only fermented.

George had a week of leave, so we decided to go to Garmisch and take advantage of an Army Learn to Ski Week. We joined up with another Arkansas couple, Betty and Dave Hendricks, for this sports adventure. Betty Hendricks, remember, had been my next-door neighbor when I was four. Who would have thought we'd reconnect years later in a foreign country. The week was amazing in many ways.

The wooden skis were way over our heads with steel edges screwed into the wood in sections. The boots were ankle-top leather lace-up beauties guaranteed to freeze your toes. Being fairly athletic, it was appalling to literally fall into my class as I made it off the T-bar lift. George had "Frau Bluker," who was determined to have her class ski better than any other. I had an Austrian instructor, who was equally competitive and his instructions of "up and down" still ring across the years. The girls were in child care, playing in the snow and having a ball. We were black and blue everywhere after the first day but took the girls sledding anyway before dinner. It was such a deal since breakfast and dinner came with the classes all at a ridiculously low price.

On the second day, we were back in the routine, ride up, fall off, get up, fall into class, get up, ski a short distance, fall, get up. You get the picture.

At lunch I couldn't find George or his class. They kept announcing a Mrs. Johnson needed to come to the aide station. I was feeling really sorry for her. Assuming his class had come in for lunch at a different time, we continued with the afternoon torture session. After class, we found his class but no George. I asked his instructor "Sunny" and was told they had paged me all day. It seems I was Mrs. Johnson!

George had gone up the T-bar with a woman who slid off her side of the T-bar, taking the bar with both of them as they hit the snow. The T-bar, spiraling from under them, hit George in the lip knocking out his two front teeth at the gum line. He had been at the base dentist most of the afternoon thinking, of course, that I was so callous and uncaring I continued skiing with my class. Poor guy was in agony. Not only were we black and blue all over, but now he had a fat lip and no front teeth. They put stainless steel temps on his teeth until we could return to Erlangen and get permanent caps.

Macho guy spent a horrible night trying to sleep through pain but braved it the next day meeting Sunny and his class on the slopes. What a trooper!

We learned to ski well enough to get down the slope, but on one run we went down a slope that literally dropped off twenty feet or so, requiring the skier to make a hard left turn. As a beginner, it scared me so badly that when I barely made the turn to save myself, my speed had picked up and to stop I ran into a fence, sat down with head between my knees, and tried not to throw up.

Looking back, it was no doubt the bunny slope!

The next morning, we got up to discover the car was completely covered in snow. At least when we fell, it was softer.

We returned to Erlangen bruised, George toothless, and in love with skiing.

A few days later, George was standing on a tank addressing the troops and spit out his front caps in front of the men. He ignored them and continued with his speech. Someone returned them after his lecture. It was only a few more weeks before he got new front teeth permanently glued in.

The hummel man was an elderly red-nosed German darling who came door-to-door with a suitcase full of hummels to sell to the Americans. The prices were much cheaper than even the PX, so he most likely went home daily with an empty suitcase. Mother Crocker made his day when he stopped during her visit.

We enjoyed participating in Volksmarches which were races or walks along a set path through the woods. Germans love to wander along the many paths through the woods, especially on the weekends. Occasionally they would organize a Volksmarch where participants could receive a medal of some sort just by finishing the route.

After one of these, we stopped at a gasthaus to have hot chocolate with the girls. We waited and waited and waited. Others were served who had come in after us, so obviously either we were *not* going to be served or the waiter was blind. We decided he wasn't blind so eventually, we got up and left. Fortunately, it was the only experience we had of not being served because we were Americans.

Cheryl was in kindergarten on our first year in Germany, and Tara was in preschool in Herzogenaurach. Herzogenaurach was the headquarters for Adidas and Puma shoes, so we drove there when we needed new running shoes.

To get to the preschool, all the little ones would line up on the sidewalk in front of our quarters to catch the bus. We moms would take turns riding to and from school. Tara would arrive home at noon sound asleep with her teddy bear clutched in her arms.

Today the thought of sending a little one that far on a bus in a foreign country is frightening.

The neighbors on a forty-five-degree angle behind us were often better than TV. The husband was a noncommissioned officer (NCO), his wife, a Native American, and both had a trigger temper. One night we heard screaming, loud clangs, and crashes. We opened the dining room sash window to discover the cause. The wife was loudly cussing between shrieks and throwing pots, pans, and all unattached kitchenware at her dodging, raging husband. We looked around and found all our neighbors in all twelve apartments leaning out the windows for a better look. The sergeant noticed them too and quickly drew the shades. Now we all had a silhouette fight to watch, but the voices were clearly audible. This happened several times a month, and we always thought he would appear with at least bandages, but he never did. He was either very agile, or she had very bad aim.

Susan and Jack Mountcastle from Richmond, Virginia lived, in the next stairwell. Susan was an accomplished artist. They were on the first floor, and we were on the second. Susan called me one day, trying hard not to laugh. Her boys, Russell and Clayborne, were near the age of our girls. Our four children were with several other young ones under Susan's kitchen window. They, no doubt, thought they were in a secret spot because they were saying every bad word they had ever heard. They would take turns saying one, giggle, say another, giggle some more. We called them in and discussed why some words aren't spoken. Busted!

We traded children with the Mountcastles to go on leave childless. Europeans didn't, as a rule, take their children on vacation; so to take them was often difficult. We kept Russell and Clay and had such a good time with them; it was a joy to trade. We planned to go north on one trip via a space available flight. The air force and army offered available seats on unfilled flights. One would sign up, and it went in order of sign up. Our flight didn't materialize for two days, so we drove back to Erlangen from Frankfurt, traded winter clothes for summer, got the girls, and went south. We had gone to Spain once before driving through France. On that trip, we had extra gas tanks on the trunk hood and bags of canned food to help us truly do Europe on five dollars a day.

In Paris we had trouble getting Cheryl out of the Louvre. She was enthralled.

I kept my mouth shut and let George do all the talking since his French was excellent with no accent.

As we went over the Pyrenees into Spain, we stopped for fresh cherries. At noon every day we would buy a loaf of fresh bread and a liter of Coke and head for the local park. We had canned meat for sandwiches supplemented with local buys.

Breakfast usually came with the hotel; in France it was fabulous coffee and the freshest of bread or rolls.

Lunch was our picnic, and dinner was something simple like an omelet.

At lunch one day, I took the girls to the bathroom at the local park. It was a small rock building housing a concrete floor with a hole in the center. Two foot pads were on either side of the hole. I had to place my feet on the foot pads while holding each girl over the hole. Don't touch anything was our motto. We were constantly amazed at the variety of bathroom facilities.

We went through a big box of sanitary wipes and could write an article about the various toilet paper offerings in Europe.

Finally arriving in Spain, we settled into our hotel on Costa Brava.

We had a wonderful week exploring the area and seeing our first bull fight.

We were a bit disconcerted to see how many Germans were there. None of them had their children but were typically pushy and rude. We felt like we hadn't gotten far from Erlangen.

When we returned, we drove through France, then Italy. Tara had a touch of food poisoning so often couldn't wait for the infrequent potty stops. We left a string of soiled panties in garbage cans along the way.

We spent one night in Milan where we forked out the most money for a hotel. The traffic was horrendous with street names changing every block. I would find one street on the map, but we would be three names ahead by then. There was much yelling in the car. The two, three, and four lanes of traffic would become six with cars cramming together all at a fast pace. It was nerve-racking.

For dinner, we drove around for a few blocks finally deciding on a Pizzeria. Inside one could point at a huge array of toppings, and the pizza would be made to order. We were in a fairly well-lit alley but worried about the Firebird's safety.

Before our pizza was served, an honest-to-goodness godfather with entourage walked in the door. We tried hard not to stare! He, of course, was served first with much scraping and bowing. We were not about to complain about our order being delayed. The pizza was worth the wait as it was the best we have ever had.

At the hotel, they wanted to put us on different floors from the girls. We were naturally appalled, so the girls slept on pallets by our bed.

Coming back to Germany, we swung through a part of Switzerland. It was breathtakingly beautiful. The Alps were awesome.

I had lamb shish kebabs for a noon meal that had bay leaf between each piece. It was overwhelmingly bay leaf. It took years for me to try lamb again. Otherwise, the food was outstanding!

We arrived back in Germany and back to the usual routine. A year later, we again vacationed in Spain after our foiled trip north.

This time we took a plane to Madrid, taxi to the railroad station, and a bullet train from Madrid to Rota, Spain. Not being familiar with bullet trains, we had envisioned a chance to buy a snack for lunch, but at every stop the train slowed down enough for people to dash on and off but never time to disembark. A very generous young couple with a bulging picnic basket shared their bread and cheese with us. It was a very kind act but also kept the whining down from our set so they may have had ulterior motives. We arrived in Rota where the weather was beautiful and balmy. Renting a Fiat 500 which sounded like a sewing machine, we crammed everything in heading north toward Fuengirola on Costa del Sol where we had reservations.

The hotel was wonderful, but best of all it was right on the beach.

As usual, we were the only ones there with children. The first dinner seating was at 8:00 p.m., so because of the children we were often the first there. We had a table we kept the entire week with the wine being corked for the next meal.

We spent every day at the beach, then exploring, and one day going to a bull fight.

The girls were dressed for dinner every night. One evening a group of English tourist had descended on the hotel and were milling around the lobby before dinner. Several older ladies came up to us and said to the girls, "What a darling party frock. Did your mummy get it for you?" The girls practically did a curtsy, their blonde curls bobbing. The ladies were enchanted. We enjoyed them tremendously the rest of the week as the girls basked in their adoring glances.

We spent a night in Malaga, walking through that delightful town and later Marbella. In Marbella we found more American tourists and huge hotels.

We had lunch one day at a seaside café where we ordered the fresh fish. It arrived on a large serving platter with its eyes staring at us. The girls went ballistic. The waiter whisked it away to return with it headless. Much better.

At dinner in the hotel, the waiter brought the girls aqua con gas or as we know it, club soda. They hated it! To this day they call club soda, Spain water.

Our children were such a rarity in the hotel the wait staff spoiled them unmercifully. If a plate wasn't cleaned, the waiter would cajole them into eating more. For the girls, it was like having several doting uncles.

The idyllic week passed much too quickly. We flew back to Frankfurt, drove to Erlangen, and back to reality.

On one occasion, George and I took the train to West Berlin when he went on army business. The train only ran at night, so one couldn't see East Germany.

All passports had to perfectly match all other documents, or we would be pulled from the train. The papers were checked at every stop the train had to make.

I stayed awake most of the night, looking out the train window at the end of my berth. There were few lights anywhere in the countryside. Even the stations where we stopped had dim lighting. There were no cars on the roads, making it seem surreal.

At each station where we were stopped, I could see uniformed police with high top boots walking up and down by the train. It was really frightening.

When we arrived in Berlin, it was the complete opposite. People and cars were everywhere.

George couldn't fly over East Germany because of his security clearance. The train was considered safer for security reasons.

Looking at the Berlin Wall, I wondered how the East Berlin soldiers really felt watching the hustle and bustle of a thriving economy just a few yards away. It was a trip I shall never forget.

The monthly coffees continued as did local drama.

The young couple in another court were trying to get pregnant, so there was a sly mention of his noon visits home. Are there no secrets?

Suzanne and Bob Steimer were a very charming couple. Suzanne was from France, so George got to practice his French, and I got great French recipes.

Isabella and Ray McMaken were parents of two teenagers who got into the usual mischief, causing even more tongues to wag.

One of George's lieutenant's wives was called on the carpet by the brigade commander's wife for not joining the Officer's Wives Club. They lived off post in a nearby village, she rode the train or hitchhiked into post for coffees, went to University of Erlangen full time, and they were on a strict budget. The OWC dues were an excess they couldn't afford.

George explained this to the brigade commander who knew nothing of his wife's demand. He asked her to apologize to the young wife. She did go out to visit her but never apologized. It amazes me we have so many of those young wives who stayed the course but, of course, many did not! It's hard not to believe experiences like this helped push them out the door.

Our stairwell alone was a small "Peyton Place."

The young German wife across the hall was having an affair with the post engineer. He would arrive during lunch, always when her husband was gone, staying an hour or so. The benefit of that was our stairwell got things fixed in a very timely manner.

The Hackenbergs lived downstairs across from the CSM and MS Lennon. They had a precious little girl named Stacey and the biggest, meanest-looking solid black German shepherd we had ever seen. He had been an attack dog, retrained. His eyes were not friendly, so we all kept our distance. They were good friends we really enjoyed.

When they moved out, Greg and Carol Ann Tillit moved in. They had no children, so she adopted mine, even teaching them to knit. Carol Ann was another home economics major, as was I, so we had a lot in common.

The Germans put unwanted items at the curb twice a year. The local paper published the streets and days items would be collected. The night before pickup, the Americans and Arabs drove around those streets, looking for free treasures. The Germans at that time had no resale outlets such as Goodwill or Salvation Army.

Carol Ann and I took the girls and made a run one night. We found a feather comforter, an inlaid sewing machine, a puppet theater, and all kinds of smaller treasures. It was all crammed in the Firebird with the girls curled up in empty corners.

We put the down feathers into twelve pillowcases we had made, sterilizing them in the downstairs laundry. We washed them twice, rinsed four times, then put them in the dryers. Feathers were everywhere! We swept and vacuumed for an hour, but we each had six down pillows!

Carol Ann and I had another brilliant idea. We discovered a wicker factory was going out of business, so we drove up to the village to check it out. We bought a large number of interesting wicker baskets for very little money, thinking we would decorate them and resell for a profit. We did sell most of them, but we weren't sure how profitable the venture proved to be.

One Halloween before the Hackenbergs left, the stairwell decided to have a stairwell trick or treat area. We pooled our candy, making bags for the children. Our upstairs neighbor was tall, thin, and very pale. We made a pseudo coffin for him under the stairs at the entrance. He wore a black suit, whitened his face, blacked his eyes, and rose up moaning every few minutes.

The Hackenbergs taped the German shepherd howling and played it in the laundry room where the dog could be seen pacing back and forth.

A long hall ran under the apartments with rooms for storage on both sides. Each room was fitted with something ghoulish. Our very tall elegant black neighbor on the third floor dressed in all black with day glow bones glued to her clothes. She danced around one of the rooms clanging a chain and moaning.

George had a rubber glove filled with ice water he used to touch the face of small children walking by.

One darkened room had greased macaroni for brains and peeled grapes for eye balls whereby children were enjoined to "feel" and touch the bowl's contents.

We were very popular that night, but most of all we had a blast!

One night during the rampage of the infamous Baader Meinhof Gang, we were sound asleep when a gang member was cornered in our stairwell. The next morning, we were stunned to discover bullet holes outside our front door where the shootout had occurred.

During this tour, I was also the Girl Scout leader for the Junior Girl Scout Troop. We met in the attic of one of the apartment houses. Cheryl and Tara went to the meetings with me where they found the attic spooky.

Skip and Scotty Clarkson were in our company, so I asked Scotty to help me with the troop.

We took the troop camping one weekend. Scotty had not had much camping experience so was a bit nervous about being in the middle of nowhere all night in a tent. Assuring her all was fine, went right out the window when the military police came by to warn us of an escapee who might be in our area. Great! Forget walking to the bathroom in the dark, so we took turns sneaking out the back of the tent trying to urinate soundlessly. We didn't want to scare the girls, but we stayed up most of the night on watch.

Scotty was adorable with long hair she wore in what we called dog ears, dimples, and a great attitude. She looked wonderful after a sleepless night in a tent, and I know the stress was all over me! I looked like I had been up all night worrying about little girls and escapees!

George received orders for Fort Leavenworth, Kansas, to attend the Army Command and Staff College. It was an honor, and we were ready to get back to the States.

Just before leaving, we ordered an open pendulum grandfather clock from a master clock maker who also was a master wood selector and wood carver. We were getting closer to departure when we had to have the clock to ship with our household goods. A call to the elder gentleman carver assured us he would have it ready the next weekend and would love some

American ice cream. We explained ice cream would not make the trip from Erlangen to Wurzburg but asked if we could bring something else. "Ya, whiskey would be nice." So we drove to Wurzburg to his home to retrieve the clock carrying a fifth of whiskey as a gift. His home and shop were nestled beside an old church. Only one room in his home was heated by a gas stove. We were seated in the warmer room and served coffee laced with canned milk. Our host seemed very satisfied with our gift. The clock was fabulous and well worth the wait.

It had at least seven different types of wood which, of course, were different shades. We have treasured it ever since and hope our German clock master had a long and profitable life. His work certainly will last through generations.

The last big shopping trip was to the Nachtmann factory for crystal wine glasses we bought for one dollar each. For retail, they were many, many times that price. These too went into the packing boxes.

Another last minute purchase we made was a wooden serving cart. The removable wheels were cleverly attached with wooden pegs. It has been used ever since.

The German moving company came in to move our items. We only "lost" two things at the other end. One was a stethoscope and the other a small fertility statue my brother, Voland, sent us as a joke, we hoped. The statue flaunted an enormous penis as long as it was tall. It had been hidden on top of the china cabinet because we couldn't imagine where else to put it. We wished the thief many, many children!

We bought the ten bottles of wine we could legally bring back to the States, packing them into our suitcases.

We were off again on another adventure. Kansas, here we come.

9 | Fort Leavenworth, Kansas
"Back to the Midwest but No Cow Birds"

WE FLEW INTO Little Rock loaded with luggage. We spent several days with my parents and George's mom. We called George's uncle Jeff Ellis, who was Mother Crocker's brother and Jeffrey's daddy. He lived in Newport, a small northeast Arkansas town. We wondered if he could get us a good deal on a vehicle. We had sold the Pontiac in Germany before we left. He answered that the "Good Ole Boy System" was still alive and well in the south so, of course, consider it done. Our frugality in Germany resulted in the ability to pay cash for a new car. The girls were getting older, so we thought a station wagon would be in order.

We were all in awe when George returned with the spacious ginger glow brown 1974 Ford Country Square station wagon complete with faux wood paneling and the "special interior." We were ecstatic to have so much room and a new vehicle.

After tearful farewells (again) and my precious mother taking one last picture of us posed by the car, probably cutting off our heads, as she always did, we were off again to Kansas. This time I knew the cowbirds didn't peck our eyes out!

The girls had their activity bag I had made with things to do to make the trip happier for us all. They again had blunt scissors, colored pencils (crayolas were verboten in the new car), plain paper pads, coloring books, sticker books, pipe cleaners to make things, a small doll with clothes, car bingo cards, and anything else I could find. Every new car we owned went through George's pristine phase, so on this first long trip the rule of no food or drink in the car was enforced with gusto. I packed a cooler and bag of snacks we ate only at rest areas and amazingly we survived.

George and a few of his classmates, Howie Kirk and Wes Clark, were below-zone selectees for the Command and General Staff College as captains, not even promotable captains, therefore low men on the housing totem pole. As usual we stayed in transit billets while awaiting quarters. We looked at the few places available on post. One was a remodeled World War II barracks featuring a steel pole in the middle of the living room and three open shelves in the kitchen. We were told cute curtains could be put over the shelves, and the washer and dryer would have to go in the dining area of the living room. No, thank you.

Our next stop was a local real estate agent to look at rentals. We found the perfect place. It was a converted barn on what had been a farm with the original farmhouse across the cul-de-sac. The owner had built the duplexes on the dead end between the barn and the house. We were delighted to find Howie Kirk and his wife, Joyce, renting one of the duplexes; so we had dear friends as neighbors.

The house was locally called the "dollhouse." It had a living room, separate dining room, and a kitchen on the main floor. Three bedrooms upstairs and a full basement that we divided between a study for George and a play room for the girls.

When the household goods finally arrived after numerous delays because the overseas containers had misplaced bills of lading and customs documents, we were in for yet another moving adventure.

Two of the shipment containers had been broken into. All of George's dress uniforms, my sewing machine, stereo components, and numerous other items had been stolen. Most horrifying of all, the full-length mink coat I brought back for a neighbor to leave with her mother for safekeeping was also missing. That phone call was very difficult! Our insurance or the government, of course, did not cover it as it wasn't ours.

Because of my crystal outlet shopping in Germany, we bought a china cabinet to have somewhere to put the stemware. We also bought a used portable dishwasher. The backyard was fenced, so we put a swing set back there and started the search for a dog.

Following an ad for Collie puppies, we went to look at them. We were captivated, but had to go through a third degree before the breeder allowed us to buy what was to be our first of five collies to date. Missy was smart, beautiful, potty trained in a day, and totally stole all our hearts. Collies are natural herders, so she kept the girls close and safe.

Cheryl was in second grade so I applied, and was hired, as a preschool teacher at the Fort Leavenworth Preschool. As a high school teacher, this was a real physical come down for me. Instead of looking up at most of the students, I was on the floor a lot looking them in the eye. I loved it! I called them my leg huggers.

Tara went half day to the same preschool, then to child care across the street, so it was great for us all. The staff at the preschool were all very, if not overly, qualified. Several had master's degree, and all but one art teacher had an undergraduate degree. I had a class of four-year-olds in the morning and five-year-olds in the afternoon.

One little boy, Charlie, was a real pistol. His parents were avid golfers. Often Charlie would get home on the bus with no one to meet him. On those days, a neighbor would feed him lunch. Needless to say, he didn't feel very grounded. One fateful day, his four-year-old mind deduced if he got back on the bus for the afternoon class, he would be in the same class. When he showed up at my door, his shocked face told it all. My heart broke as I hugged him, assuring him all was well. Inside I was so angry at his parents but never got a chance to vent since, as far as I knew, they never came to any school functions.

Wes and Gert Clark's son, Wes, was also in my class. He was very smart and a joy to teach. I was reading the class a book about helpful bugs, and little Wes said, "Yeah, and aphids are not good bugs." No one else in the class had ever heard of an aphid. Thus a more in-depth discussion ensued. The first day of class, Wes arrived in his English schoolboy outfit. As they had just come from England, he was perfectly dressed for an English school, not Kansas. In the circle all the little boys sat together with their blue jeans, knit shirts, and tennis shoes all similar aligned. Then there was Wes in shorts, knee socks, and leather shoes. That first night I called Gert and suggested she go to the PX and get the boy some jeans, T-shirts, and tennis shoes. The next day, Wes arrived grinning from ear to ear. He sat in the circle, swinging his new tennis shoes from side to side absolutely in heaven being one of the guys.

Very intelligent children can often get obsessed with a subject until they exhaust all the knowledge they can glean. Wes first did this with volcanoes and dinosaurs. At open house, all the class artwork was displayed on the walls. Among the collection of sunshine, horses, dogs, cats, houses, and people were five volcanoes with various dinosaurs on them. Wes could tell you all about every dinosaur that ever lived. Gert had taken him to a museum in Kansas City to see the dinosaur display and encouraged his interest. Big Wes asked me if that was normal. I assured him it was very normal for a highly intelligent mind and as always, soon the volcanoes were replaced by the next big interest.

There is a phenomenon I have discovered among military wives. This doesn't apply to all, of course, but to too many. One's worth is judged by what you do for a living or the rank of your husband. At the beginning of every month, tuition was due for the preschool. Most parents came to the office to pay or mailed it. Mrs. Revelto, a teacher of three-year-olds with a master's degree, and I were standing at the classroom door with students to be picked up as moms drove by stopping at the appropriate door to retrieve their darlings. A mom, whose husband was a student at Command and General Staff, as was mine and where Mrs. Revelto's husband taught, pulled up and waved her tuition check at us. We assumed she wanted us to leave the children, cross the street, and get it; so we pretended we didn't see her. She waved even more frantically, looking increasingly furious at our lack of attention. Finally, she put the car in park, got out, and stomped over to us, practically throwing the check at us. I asked sweetly if she would like us to see that the registrar received it. She spat that that would be correct and peeled off. Perhaps she was having a bad day! "Bless her heart," we said the "nasty nice" together.

The men had lots of free time, so the golf lovers and occasionally the wives spent many enjoyable hours on the golf course.

After three years of pommes frites and bratwurst and other glorious German food, I desperately needed some form of exercise. I called the

Leavenworth Parks Department and discovered they had two classes that sounded interesting. One was a belly dancing class and the other a karate class. The karate class was at a local high school gym, so I went by to observe and determine if it was for me. The instructor was a Korean ninth-degree black belt, just six months in the US, and an instructor at the University of Missouri in Kansas City. He was teaching karate in the evenings to make extra money.

The class was two hours long with a ten-minute break in between where students could rinse their mouths with water then spit it out. Discipline was a key word. At the end of two hours, the class took off their gi shirts and literally wrung the sweat out of them, thus I was hooked. Just what I needed, a really great workout.

Twice a week, I donned my gi with white belt and went to torture class. Master Chung had about thirty students when I started. We would line up by rank, white belts in the rear, and practice stance, kicks, punches, and blocks ad nauseam. I had stumbled into the sport that was perfect for me, and I loved it. If my stance was off, Master C would walk along behind us and kick a leg out from under me then make me do pushups as punishment. You only messed up once. The constant repetition made all movements automatic, which one wanted, if needed. Every week I'd get home and ask George to grab the lapels of my gi hoping to practice the latest take down. He would take me down instead. After about three months, I asked him to grab my gi and when he did I took him to his knees. Whooping and hollering was definitely in order. I earned yellow belt in the World Tae Kwon Do Association and truly earned it. By the end of that year, there were only about five students left in the class, and I discovered I was pregnant, so my sparring days were over for a while.

George's advisor turned out to be his former brigade commander who was the one who was too drunk in Germany to troop the line at his change of command. He was a very intelligent man who we hoped had controlled his drinking problem. We had a party one evening and invited them to join us. The self-serve bar had been set up in the kitchen. The colonel's first drink was a water glass of straight scotch weakened with a few ice cubes. He obviously still had a serious problem.

We enjoyed several visits with relatives who lived in nearby Kansas City and Independence, Missouri. On one visit to Aunt Muriel and Uncle Wilber Herrin's farm, we took Missy who went nuts at the sight of cows. All the aunts and uncles came for a huge family meal; we picked mushrooms in the woods and generally enjoyed a wonderful day with family.

Other friends from Fort Bragg, Mark and Jo Ponzillo, were also at Leavenworth, so we got to renew that friendship. One of the many pleasures in moving so often is reconnecting with old friends.

Orders came for George to attend graduate school at Duke University in Durham, North Carolina, before going to West Point as a tactical officer. Knowing we would only be there a year, we rented a townhouse in Durham where most of the army students stayed. We heard it was very nice but small.

A group of female packers packed us up from Leavenworth which gave us a false sense of security. We had all the boxes marked silver and china put in the attic at Durham, knowing we would really use them at West Point. It would be another year before we realized the silver boxes held books, motorcycle helmets, and other heavy stuff. We had settled with the moving company over the few broken items so at West Point we had no recourse but to accept the loss. All the wedding silver and china was stolen by double-tagging boxes. As I said before, you learn something every move!

10 | Durham, North Carolina
"Grad School and Baby Boy"

AS WE SETTLED into life in a tobacco and college town, George went to classes and enjoyed his advisor, Dr. Colver, who was truly a class act. One night, he came home amazed at one of his professors who claimed disciplining a child was terribly harmful to that child's psyche. I told him either the professor had no children or his children were totally out of control. The next day he came home to share that the professor's wall held pictures of their dogs. Enough said.

For me, a paper would require loads of research and revising, but for George it required a couple of hours resulting in an "A." He therefore had plenty of time to pursue other interests. We went camping one weekend in the North Carolina Mountains, got rained out, so packed up the wet tent and on the return trip discovered a 1940 Ford for a great price. George returned the next week, bought it, and made a deal with a local garage to use their empty space to work on it. The good old boys were a huge help making suggestions and sharing suppliers of old parts. He stripped it to the frame, and at the end of the year it was fully restored to its original gleaming beauty.

I worked out with a karate class for a couple of months to stay in shape, but when the belly grew bigger it was time to quit. The complex had a pool, so we swam, and the girls took swim lessons.

George was promoted to major there, so we had an impromptu party to celebrate. Normally when a soldier is promoted, a superior officer has a ceremony where friends, family, and coworkers are invited to attend. So far, he had not been officially promoted in public by a superior. This time he read it in the army times.

Tara started first grade there and Cheryl third. I applied to substitute and was asked to substitute for a fourth-grade teacher who had suffered a heart attack. It was the first time I had been in a classroom with absolutely no free time. That was a terrible situation to be in while pregnant. The bigger the baby grew, the more often I needed a bathroom break. Even at lunch, we were with our class. I had to ask another teacher to keep an eye on my class as I dashed to the little girl's room.

Sadly, the teacher I was replacing died in the hospital, so my subbing became long term. She had taught for forty years and had never thrown anything out. It was a daunting thought to clean out the closets, so I chickened out and left it to the next full-time teacher. In my seventh month, the OB doctor at Duke determined me to be high risk, ending my teaching.

On February 1, 1976, I had horrid back pains but was sure they weren't labor. The other two children caused labor pains in other places than my back. We called the doctor who said, "Get in here." We did get in, and we waited, and waited, and waited. I walked the halls reading an entire Ludlum book while George visited with other expected fathers. He congratulated them on their newborns and welcomed the new group of fathers-to-be. Finally, when they determined our baby was breech and in fetal distress, they set up for a caesarean section. George was allowed to scrub and observe. I tried to stay awake, but the last I heard was the discussion of what everyone wanted on their pizza.

Brackett Scott was finally born with much joy in his arrival.

I had incredible care at Duke. The nurses could not do enough for me. George and the girls got to come in and hold the baby. George even got to visit Brackett in the nursery. On about day four, one nurse asked me what George's specialty was but when I replied, "Infantry" that didn't seem to compute. For four days, the staff all thought he was a doctor and gave him free reign in the hospital. They certainly weren't mean to me after that, but all the extra visits stopped immediately.

Again, Mother came to help out when Brackett was born, providing much-needed help. She cooked, cleaned, and washed clothes allowing me to tend to the baby. With the girls in school, I could devote all day to the baby, then shower the girls with attention when they got home. Mother stayed just long enough to get me on my feet.

George's mother called to announce she was coming. I asked her to wait a few weeks until my strength returned. She refused to wait and announced when she would arrive.

She came loaded with gifts for the children hence the nickname we had given her, Bon Bon. She wanted to go shopping immediately, so I would drag myself out the door with the baby, drop her at the outlet mall or shopping center, nurse the baby in the car, then meet up with her some place.

Unlike Mother, all she wanted to do was play with the baby, expecting me to do all the cooking, cleaning, and washing. When the time for her departure rolled around, I was so exhausted I was counting the hours. The morning of her departure arrived. She heard the doorbell and raced down the stairs, slipping on one, sliding the rest of the way, pulling the ligaments in her knee.

We were horrified she was hurt and doubly horrified her stay was extended. She was taken to the hospital where she was given crutches and told to stay off it a few days. I, of course, waited on her for another week until she was well enough to travel.

After her departure, it took a week to have enough energy to move. Several of us began walking in the early mornings pushing strollers. That helped build up some stamina, and Brackett loved being outside.

The girls were thriving in school and loved reconnecting with Russell and Clayborne Mountcastle who also lived in the area. They would spend two years at Duke while Jack finished a doctorate then come to West Point where Jack would teach.

Too soon, we got ready for yet another move, this time to West Point.

George in Vietnam. Vonda using make shift shower at the lake.

Vonda and Cheryl returning from Panama

Fort Benning. George, Cheryl, Tara, Vonda

George in Vietnam again. Tara, Vonda and Cheryl ready for church.

R and R in Kauai, Hawaii. George and Vonda.

George with the Charlie Brown Tree

Vonda, Dad and Mom Jones in Paris, France

Tara and Cheryl in Spain

Tara, Cheryl, Vonda, and Dad Jones
in Front of Quarters, Germany

Vonda, Tara and Cheryl in Germany

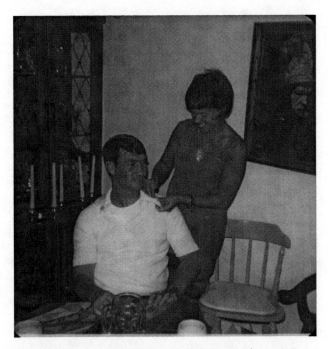

Vonda promoting George to Major in Durham, NC.

George and Brackett in Durham, NC.

11 | West Point, New York
"Living in a Museum With John Q. Public"

GEORGE WAS GIVEN July 1, 1976, as a West Point reporting date, arriving to discover everyone was off until the sixth.

George stayed in the barracks until everyone returned to duty, then was given all the cadets involved in the 1976 honor scandal to corral.

That year, in order to get quarters, one made a trip to West Point, if possible, to look over all the available housing you then ranked according to your preferences. A huge gathering of incoming personnel met in an auditorium where names by date of rank were called out. One stood and stated your housing preference. On our long list, we jokingly put Quarters 1 as our first choice. We didn't get it. We did, however, get one of our real first choices, Quarters 3034B in a cul-de-sac in Stoney Lonesome housing area. It was the newest housing and on top of a mountain above the football field. Redoubts from the Revolutionary War were scattered around the mountain and were a huge draw for the neighborhood kids.

Since the quarters would not be available until August 1, the kids, dog, and I went to Arkansas, staying most of the time at Mother and Daddy's lake house, "the Jones Jurisdiction." We visited with family, doing fun things like digging for diamonds, peach picking, and swimming in the lake.

George called with the great news that the quarters were available, so we crated Missy, packed up all our suitcases, a stroller, car seat, etc., etc., and headed for the airport looking much like Oakies during the depression. Herding the girls with baby on hip, we boarded the plane for yet another move.

George met us at New York, La Guardia Airport, where I was welcomed to the graciousness of the north by a porter who laughed at my five-dollar tip. George doubled it, gave me a look of "You were kidding, right?" And the porter left only partially pacified. In hindsight, we did have six suitcases, a stroller, car seat, huge dog crate; and each child had a backpack and the "inevitable, standard keep-busy-on-trip sanity bag," dragging on the floor. Therefore, in his place I too would probably have laughed at even ten dollars.

We were to stay in guest quarters at Fort Stewart over the mountain from West Point. As we unloaded the dog, who was dragging her leash and started grabbing a suitcase each, the dog ran ahead and was greeted by a very surprised skunk at the door. One doesn't surprise skunks without consequences. George had to drive all over the area looking for a store that was open and sold tomato juice.

Missy was skunked in the face and leash, so her first reaction was to rub it off. We waited outside until the tomato juice arrived. We managed to keep her head up as we rushed her inside and to the shower where we doused her in tomato juice and tried not to gag. Tomato juice really doesn't work very well.

After a few days, we were able to accept quarters 3034B and our household goods. The neighbors on both sides, upon hearing my name was Vonda, thought I might be German. It is a Welch name but no matter. When we met them upon our arrival and the first "It's so nice to meet y'all" was spoken, both couples let out a whoop. Linda Roebuck was from North Augusta, Georgia, and Marge Kirkegard was from lower Alabama or "LA" We three southern girls were to form a close bond among our overwhelmingly Yankee neighbors.

The year 1976 was the first year for women at West Point, and George was the tactical officer for Company A-1 in First Regiment. His company had some of the women assigned to it.

I asked if I could work out with the cadet karate club because Master

Chung had told me to check. Master Son was the instructor at the Academy and not only did I have his book, but he and Master Chung were acquaintances. It never occurred to me what an unusual request it was, but they readily agreed, mainly so the cadets could get use to having a female in their midst. I was a green belt going in, so I wasn't a novice.

There were about one hundred cadets in the karate club, and they worked out several days a week. The work out began with a mile barefoot run on the suspended track at the old gym, then sparring practice, repetition of moves, karate practice, then the end run outside up the mountain around Delafield Pond and back. The first few weeks were brutal. I hurt everywhere and always brought up the rear on the mountain run. Every day I gave thanks for Master Chung and his two-hour workouts with no water.

Soon after the year began, Master Son was replaced by "Tiger Kim the Korean Fighting Machine." All of these men were ninth-degree black belts and the training, so far for me, was unbelievable.

After the first year, the cadets forgot I was there, so they would talk about things as if I was another guy. If it was important, I'd tell George but never revel where I heard it. Occasionally, those problems aired would be fixed. I would go to competition with the team and had several memorable occasions.

George and I drove part of the team to one competition where I was the first to compete. It was billed as a no contact but in reality was full contact. None of my punches were being credited, and we were all getting frustrated when about that time my opponent landed a blow to my rib cage, and we all heard it crack. Then and only then, when she was awarded the point did we comprehend what kind of tournament this was. We had been trained to stop the blow a hare's breath from an opponent's body, which took far more control and expertise, but now we knew. I know why fighters can fight with injuries because you are so focused; the pain is put away for later. I got in a few revenge blows before the bout was over, bowed respectfully, sat down, and then the tears came. Master Kim came over and asked if I was all right so naturally I responded, "Of course, just fine." He later told George, "Too mucha contact."

We were all so unprepared for the full contact that George drove the van and I the station wagon full of injured cadets directly to the infirmary at West Point. They taped up my rib, set bones for the guys, then we dropped the cadets at the barracks. Tiger Kim assured us he was misled, and I knew that he was.

Another tournament, this one at Princeton, was really fun. After training with cadets, I was in incredible shape for an old mother. George marveled that I could do one hundred fingertip-and-knuckle push-ups. I was to spar with a Japanese girl, and as we entered the circle and bowed, the Princeton crowd started chanting "Piece of cake! Deck the old lady." I really didn't think I looked that old. The cadets were all grinning from ear to ear. She never landed a point as I beat her in record time. The Princeton crowd was quiet, the cadets whooped, and I grinned.

The Nationals were held in Madison Square Garden, and I went with the cadets to compete. We all competed in the preliminaries in the morning where most of us progressed to the finals. Grand Master Chung was there as a judge. He took me aside before the finals and asked, "Are you going to win?" I answered, "I'll do my best, Grand Master." He yelled, "NO!" "Are you going to win?" I yelled back, "Yes, Grand Master, I am going to win." He nodded and said, "Yes! Always the positive up here." He said this as he tapped his head. It was a lesson I've never forgotten. I called George to let him know that I was in the finals, and he said he would come to watch. I didn't see him when my turn came, but assumed he was in the audience. I won in forms and sparring and was thrilled beyond measure with two first place trophies, but was so disappointed George hadn't gotten there in time to see it. It took a while to quit mentally listing all the times I was there for him.

Shortly after Tiger Kim began teaching at West Point, he changed the forms. I was scheduled to try out for black belt, so I had to learn all the new forms. One of the cadets, named Greg, who was trying for second-degree black belt agreed to work out with me in the gym after hours. For weeks we sweated and practiced until we felt confident of success.

The big day came, and I blanked out on one of the katas so didn't make it. I was hugely disappointed but determined to make it next time. Greg did make it, so that was a good thing. I doubled my efforts and by the time testing came around again, shortly before we PCS'd, I could have done all the katas with a lobotomy. To pay back getting to work out with the men, I washed and ironed all their gis before competitions. In return, they let me watch the Bruce Lee motivational movies before we competed. Those were my karate highlights so back to our lives in Stoney Lonesome.

The girls were in Girl Scouts, so rather than lead a troop as in Germany, I helped Amy Robinson with the Junior Girl Scout Troop. We took the troop camping one weekend in the woods on post. They pitched their tents in a circle, and Missy was up all night circling each tent protecting the girls. When we hiked back home the next day, Missy collapsed in the living room and slept all day.

The girls were active in Sunday school which was lead by cadets. The young men were marvelous role models for the children and young enough to remember how to have fun. One Sunday, Cheryl's teacher asked if he and another cadet could take the class swimming after church. We all agreed because the cadets were all so honorable, right? By four, the phone lines were hot between the parents trying to find our delinquent children. We called the post chaplain who immediately got on the trail of the missing Sunday school class. Around five thirty, they returned stunned that we were worried. They had gone to the pool to find it closed so took the class to the movies to see *The Last Remake of Beau Geste*, which was a movie to which none of us would have taken our children, and then they had gone for ice cream afterward. The cadets were counseled, but our children still remembered the movie and fun time.

Cheryl was in fourth grade and still remembers the Ten Commandments as the cadets taught it.

The Shinseki family lived up the street as did the Forepaws, Mountcastles, and several other old friends.

Part of the duties of a tactical officer at West Point was to be a father-type figure dealing out discipline and guidance, thus the master's degree in counseling. It was expected that we would have cadets in our home on various occasions. Also we were to have the firsties or seniors over for dinner to graciously give them experience in eating a meal with senior officers. Many tactical wives chose a simple meal they served everyone. Spaghetti and lasagna were big favorites. Never taking the easy road and having that home economics degree to uphold, I chose to educate. The cadets came from all backgrounds and areas of our nation as well as other nations. I planned menus that would introduce them to foods they may not have experienced and invited two at a time since our table sat four. One night we had beef fondue, so they cooked their own meal, another we had chicken curry, and so on. We tried to get them to relax by explaining the "tie in the soup" award to the first one to dip his tie inadvertently in the soup. I had at least three courses, so they had to learn the silver etiquette as well as keeping their tie clean. We really enjoyed those evenings, and most of the cadets seemed to also. One cadet in particular was what George called his diamond in the rough. After observing him pull a chair up to the buffet table for a class party at the house, I called him a social piece of coal. When he came for the obligatory sit-down meal, I served steak and potatoes knowing he would like those and probably be rudely verbal about something he hadn't before tried.

Zig Roebuck, next door, said as a cadet he learned the etiquette of bread eating. Breaking off a piece of bread, butter it, and eat it in one bite rather than buttering the entire roll and biting off it. He was very impressed with his date (later wife), Linda, who ate hers properly. Of course she did, she was from Georgia.

The big parties were encouraged for certain events. At Christmas we had the plebe class, ring weekend for the juniors, a just because for the sophomores, and the first class graduation. Imagine having between twenty and thirty starving men and now women in small quarters to eat. I bought huge pots to cook in and learned to cook en masse.

The plebe class of 1976 had the first women, so I felt their pain. Being with the karate club where the male cadets openly voiced their opinions was an eye-opener.

The cadet meals were over five thousand calories per day. Women's metabolism is often slower than a man's, so the women who had tailored uniforms to fit when they entered the academy now had what was despairingly called the "Hudson hip disease." Many of the females' back jacket vents literally stood out rather than lay flat over the bottom.

A lot has been written about the angst that occurred by the staff determining bathroom configuration, length of skirts, length of hair, makeup, weight of backpack, number of pull-ups, perfume usage, how lingerie should be folded in the drawers, and on and on. It took several years to work some of it out, but that first class of women deserve medals for sheer willpower as well as enduring a mental war.

As I've said before, having brothers and an outdoorsman father made me tough in many ways, so the few women who whined about the small stuff really made me angry for the tougher majority.

At Christmas we entertained the thirty plebes at the house. The girls and I baked hundreds of Christmas cookies that the cadets decorated. The girls chose the winner of the various decorating categories. Unfortunately for Cheryl and Tara, it was three years before they got to decorate Christmas cookies or decorate the tree.

To get in the door, the plebes had to bring a homemade ornament. It was a great ice breaker. Thirty plus years later, we still have some of them. One year a very creative young cadet brought strips of white paper and taught us all how to make origami stars.

Besides decorating cookies they pulled taffy, decorated our tree, and ate everything in sight.

Somewhere along the way, we were given the recipe for individual English muffin mini pizzas. The cadets loved them, so the oven was kept hot as we stuffed pan after pan of them in to cook. Here's the recipe should you want to try them.

INDIVIDUAL PIZZAS

3 (2 ½ oz) jars mushrooms	¾ c chopped onion
1 ½ c sharp cheddar	1 c mayonnaise
1 ½ c Swiss cheese	6 TBS chopped black olives
1 c chopped salami	¾ c pepperoni

Put all ingredients in a food processor or grinder. Spread on English muffin halves. Bake 450 degrees until cheese melts.

These parties were times to really get to know the cadets, and they were often very open with their concerns, at least to me. I asked the female cadets why they didn't take more pride in their natural beauty. They eyed each other then told me why. No makeup kept them from being written up for excessive makeup, perfume even sprayed in the air and walked under was an automatic gig for excessive use of perfume, and anything used to enhance their beauty was excessive. It was much easier to take no action than to endure the constant vigilance of some upperclassman determined to run them out. Every tiny infraction was magnified into major offenses. Fortunately, not all male cadets felt that way, but the enthusiasm of the few surely made it seem like the majority.

The second summer, George was tasked to escort the cadets going to airborne training at Fort Benning, Georgia. The kids and I packed up to go to Arkansas for vacation. While at Benning, George had a week off and had as a fluke put his name in the pot for a beach cottage on the military part of Destin, Florida. His name was drawn, so we were thrilled. We borrowed Daddy's station wagon, packing it to the roof with necessities for a week at the beach. George's mother wanted to go, so we were really crammed but excited about the trip.

The cottage was really neat, and we filled it to overflowing. The water was shallow for a long way out which was perfect for the kids.

The week flew by and before we knew it, we were on the road again returning to Arkansas and George was heading back to the cadets at Fort Benning.

Somewhere in the middle of Mississippi, a tire went flat. We hadn't seen a house for miles, but fortunately the flat occurred within view of a small clapboard house sitting in a grove of pines. Several people were sitting in the front yard watching us unload suitcases and beach toys to get to the spare tire. The menfolk ambled over, asking if we needed any help. Trying to look helpless, we assured them we could sure use some. They had the tire changed in record time. We had to force them to take money for their efforts coupled with profuse thanks!

George was asked to try out a new tactical officer approach which was to have his office in the barracks area. As a cadet he had tried most, if not all, of the creative verboten activities of the long line of cadets. Many cadets, for example, kept an unauthorized popcorn popper hidden somewhere in their room. George's had been behind a loose brick in the historic old barracks. Therefore, he was savvy to most of their tricks.

The cadets began calling him Darth Vader because they swore he swept down on them with uncanny ease to confiscate the offending item or the offender.

We hung a full-size poster of Darth Vader on the inside door of the guest bathroom downstairs. Occasionally, a yelp could be heard during cadet parties.

We were inadvertently to blame for the cessation of the very convenient transport of cadets to quarters. One fateful party evening a two-ton truck full of cadets, driven by a cadet, caught the curb coming into our court and overturned. No one was seriously injured, but we were all scared to death. The academy said never again and rightfully so.

West Point was like living in a museum especially in the summer when what we call "John Q Public" came en masse to experience history. The young women were hilarious to watch. They had dressed to impress cadets, not to tromp up and down mountains. After lunch and on into the afternoon, the girls looked increasingly bedraggled. Most would be carrying their high heels and limping, not creating the look they had envisioned just that morning. What were their mothers thinking?

Football weekends were a favorite of ours. We would get a sitter for Brackett, usually a delightful young lady from Lady Cliff College which was located outside the front gate of West Point.

The girls and their buddies would plan to sit together in the peanut gallery which was a designated section in the end zone for children. They loved it! Armed with a backpack full of snacks and drinks they were ready.

The adults sat by class. The class of 1966, George's class, was almost in the nosebleed section. We had to watch the children with binoculars.

To get to the game, we stood on the sidewalk in front of the court to catch the post bus that took us all down the hill to the stadium. The return trip was the reverse and almost as much fun as the game.

To make some extra money, I substituted at Highland Falls High School in the adjacent town of Highland Falls. The first two classes for which I was called were fine, but the third was a definite challenge. The industrial arts teacher was absent, leaving me directions to let the boys read *Popular*

Mechanics magazines. Since all the magazines were well used and very dated, I supposed he was often absent.

After introductions, the usual "get the sub" routine began. One very big boy stood up, went to a wall phone, and dialed a number. He supposedly placed an order with McDonald's, so I said, "While you are ordering, I'd like a chocolate milk shake." He slammed the receiver in the cradle and said, "Damn, she knew." The phone wasn't connected obviously, and McDonald's doesn't deliver. The next day, I took in *Black Belt* magazines and some of George's car magazines. The boys grabbed them and one finally asked, "Does your husband do karate?" I said, "No." He waited a minute or so more and asked, "Your kids?" Again, same answer, "No." He waited another few minutes mentally eliminating names. "Do you?" "Yes," I replied and continued with my reading. After they perused all the magazines, they again became restless and started acting out. I asked if they wanted to talk about anything. I was willing to talk about anything at all. One student said, "Yeah, sex!" "Okay," I said. "You start. What do you want to know?" They dove into a lively discussion, and it was amazing how much incorrect information they thought were facts. No wonder there are so many teenage pregnancies.

There was only one really bad experience with the boys. One young man was high on drugs when he came in, and the other guys clued me in which I really appreciated but had already deduced.

He slammed out of the classroom, and as I followed he locked himself in the dark room down the hall. I asked a janitor for his keys which he handed over with a grin.

After unlocking the door and turning on the lights, he was found terrorizing a young female. I got him in a hammerlock and marched him up two flights of stairs to the principal's office where he was taken off my hands. For the rest of the time I substituted there, the industrial arts boys would stick their heads in my classroom and ask if I needed anything or if anyone was giving me problems. I really liked all the industrial arts bad boys but hated that they got nothing out of the class. I never saw a lesson plan and wondered if the teacher ever had one.

West Point has a ski slope which is rather small but still a slope. We got yearly passes, $35 for the season for the family, put the girls in ski school, bought Brack the smallest skis and boots made, and discovered the new shorter modern composite skis were leaps and bounds better than those horrid long German skis. We could immediately ski better. Every weekend during ski season and most nights during the week, we were all on the slope. Brackett never learned the wedge because at two he was so close to the snow he just paralleled naturally.

The girls had a blast with their friends and learned very quickly.

George and I decided to take the Qualified Amateur Ski Instructor's (QUASI) course so spent several weeks learning technique from instructors from Stowe. Our favorite was noted instructor, Jim Cardnelle, and the most outlandish was a fellow called simply "Butch." At the end of the course, we all went to Stowe for the weekend for final testing. The Knapps went with us, and we had a fabulous time. On the way back, the roads had iced over, and we were literally gliding down the road with no traction. The angel was definitely on the roof on that trip. The Knapps were asleep in the backseat and missed the white knuckle praying in the front. From then on, we bought used studded snow tires which made all the difference.

Every winter, there we spent a week of leave skiing at either Stowe or Killington. It was so expensive for five of us to ski that we cut cost by staying in the cheapest motel we could find about five miles from the slopes. We took food to fix lunches as the food at the slope side lodges was very expensive. A thermos was always happily filled with hot water by the motel owner, and we took instant soup and ramen packets to make instant hot lunch. We put Brackett in child care ski school, picked him up at noon, and skied with all the children in the afternoons.

We never really used our teaching skills except for one class I taught to enlisted personnel from Fort Dix, New Jersey. It was great fun, but several of our group were serious about teaching and continued to become certified ski instructors. One of those was Sally Elliott. She and her husband, Torch, were part of the weekends at the ski lodge group. Sally brought her newborn in an infant seat. Everyone took turns watching her. Several of us often took a crock pot full of dinner to plug into a socket at the lodge, and by five it was ready. The Elliotts and their brood would remain dear friends long after retirement, and Sally is still teaching us techniques to improve our skiing.

One weekend, we went with the West Point Ski Club to Waterville Valley, Vermont, where the Kennedys skied. As we drove up, it was raining on the slopes, but we hoped the next day would bring snow. It did but under the snow was solid ice, so the skiing was challenging to say the least. One learns to use the ski edges skiing in the northeast. We went in for lunch before someone got killed, and when we came out, George couldn't find his Rossignol ST Comps. Someone had stolen his skies. We never went back.

One winter, it snowed so many feet that the cars were buried and classes halted. We skied to the ski slope, skied down to the lodge, and had a fabulous day on the slope. When we went home, we took the lift up and skied back home in our earlier tracks.

Shopping was another adventure in New York. The sales tax was twelve percent in New York and only six percent in New Jersey, so the three southern girls would drive to Paramus Park, New Jersey, to shop.

Marge Kirkogard had gone alone on one occasion, and the saleswoman in the Bloomingdale's handbag department had been insufferably rude. When Marge stormed back to share her experience with us, we vowed to go the very next week and avenge her. We reacted like teenagers.

We got all gussied up and drove to the scene of the crime. We went into the handbag department, ascertaining the saleswoman was the same and picked up every bag there. We opened each one constantly commenting on them. We, loudly and in our most southern of southern accents, stated that the prices were outrageous. Walmart had the same bag for a fraction of the price or the construction was flimsy or they were somehow flawed. The saleswoman kept asking if she could help, we assured her we were just looking. Often we would ask her if she actually sold any of them. Finally after every single bag had been picked up, opened, found wanting, and put back somewhere else, Marge said, "Girls, let's go upstairs. I heard they have a sale on energetic shoes." We left single file, and as we rode the escalator upstairs we looked back at the saleswoman who was lying across a table full of handbags. I couldn't tell if she was crying or not. Let this be a warning to all, never be rude to customers. You may think this was very cruel and just downright mean of us, and you are probably right, but it did feel good to avenge our friend.

On another southern theme, Linda Roebuck called us one morning and asked a favor. She had browbeaten the produce man at the commissary into ordering a case of turnip greens. Now, that is not a staple at northern tables, but it certainly brings a tear to a southern eye. She asked us to go buy some and make sure he knew how much we appreciated his stocking it. We assured her we would, and we did. They were great, but the next week he ordered them again, as well as several more weeks in a row. We all had turnip greens in our freezers, and the families balked at eating them at every meal. We finally quit buying, and he quit ordering.

George's regimental commander was Colonel Mark Sisinyak, then Colonel Bob Joseph.

The Moscotellis came in next. Bob and Bonnie were a great team. Bonnie had been in the military herself, and they had two children. Bonnie is a free spirit, and on one occasion when she was told what to bring to a ladies function she really wanted to make peanut butter and jelly sandwiches cut into cute shapes but relented and made nastursum sandwiches instead. The general's wife who was hostess at that party, after the guest left, bounced out of the house in her tennis togs announcing to the colonel's wives to close the front door after they got the kitchen cleaned up. One is forever in awe of the occasional officer's wife who is all about me, myself, and I and thinks her husbands' rank sits on her own shoulders as well as his. Fortunately for Bonnie, the hostess and her husband soon departed.

Before the plebes come in every year, the upperclassmen practice their first day events called "R" day for Reception Day. Volunteers are requested to play the plebe parts. Bonnie and I were two of the volunteers. It was a great eye-opening experience.

I had a great time. As we were marched into one building, I asked if my momma could bring up my TV later. The cadet glared at me, but his eye had a twinkle and he told me, "No, there will be no TVs."

We learned how to answer, "yes, sir," "no, sir," "no excuse, sir," "square corners," and "march." When they marched us upstairs in the barracks, Klenny Brundage, a huge football player, took charge of us. Klenny did *not* have a twinkle in his eye when he yelled at me to "Smirk off, Crocker." The grin was immediately wiped from my face, not to reappear until Klenny turned us over to someone else. He scared us to the point one teenage volunteer broke into sobs. I think they have plebes who cry during the real first day.

George had told me stories of his parents taking him up there and his first days, but physically being in that practice made it real for me.

We had one couple in our court that had no children. They did have a beautiful car. Brackett, who was only two, and Larry and Fran, Donathorne's son, had watched him every weekend wash and polish his car. They decided in their two-year-old minds it would be really kind to help him out, so they scooped up mud in the street and rubbed it all over the doors of his car. We heard his roar from inside our house, rushed out to find our sons sobbing. Their good deed was not appreciated, and it cost both families the price of having our neighbor's door scratches buffed out.

The Department of Tactics Division of West Point was the regimental commander and company tactical officers. The academic side was, of course, the academic instructors. Many of the instructors were permanent. There was some discomfort among the children of the two departments. The tactical side was literally on call 24/7 and the academic department only for the classes they taught and the time to prepare. Some of the older kids threatened to make T-shirts for the Tac kids that said, "My dad's a Tac, if you see him tell him hello for me." Their hours were very long twelve months a year.

Our girls and the other neighborhood kids decided to make a tree house in the woods behind our court. They scavenged wood, nails, and fabric from all the families and began the construction. With no adult supervision, they did an amazing job. The problem was their plans grew into epic proportions. One story became two, then three, then four. When a classmate fell out of an upper story breaking an arm, it had to be demolished.

Because it was such a safe environment for them, we all allowed them to roam in groups all over the mountain. They had wars using the redoubts, played hide-and-seek, and unbeknownst to all parents on occasion they would walk down into the town of Highland Falls for a snack.

In the winter, we could watch deer feeding in the woods behind our quarters. They would use hoofs and antlers to move snow to get to the grass. Missy would go nuts!

The first spring there, I prepared a little garden in May. Before it could be planted, it snowed a foot. Welcome to New York spring time.

We had looked for a piano for the girls to take lessons and found one for $100. It was old and looked awful, but was a classic pre-World War I Ludwig upright model. So I took it apart, stripped it on the kitchen floor, shellacked it, and put it back together. We found a piano tuner who rebuilt the soundboard. He was amazed at the name on the piano lid as his father had, years before, worked for that company in New York. Although an upright, it had a full baby grand-sized soundboard. Even the West Point bandmaster was impressed with its full sound and tone.

The girls learned to ice skate on Round Pond on our last winter there. It was the beginning of a lifetime sport for both of them.

Back in Arkansas, Daddy was diagnosed with colon cancer. In their usual stoic way, we weren't told until the surgery was over, and he was well on his way to a full recovery. They came up to visit once while we were there, and we had a great time sharing the area with them.

Mother Crocker also paid us visits and, of course, enjoyed area shopping.

One night, we were awakened by what sounded like gunshots. We opened our bedroom window to find Marge's husband, sitting in his window wearing only BVDs taking pot shots at a big tom cat singing on a fence post.

Another night, George went out to take some trash to the enclosed trash container built into the front of our quarters. I heard yelling and stomping, so I rushed to save him. I found a hilarious sight. A mother raccoon and her children had made their way past the steel door on the trash enclosure. They were deep into the main course when George rudely interrupted them. The raccoon family scattered. George had grabbed the closest weapon, an umbrella, which he used to poke any raccoon he could reach. While he was poking and yelling, one baby got so scared he ran for the darkest hole he could find. Unfortunately for George, it was his pants leg. Now, he was yelling, poking, and dancing. The entire raccoon family finally got organized, scurrying off into the night. After that we made sure the steel door was securely shut.

As we were preparing to PCS to Fort Bragg (again) putting George in a state of euphoria, a very upsetting event occurred in our court.

A couple we had grown to really like were acting strangely. She had just had their third child. He drove up in a new red car, and when we said something about it, the wife stated it was a surprise to her as well. In the days that followed, the story unfolded. The husband had been having an affair with the wife of another instructor. We had, of course, noticed the other wife dressed very provocatively, but she had said her husband preferred her to do so. Not that we asked, she had offered the information. Our neighbor having found receipts and tickets to places she hadn't been, followed him one night with another wife as backup. They saw his car at a motel, went to the manager, got a room key, and walked in on him. The husband and the other woman were in bed drinking champagne. She said she told him if he wanted to see his children again, she would talk to him at home. When he arrived later that night, they agreed to remain in the same house until he PCS'd but then go their separate ways. They had lived with the stress for weeks before anyone knew. The other husband had such an ego he never suspected his wife. We kept in touch with her for a while after we all left. She went back to school, got a good job, and was doing fine. She also taught weight watchers, lost all her after baby pounds, and looked fabulous. All I could think was "you go, girl!"

Our Collie Missy loved to chase the deer that forged in the woods behind our quarters. She slept at the top of the stairs every night to protect us all. We loved her as much as she loved us. One day we called and called, and she didn't come. We searched everywhere for her to no avail. The next day, the military police called to say they found her body near the cadet parking lot at the foot of our mountain. We surmised she drank antifreeze a cadet had dumped. It was an incredibly sad day. We heard her for days but only in our minds and hearts.

Mark and Jo Ponzillo came to visit one weekend, and we enjoyed the visit tremendously. As they were leaving, we heard a loud speaker from his car blasting his parting works, "I am the infantry, follow me." It was so Mark Ponzillo; we grinned all day.

George received his report date for Fort Bragg. I had hopes that things had changed there for the better. It certainly could not have gotten worse. He was deliriously happy. I was dubious.

Once more the packers arrived, only this time we hired a cleaning team. The joy of walking out the door without the usual broken nails, wrinkled skin, and cuts and bruises from cleaning quarters was without match!

We piled in the station wagon and headed south.

12 | Fort Bragg, North Carolina
"Hooah x Two"

AFTER A SHORT stay in the usual transit quarters, we accepted quarters in a fairly new subdivision Yadkin North, now Biazza Ridge, on Fort Bragg. Here we were again on the only post to which I had never wanted to return. There was a light on the horizon when we noticed the absence of the Ku Klux Klan sign outside Fayetteville. There was hope here!

The quarters were one-half of a duplex with a small grassless chain-fenced backyard with a view of the neighborhood playground. The back view was perfect to watch our crew at play. The past occupants had an anger management problem as the walls had several holes punched into them and then badly patched over. The downstairs contained a kitchen decorated with green fern wallpaper and a den of sorts. The wallpaper was a real advantage as the other wallpaper options featured huge orange and yellow flowers. The living room slash dining room opened onto the concrete slab covered back porch and minuscule backyard. We were thrilled. The past occupants had animals that destroyed the yard with urine and feces, so my first project was to make a raised bed on one side for flowers and treat the soil in the yard to accept grass seed. It took a year to get it to the point grass would really grow.

The three bedrooms upstairs were more than adequate, so we jumped in to decorate yet another house. The household goods arrived without many problems, so the beginning here was auspicious.

In our court of six duplexes we had over thirty children. Next door the Fontenots had four children, two who were the ages of ours.

Russell was a very studious jag (attorney) who looked the part of a college professor. His wife, Martha, had a fabulous voice, played a mean piano, and became a very good friend. During our time as neighbors when it got too stressful for either for us, we would leave the kids with their fathers, get in one of the cars, drive to the nearest Dairy Queen, and indulge in an ice cream treat. Once we commiserated over calories, we felt revived, so returned home all smiles. She was such a good friend that she even agreed to accompany my Girl Scout troop to a horseback riding field trip although she had never been on a horse. I'm sure she never rode again as about half mile from the stable, her horse quit holding his breath and her saddle literally slid sideways with her attached. She landed hard. Another mom stayed with the rest of the riders while I walked, and she limped back to the stable leading both horses. She was a real trooper.

The Saffos and Leides were in the next duplex, both with children. The Saffos children were more the age of ours, and the girls were quickly friends with them as well. While we were there, Carl Saffo died of sickle-cell anemia and devastated the entire neighborhood. They were a great family. Jack Leide's children were younger, but George still sees Jack on occasion. They too were a great family.

On our other side were older boys who soon left for India. Next to them the Inderlands and Robinsons. Shannon Inderland became one of Cheryl's best friends. The entire neighborhood teemed with children. The junior high on post was excellent, so the girls were very happy there.

As in all social environments, there are vastly different financial levels. In the army, this is also true. At Fort Bragg, the paratroopers received jump pay which was one hundred and ten dollars more a month for officers and fifty-five dollars for troopers. There were other groups who received stipends for various jobs. The doctors made more as did the air force pilots. Some had family money. Also, there was a distinct difference in what each family felt was important.

During these years, Calvin Klein jeans and Izod shirts were the fad and must-haves for junior high girls. Our girls had one pair of jeans each and two or three shirts. Other girls had multiples of both. Cheryl and Tara knew if they wanted to wear Calvin Kleins daily, they had to wash them daily. One morning Tara came downstairs with dirty Calvin Kleins; I refused to let her go to school that way. A meltdown occurred, and she knew her life had ended. "What can I wear then?" she wailed. I suggested she wear a pair of cute jeans with colored stitching on the pockets that Martha's mother had sent them in a box from Montgomery Ward. The Fontenot girls couldn't wear the one pair, so Tara had inherited. "What will I tell everyone?" she wailed. You tell them that they are La Coeuler Jeans from France; they are the latest fashion statement and ask if they have a pair. She trudged off to the bus knowing her life had ended.

When the afternoon bus pulled in to disgorge our court, she was all grins. I asked how it had gone. She said she had told the girls exactly what I had said after they snidely asked her what those jeans were she had on. All day they asked her where she had gotten them, and she refused to say, just appeared amazed they didn't have a pair. Finally, one of her friends kept at her on the return bus ride and she exploded with, "Okay, you want to know! I'll tell you! They came from Montgomery Wards!"

That was a lesson she never forgot. In later years, the girls began many fashion fads from bandanas as belts to applying makeup to the area behind and below the earlobe to match their eyes.

I began making wooden marionettes that were simply strung but loaded with personality. I copyrighted the design and called them VJC originals. Each marionette was signed and numbered. I sold them at a local craft show and did fairly well. Someone told me about the Southern Living Christmas Show in Charlotte, North Carolina, so on our last year at Fort Bragg I applied to sell at that juried show. They accepted my application, so I began making them in earnest. The show was nine days long, so it would be brutal. George's West Point classmate, Charlie Chitty, and wife, Kaye, lived in Charlotte; so I asked if they could put me up at night. The show started at 10:00 a.m. and lasted until 9:00 p.m., so the days would be long. They were most gracious, so we loaded the station wagon with boxes of marionettes, a cash box, receipt book, and a week's worth of "work clothes."

The show supplied credit card machines, so that was a huge help. A friend, Paige Kellogg, agreed to come over and keep the kids before and after school until George got home; so off I went.

The booth was set up quickly and stock hung. Nightly I would drive over to Charlie and Kaye Chitty's house. They were kind enough to allow me to sleep in their guest room and kinder still to have a glass of wine ready when I dragged my poor feet in the door. We would rehash everyone's day, and then I would collapse into a deep sleep until early the next morning when it began all over again.

It was great fun prancing the goat around and having it talk to the little children. The marionettes were so popular that I almost ran out of stock halfway through; so I made a mad dash back to Fayetteville, spent most of the night putting more together, and drove back to Charlotte before the show opened the next day. En route, I was breezing along and out of nowhere I heard a siren then saw the flashing light in my rearview mirror. I pulled over, and a state trooper told me to pull into a parking lot which I did, of course. He was a very tall man who kept looking at me in a strange way. He asked if I had been drinking. I assured him that coffee was all I had had for weeks. He said, "You look like you are on something or hungover." Thanks a bunch! I gave him a rundown on the week, where I was going, and why the run to Fayetteville. He was most sympathetic but not enough to just give me a warning. Ticket in hand and promises of giving him a deal if he brought his children to the show, I drove much more slowly on to Charlotte. At the end of the nine days, I had money in my pocket and only a few marionettes left. George and the kids drove down to help me pack up and go home.

One Christmas, the girls and I decided to go for the house decoration award. We piled white plastic bags stuffed with newspaper to simulate snow all over the front flower beds. They were stacked to appear as snowdrifts. If you got too close, they looked like someone dumped their garbage in our yard. We used cardboard cores from rolls of carpet painted white with red ribbon stripes to hopefully appear as giant candy canes. With these, we fashioned our doorway arch featuring a Santa's Workshop sign. We won! I don't really think there were that many people entering, but it was fun.

Missing our collie, we tried to find another one. We decided on a cute puppy from a breeder close to Joe Don Danny's truck stop on Interstate 95 near the South Carolina boarder. Most of the North Carolina collies we looked at appeared to be fairly small. This one was no exception but was a frisky little bundle of fur we named Duchess. After a few weeks of her frisky ways turning into manic frantic behavior, we realized she needed lots more room to run than we had. George's Russellville High School classmate, Randy Flannigan, and his wife, Neila, lived on a farm in Mountain Home, Arkansas. We were planning our annual trip home and asked if they would like a collie. They were thrilled and met us at the lake house to get her. She was in doggy heaven on the farm and lived a long and happy life there running to her heart's content. Subsequently, any hyper dog to us is a Duchess. We still laugh about her frantic running in circles in our little front yard.

George was S-3 of I-504 for about two months then became First Brigade S-3 for about a year, then XO for the last fourteen months of our tour. When the Fergusons left brigade command, the Boylans took their place. Peter Boylan was a very intelligent man, who loved word games and other mental challenges. Kathy Boylan was always up for some fun and strongly believed in forging strong group comradery by doing things together. Of all the wonderfully talented ladies I was privileged to work with through the years, Kathy taught me the most.

The Boylans had five children who were all active, smart, and varied greatly in personality. Their differences were celebrated rather than discouraged, and that philosophy was carried over to the brigade.

The HQ group had a monthly coffee just as each of the battalions. At these coffees, which were held in various homes, concerns were voiced, projects undertaken, and spouse bonding occurred. The 82nd Abn Division had a luncheon about twice a year with brigades taking turns hosting. Extra events occurred when the need arouse such as the changing of the division commander.

General Meloy was departing, so a farewell luncheon was being planned for Hatsie Meloy. Hatsie had commissioned a friend to design and produce a scarf with the 82nd patch in red, white, and blue. It had been a huge hit. Our brigade was in charge of the entertainment. Kathy had the idea of a huge scarf with double A's in a perfect replica of the original. We made it at her kitchen table out of yards of old semisheer drapes, and I got to be the one prancing by Hatsie slinging the twelve-foot-long scarf over a shoulder to trail dramatically behind me. It brought the house down because we all had one of the scarves, and I'm sure some felt pressured to buy one.

Kathy was big on celebrating the top ten birthdays. The top ten were the three battalion commanders and wives, the executive officer and wife, and the brigade commander and wife.

The group met every month for dinner and games in someone's home. The birthday celebrations were surprise events that ran the gauntlet from a kazoo band with nine of us as the band members marching down a Fayetteville street to the birthday person's home to a supposedly routine check on the troops trip that arrived in a field where the top ten awaited with a surprise birthday picnic. All of these really fun ideas were filed away to be used later when George was in command.

Truly the group that plays together stays together.

13 | Washington DC
"A Different Army Experience"

GEORGE RECEIVED ORDERS for the Pentagon. That is a dreaded assignment for officers who love being with troops. It was, however, one of the blocks to check for being well rounded, so he was getting to check that block in "DCSOP's" or Deputy of Chief of Staff for Operations and Plans. Now it's called Army G3. George was to be a force structure plans officer.

We went up to DC to find a place to live and spent one day with a real estate agent we really liked. We were obliged to rent as it was 1980, and the prime rate was 17 percent, thanks to the Carter Administration inflation. So we could not afford to buy. She showed us so many houses that they all began to blend. The housing sales market was dismal, so we were even offered new unfinished homes to rent where we could decide carpets, room colors, cabinet finishes, etc. We really liked the one house that was, of course, at the top of our price range. It was one block from Oak View Elementary and Robinson High School and a block from the bus stop for George. The house had been built by a builder for himself who then changed his mind, selling it to an army officer stationed in California. The backyard was huge and the house wonderful. The first floor had a large sunken living room, half bath, separate dining room, and a large kitchen off a sunken den. The den had a fireplace and doors onto a patio in the back. The basement had large walk in closets, a recreation room opening to an outdoor patio, large laundry room, guest bedroom and bath, and a lit alcove, possibly for painting. Upstairs featured four bedrooms and two baths. We choose it, but until we saw it again I was sure the kitchen had a brick floor. Always take copious notes when house hunting.

Before we left Fort Bragg, we gave away our old couch, bought bedroom and living room furniture in North Carolina, and had it shipped to the DC address. We also ordered a beautiful reversible fabric. We made four nine-foot tall hinged screens from plywood and molding, covering the plywood with the fabric. The sunken living room was too big for our meager furniture, so the screens helped fill an entire corner.

The move went fairly well as moves go. No major losses or stolen silver.

There also was no sense of comradery found on an army post. Everyone lived so far apart, and many of the wives worked to make ends meet. The DC area is not a cheap place to live. Therefore, there were no monthly coffees, fun gatherings, thrift shop duties, etc. About once a year, someone would have a gathering, but few of the wives knew each other.

The girls had just started to skate and compete at Fort Bragg but were also in other activities. In DC, ice skating was so much more expensive; that was their only sport.

School was another huge adjustment. Robinson High School was so large that the student body was divided in half alphabetically, so it had two separate staffs, one for each half. The first time I went into the school, the total lack of supervision and staff control stunned me. Teenagers were necking in the hallways, eating and drinking in the classrooms, boom boxes were blaring, and students were everywhere besides class during class time. At our first PTA meeting, the principal took questions from the audience. A parent voiced concern about drugs in the school, asking the principal to comment. He assured us all there were no drugs in the high school. Another parent stood up quickly, yelled, "Yes, there is. My son is in jail for selling here." The principal quickly moved on to another subject totally ignoring the outburst. It was alarming to us all. His philosophy was to have a relaxed, anything-goes atmosphere to prepare them for college where they would not have supervision.

Brackett was in his second semester of kindergarten with an exceptional teacher. His next to nothing education at Fort Bragg the first semester was not only made up and surpassed, but he truly bloomed in her classroom. His teacher had been a teacher of the year in Virginia, and we understood why.

Tara was in the last half of the sixth grade and having trouble with the transition. She made it thru the sixth grade but not without some battles. When she went over to the high school the next year, she settled in much more easily.

One day, Tara met a friend from down the street, and they were walking across our yard to walk the few blocks to school. She had dark blobs on her ears, so I called her back inside. She had wanted to pierce her ears, I had said, "Not until you are sixteen." She had used an ice cube and a needle to pierce her own ears and had thumb tacks stuck in the holes. I lost it! I made her take them out, put alcohol on her new holes, and go to school, promising when she was sixteen, I would take her to get her ears pierced, and I would get mine done too. She tearfully agreed but had to stomp out of the house to make a show for her friend.

Both girls spent that summer at the ice skating rink. They had a 4:00 or 5:00 a.m. ice time followed by classes most every day. They took breakfast and lunch in a cooler. Cheryl got a job working there with her best friend, Heather. Cheryl was on the Fairfax ice dance team, and they both competed. We spent many hours watching practice and competitions. I learned to make skating costumes from leotards. As with any sport there are "skate moms" who yell at their darlings, giving advice, criticizing, critiquing, and asking the other moms probing questions to determine standing, I suppose. Since my skating skill included being able to hold on to the wall while trying to stay upright as I circled the rink, my girls were never embarrassed by my help. Sometimes I know enough to keep my mouth shut.

I decided to do another year at the Southern Living Christmas Show in Charlotte so had spent a year getting enough marionettes finished to last the entire nine days. A few days before I was to leave, the panic set in because the downstairs bedroom bed was covered with unstrung marionettes. The next morning, when I went downstairs they were all hanging from a bar in the huge laundry room. A miracle had occurred, the elves had visited, or it was a mirage. In reality, our Tara had stayed up all night and strung them for me! What a precious gift!

Cheryl was taken out of school for a week to help me sell. She had a real knack for setting up the display but was quickly bored by playing with the marionettes to entice buyers. Most of the food vendors had free samples of food, drink, and wares; so she ate most of her meals on the ramble. It was helpful to have her there, but when George brought Tara and Brack down and those two started playing with my stock, the sales skyrocketed. I learned where my children's talent lay in the merchandising field.

On my birthday, George was TDY (temporary duty) somewhere so I was alone feeling sorry for myself because no one called! Birthdays are not huge on his list, but they are on mine. My younger brother, Lyn, called that afternoon and at 11:00 p.m., Mother and Daddy called. George called later than that. When Cheryl and Tara came home from school, Tara handed me a bouquet of flowers she had picked in the front yard of the model house for the neighboring housing development, and Cheryl asked if I could take them to the mall to get me a card. Oh, and could they have some money for the cards. It crossed my mind to repay the courtesy on their next birthdays. A homemade card made before the day would have been treasured. Welcome to teenage years!

I began having female problems with one menstrual cycle followed closely by another, and the flows were heavy. The OB-GYN at Walter Reed said the uterus had to be removed as soon as possible. The next week, I was in surgery. Mother took time from teaching and came to help. She was a lifesaver as she cooked, cleaned, corralled the children, and kept everything running smoothly. She stayed for five days, and the day she left, I felt really badly. By that afternoon, I literally crawled to the bathroom, had a fever, and stayed in bed in pain. When George got home he called Walter Reed, put me in the backseat of the car, and drove back to the hospital. I remember very little of that ride. An infection had begun internally where the surgery had occurred. I spent the next ten days in the hospital on IVs and antibiotics. The only good thing was the weight loss!

Lyn was playing with the Claude King tour (Woverton Mountain fame), and they were coming to DC. We offered hospitality which they accepted, so late one night a huge tour bus pulled up in front of our house, and the band filed out. We showed them the sleeping options and, not surprisingly, Claude took the big downstairs bedroom as the rest of the band spread out to the other options. They spent the next day buying guitar strings, stocking the bus, and washing clothes. A rather large member of the band was swinging on a pappy dad, a sack hung on a rope from a tree, when the rope broke. He was okay but was mortified. No amount of assurances that it was only a rope and certainly no big deal would suffice. They played at an NCO (Noncommissioned Officer) club that night, so we went to hear them play. Our older brother, James Voland, was stationed near DC as well, so he also went. At one point, Voland and I were dancing with each other, and Lyn almost missed a beat. He had never seen such a sight. He still talks about how startled he was to look up to see his siblings dancing with each other.

The year and a half in DC ended, and George was once again assigned to Fort Bragg where he was to be a battalion commander. We were so excited, not only to be returning to Fort Bragg and the 82nd Airborne Division, but also for him to get a command position with troops.

George was promoted to lieutenant colonel by General Gary Luck at the Pentagon. The only time up to then he was promoted in a proper ceremony.

When he was promoted to first lieutenant, he was on an ambush patrol in Vietnam. He got a radio transmission, "Be advised '36' is an Oscar-2."

The promotion to captain occurred one Saturday morning in the I-325 at Fort Bragg. He was told to report to the battalion commander in his office who unceremoniously got up, pinned on a pair of captain's bars borrowed from his adjutant. The adjutant quickly took back his bars, so George returned to the company he was commanding, still a first lieutenant.

When he was promoted to major, he was in graduate school at Duke and read about it in the *Army Times*.

George was delighted General Luck could promote him as he held the general in such high regard. General Luck was later to be Fort Bragg and the Eighteenth Airborne Corps commander when George commanded the 82nd First Brigade. Small world.

14 | Fort Bragg, North Carolina
"Hooah x Three"

WE HAD NEVER bought a house before but thought this might be the time, as interest rates had dropped from 17 percent to a mere 11 percent. We picked a realtor at random, and she agreed to show us as many houses in our price range as possible in a day. We told her we had eclectic tastes but needed a formal living room, dining room, a den, four bedrooms, and two baths. Our living room was all pastels with oriental rugs. We knew we were in trouble when by the third house none of them met our request. The fourth house was a deal breaker. She took us into a log home, told us to just shut our eyes so we wouldn't see the pine paneled ceiling and walls. We couldn't imagine a house farther from what we requested. It was about noon by then, so we told her we would think about them and call her if we needed to see anything else. Thank you, very much. We remember her name to this day and the annoying rabbit twitch of her nose!

We immediately called another company and spent the afternoon with a realtor who knew how to listen. We found the perfect house just to discover it had sold that morning. The realtor suggested we contact the builder and check on the cost of building it.

We did, found a great lot, and contracted to have the house built. I made a few adjustments to the plan including reinforcing the garage rafters to support a room above and opening a wall between the kitchen and the den.

The kids and I went to Arkansas to wait out the summer. The house was supposed to be finished by August. George lived in the BOQ (bachelor officer quarters) on post and occasionally went by to check on the progress of the builder. By August, it wasn't close to being finished.

School started the end of August, so we drove back to Fayetteville from Arkansas, a thirteen-hour drive. George found us a short-term lease apartment not too far from the kids' schools. It was an eat-in kitchen den combo with two bedrooms and a bath. The girls shared one bedroom, George and I had another, and Brackett slept on the couch in the "den, living room, kitchen combo." The girls caught a bus to school, but I took Brack every day. The cramped space got smaller and smaller the longer we were there. September slipped into October, and we were getting less and less understanding about the delay. Finally, the builder said he would lay the entrance floor then finish other small things after we moved in. The lawn had no dirt on it, just sand, and he had put some seed out. The contract stated he would put good soil and lay sod. The two windows in either end of the room over the garage weren't in, and various other "finishing touches" were lacking.

We called and asked if he wanted to close the sale as he had built it supposedly with his money he used to build while waiting on more favorable loan terms. He said, "No, not yet, because the points aren't in my favor." We asked about money for the month living there while he completed the detailing. His answer was always, "You don't owe me a thing."

Several times he brought prospective clients by to go through our home to show off his work. We were happy to accommodate him as he hadn't wanted rent before closing.

I had gotten a job teaching at a junior high school in Fayetteville which added even more complication to our daily life.

George's battalion was alerted, then locked down to deploy to Grenada on Operation Urgent Fury to rescue American medical students. When a unit is locked down, that is exactly what happens. They are locked behind chain fencing, getting everything ready to go on a mission. By locking down, control over communications to the outside world is controlled, thus offering security of the mission.

The builder called the day they were locked down in a panic to close. I told him it was impossible, but he insisted on going over to Green Ramp and giving George the paperwork through the fence. I explained that it was impossible, and he would have to wait for George's return. He called daily insisting we mail it, send it by courier, etc. When George finally returned after the battalion successfully rescued over one hundred students, we sat down with his attorney and closed on the house. The closing was unprofessional; they had the wrong price and wrong payments for starters. Also, by North Carolina law, a veteran using a VA loan was to be represented by counsel. The builder's attorney stated he would get us our counsel and save us the fee. We thought it odd with a potential built-in conflict of interests but trustingly proceeded. We had never bought or built a house. One line on the checklist was to ask the builder if any other rent, fees, or monies were owed; answered "none." He and his lawyer later lied under oath about this. We thought that was the end of it but would discover later to our amazement, it was anything but the end.

Throughout that winter and into the spring, we settled into the house and the battalion.

George had taken the battalion from a bachelor, so the executive officer's wife had run things. A new executive officer (XO) and his wife came on board about the time we did. Larry and Mary Lou Tatum were a great team, and I was so glad to have a competent wife to walk into the fire with me.

At my first coffee, I was told that a certain lady who was not a fiancé but a girlfriend of a company commander always came to the coffees and paid her yearly dues. I personally didn't care who slept with whom or about anyone's living arrangements, but the coffees were for spouses and often things were discussed and decided that required that legal marriage document. I told them that she was welcome at every social event we had as his date, but she could not be an official dues-paying member of the wives' coffee group; and we would refund her dues money. I called her and explained. I obviously did a bad job as she didn't speak to me again for several years even after they married. Mary Lou's favorite new saying was "Better you than me!"

The wives' group hadn't had much structure, so Mary Lou and I had to gently bring it around to a cohesive group.

The army had not deployed to combat since Vietnam, but had spent the intervening years rebuilding itself. Sadly family support was totally neglected. There were no standard operation procedures (SOPs), nor any guidance on how to inform and care for wives when the husband's unit deployed to combat on short notice.

This omission was particularly egregious in the 82nd Airborne Division, as no notice warfare and rapid deployments were the 82nd's reasons for existence.

Grenada was the wake-up call for the army.

When the men were deployed to Grenada, we got a roster from the rear detachment and called everyone on it to determine who had a wife and who didn't. We ended up with a list of our first family support group members.

We called them all and set up a meeting in the chapel. At that meeting, we compiled a list of wives in each company so if we needed to disperse information we could do so quickly. Each company commander's wife and first sergeant's wife started the chain after a call from me. Everyone had my number and their company commander's wife's number.

I decided we needed to call the company commanders' wives together to get their feedback on how to merge our new group into a cohesive team. I invited them all to lunch at the Officers' Club. One wife was very late, so we went ahead and ate then began the meeting. Everyone voiced their opinion, and we were getting on a common ground when the latecomer appeared. I explained what we had done so far and encouraged her to get something to eat. She narrowed her eyes, leaned across the table, and told me she had no intentions of doing anything. Her husband was in the military, not her, and she would *not* be told what to do. She turned on her heels and marched back to, I suppose, selling Mary Kay. She was right; she rarely did anything, so the company wives had to take up her slack and did so with enthusiasm. Her attitude and rudeness did much to cement a bond of friendship between the rest of us.

During these stressful "no-husband" times, the phone would often ring throughout the night. Usually, it was a young wife who was scared or lying awake thinking and needing guidance. The only company commander's wife who took her phone off the hook was, you guessed it, our rebel wife. So her group all called me. Thanks ever so much!

We elected officers of our new little family support group and a corporal's wife, Sybil Sosaki, was elected president. She was fabulous. She had a master's degree and worked full-time in downtown Fayetteville. Take that stereotypes!

We had planning meetings every few months to plan several months in advance. One such meeting was at our house. I asked everyone to bring a vegetable for the soup. I put a roast on to cook early that morning, so when the ladies arrived we chopped all their gifts and added to the pot. Those who brought children sent the kids upstairs for my girls to babysit. By the time the meeting was over, the soup was done; we ate and visited until late in the evening. Those meetings were held while the men were gone on assignment or in the field. The group was composed of wives of all ranks from private to lieutenant colonel.

As a family support group, we sponsored a trip to the outlet mall in Burlington, North Carolina. To fund it, we had a bake sale near the troops. Everyone knew they were always hungry. We rented a bus, paid one of the husbands, who had the appropriate license, with lunch and provided snacks for going and coming back. Coming back, we stopped at McDonald's for supper. Husbands were warned to fix dinner if they wanted to eat as we would be late. On the return trip, we always had show and tell. As everyone shared what bargain they had found, someone always asked, "Where did you find that? Can we go back?"

One of our more energetic officer's spouses, Donna Parker, Lieutenant Phil Parker's wife, was a true free spirit. On one of our first family support group meetings, she sat on the floor in the aisle with her baby in her lap. That simple gesture made everyone feel relaxed and the husbands' ranks all but disappeared. She was a treasure!

The brigade formal was to be our battalion's responsibility, but our men were in Grenada, so we gathered the men who remained and some of the wives. We made the plans in case the battalion didn't get back in time.

Several themes were suggested, but the one we all loved was a beach Christmas which was suggested by one of the rear detachment men. The possibilities abounded!

We had thirty round tables seating ten each so two of the rear detachment men cut four-foot branches in the woods, cemented them into large coffee cans, and sprayed them all white.

After sharing our plan with my teaching buddies, we planned an overnight to Myrtle Beach, North Carolina. We stayed with a friend of one of the teachers. The next day we spent two hours picking up buckets of shells and drove back to Fayetteville with our bounty.

One of the men drilled a small hole in each shell. The battalion wives dipped each in glue, then white or silver glitter. A silver ribbon was run through the hole and then hung on the painted branches. The cans were covered with white paper tied with large silver ribbons. Votives in faceted plastic cups were lit under each tree. The trees were placed on mirror tiles so the total effect was a forest of white trees glittering in candle light. It was spectacular.

Large sprayed trees with twinkle lights banked the entrance to the dining room.

The trees were stored afterward and used repeatedly with other decorations for other occasions.

We took on service projects too. One was to improve the atmosphere of the mess hall. We had raised money with bake sales so we bought plants. We decorated day rooms at Christmas, and the big one was the redo of the nursery at the brigade chapel. We begged carpet samples to lay a colorful mosaic on the concrete floor, painted the walls adding colorful drawings, got a donated rocker, and decided to ask a large store specializing in baby items to donate a baby bed.

On a cold rainy day, Mary Lou and I drove downtown to the store and asked to speak to the owner. She came out and listened to our request with impatience. It is true we probably looked like wet scavengers, but she had obviously had a very bad morning. Her mouth became a tight straight line, and she grabbed a set of baby sheets, literally throwing them at us.

We were too stunned to react. We mumbled thanks and left. Sitting in the car, we stared at each other openmouthed.

By the time I reached home, I was smoldering. I boxed up the sheets and wrote her a letter telling her we couldn't possibly accept the sheets so ungraciously given. We assumed she had had a very bad day, and that should any of the thousands of army wives come into her store, we hoped she would treat them with more courtesy.

I mailed them back to her adding our joint return address label. The very next day, we received an apology. At the next commanders' wives meeting, I mentioned our experience to all, and the division commander's wife was livid. In business it is always wise to treat everyone with dignity even if they do look like a drowned puppy.

We hadn't been at Bragg long before, again, we had to work our day at the thrift shop.

I had been there at least three hours when it was announced a car was on fire in the parking lot.

About ten minutes later, the more frantic call announced the burning car was small and blue.

My little Volkswagen Rabbit was small and blue. I grabbed my purse from the hidden shelf, dug out my car keys, and dove out the door.

I unlocked the hot door handle so a fireman could pull it open. Smoke boiled from under the hood and into the interior.

I jumped in and put the car in neutral. Firemen pushed it to the center of the empty parking lot as I dove out thinking it may explode any minute.

I went back inside to call George.

He was in the field, so someone in the office answered the phone. He asked if he could take a message. "Well," I said, "you can tell him our car just burned up in the thrift shop parking lot."

There was a pause then he emphatically state, "No way am I telling him that!"

"Just have him call me," I suggested.

When he got back and the USAA insurance adjuster checked out the car in the post impound lot, he was calmer when we were told the car had spontaneously caught fire after sitting for that long. Thank goodness we weren't in it at the time of combustion.

I taught at Douglas Byrd Junior High. The first year I had one seventh-grade science class, an educationally mentally handicapped (EMH) science class, and ninth-grade physical science. The seventh graders were on an emotional roller coaster. How my mom could teach only seventh graders, I could not fathom. The ninth graders were great, and I dearly loved the EMH class.

Our EMH classroom was a really fun place to learn. Different types of clouds hung from the ceilings, student artwork was everywhere, and a pet gerbil was loved by them all.

For the most part, the teachers were great, and several became very good friends. Linda Sherriff, the home economics teacher, lived with her mom and sister taking care of both. She was blessed with a great sense of humor and a strong work ethic. Karen Asbury taught English and was a partner in crime. We did not have to have our jobs to exist, so were more ready to buck the system when need be.

The second year I only had ninth graders and was *so* grateful! I also was the girls' track coach, which meant longer days during track season and a few dollars more per month. At least once a week, a parent wouldn't come to get a child for one reason or another or no reason, and I would drive them home. This made for very long days.

During all this, not only did we have extra duties at school such as attending ball games, but the battalion, brigade, and division also had functions as well as the FSG activities. Time became a priceless commodity.

Jim Johnson commanded the brigade when we arrived. His wife, Edna, was a treasure.

Just before George assumed command, Terry Scott took the brigade with his wife, Carol. They were from Texas, but we didn't know them well yet.

For my birthday one year, the company commanders' wives decided to have a dinner with entertainment. They reserved a room in the Barn which was still one of the few places in Fayetteville that had tablecloths. They also invited Carol Scott, the new brigade commander's wife. Dinner was wonderful, but toward the end I noticed all the waitresses were coming into the room and hanging out around the walls. It soon became apparent why!

A very handsome, well-built young man came in the door in a three-piece suit carrying a rose. *Oh, how sweet!* I thought. A rose! But no, that wasn't all! He came to my chair, handed me the rose, and said, "Happy birthday." And he began to undress! I didn't know where to look. Never having been to a strip club for girls, I was at a loss. In college at the University of Arkansas, I had gone to Dallas a week before the Cotton Bowl as part of a prebowl activity week. I was head cheerleader that year; so the team, band, and cheerleaders were all in town together.

One night, we went with four of our football team members to a strip club and saw Chris Colt and her 45's perform. There was much whopping and hollering, but Chris was getting on in years, and I honestly didn't see what the fuss was all about.

This, however, was way different! The girls were whopping and hollering, and Donna was yelling at me to put money in his G-string. I didn't dare glance at Carol, afraid she would have already fainted. I rarely blush, but they say I was really red. I kept looking at his face, not daring to put money anywhere. Since I couldn't make myself look down I would have missed and made it all even more embarrassing. He did his little dance and left amid the roar of applause. I did give him a weak "Thanks" and clapped with the rest. He deserved the applause for his nerve if nothing else.

Carol, when I did look at her, was cheering with the rest; so that was a relief.

After that, at the next coffee we had a chat about appropriate and nonappropriate activities. Not that it would have swayed this group!

It turned out that it wasn't Donna's idea but Mary Lou Tatum's, so revenge seemed appropriate. We celebrated Mary Lou's birthday at my house. One of the girls taped the music to the stripper, Penny LaFaro's husband, Guy, agreed to be our surprise guest entertainer; and we lay in wait. We gave each other silly gifts for birthdays, so I told Mary Lou hers was an enormous surprise. She sat in a big center chair, the music started, and Guy came in the room with a trench coat. He danced up to her flashing her with his camouflage swim trunks, and AAs cut into his chest hair. He slid out of his trench coat, sat on her lap, and sang "Happy Birthday" to her. This time she was red. We all sang, "Pay Back Birthday Girl."

In every unit, there are women with amazing talents and stories. I was always in awe of each of our young wives. It was always my goal to form a close family within the military unit. Most of us were far from family, so we had to rely on each other for support in times of need.

One thing I did outside of the military community was joining the Christian Women's Club of Fayetteville. They had monthly luncheons, usually at a country club, with a lay speaker and a guest inspirational speaker. These were informal luncheons where I met many lovely ladies from the Fayetteville area. The creative centerpieces were worthy of applause. At one luncheon, the lay speaker whose name I have forgotten but the guest speaker was a lady who told the story of being struck by lightning camping on an island in Minnesota. She and her husband were quickly boated out by other members of their camping party. Upon arriving at the emergency room, they were put in the same room as they weren't expected to make it. They had prayed together and did survive, but the wife still had the hand print of her husband on her back where the bolt of lightning went from him through her. We are told God doesn't give you more than you can handle, so it occurred to me that I had led a very gentle life to date, so perhaps I wasn't such a strong person after all. I had not had any huge events to survive. I would remember these thoughts later and understand that up to date, I had not been shaped enough to endure the fire that was to come.

Cheryl and Tara were students in Pine Forest Junior High and Senior High School. Brack was in elementary, and all were doing well academically.

The girls were both in Girl Scouts and Brackett in Cub Scouts. For two summers, I joined a friend, Donna Lampkins, in running the area summer Girl Scout camp on post. One year, the main tent had to be moved two feet because we were too close to the nesting tree of a red cockaded woodpecker. They were on the endangered species list which played havoc with our camp but mostly the training for the troops. The birds had flourished amid the training for years, but suddenly all activity had to work around their habitat.

Tara and a friend went roller skating one night for her birthday. George was gone with the troops on an exercise. He always seemed to be gone when disaster struck. Someone knocked on the door, and I was surprised to see a police officer standing there with his blue lights flashing from our drive. A quick glance around assured me every neighbor had their blinds opened enough to check it out.

Having teenagers, a cop at the door can only mean a "heart-in-your-toes" reaction. He asked if Tara was our daughter; I assured him she was and inquired if she was all right. He said, "It depends." And he led me out to the patrol car. She and a girlfriend had drunk straight liquor in the skating rink parking lot and were both skunk drunk. Tara had thrown up in the backseat of the patrol car and couldn't stay on her feet. The girlfriend had been rushed to the emergency room to have her stomach pumped. Tara was on her hands and knees in the yard, so I suggested she crawl into the house. Cheryl came out grinning from ear to ear to help Tara get in the house. I said, "Let her crawl in!" It took me several trips and a full can of Lysol to clean up the cop's backseat.

Tara made it to bed and was not only hungover the next morning, but also horrified her friend was in the hospital! The girlfriend's mother called and said they didn't keep alcohol in their home, so obviously it came from our house. They would insist the girls not spend any more time together. The friendship was ended. I agreed.

Since Tara has since been a detective SGT in the Honolulu Police Department serving for seventeen years, I wonder what the arresting officers would have thought of that.

Tara told me years later, the liquor was provided by the other girl, but she didn't say so to protect her from her parent's wrath.

The brigade left for an exercise which included a jump into Fort Stewart, Georgia. Watching the men jump always made me hold my breath until all the jumpers' chutes opened. They usually jumped at night, so we didn't watch very often. You can't fixate on the "what ifs" when your love does dangerous things. You would go mad in no time, so I just trusted God would take care of him.

One night about 3:00 a.m., the phone woke me from a sound sleep. It was the battalion chaplain calling to say the air force had dropped the entire battalion in the trees. The brigade commander, Terry Scott, had a broken back, and George was in the emergency room at Stewart with a collapsed lung, broken scapula, crushed right wrist, broken ribs, and maybe other injuries. He had landed in the highest pine tree in Georgia, tied his reserve to the limb to climb down, put on his gloves, leaned down to repel using his reserve when the limb broke. He landed on the canteen on his back. It was a miracle that he wasn't killed.

I woke up the girls, told them what had happened, gave instructions for caring for Brack and each other, left my lesson plans with a fellow teacher, and drove out of Fayetteville heading south, praying the whole way.

A couple I did not know offered a room in their quarters for me when I needed sleep.

I arrived at the base hospital to find George awake, drugged, and in agony.

The anesthesiologist had planned to leave the next day for vacation. He cancelled it and put a reclining chair next to George's ICU bed, where he set up his twenty-four-hour vigil. They let me in occasionally to hold his uninjured hand and tell him how much I loved him. Otherwise I claimed the couch outside the ICU. Fortunately, the ICU was state of the art at the time.

The admitting doctor was Chinese and had put a drain in George's chest cavity to drain the blood from the punctured lung. He had put the drain in too high, so the chest cavity did not completely drain.

Because the injured and bleeding lung was filling with blood, it induced a syndrome whereby the bad lung fooled the good lung into also filling with blood and fluid. George was literally drowning in his own blood.

The doctors quickly decided he must be tipped up on his side so the blood and fluid would reach the drain pipe. He was given a massive shot of morphine into his spine and then turned on his side.

You could hear the broken ribs crackling, causing untold agony to my love. I wanted to hit the doctor and ask to see his medical degree. The anesthesiologist interceded and said he would take over. George was in such agony after the incompetent manhandling they upped the morphine. He got very pale, skin became cold and clammy, and his eyes started to glaze over. We all yelled about the same time to stop the morphine. They sent me out, got him stabilized, and the Chinese doctor was replaced.

The man in the next ICU bed died a few minutes later which didn't help the morale.

Despite almost killing George with an overdose into his spine, the little teapot tip-him-over-and-pour-him-out strategy worked. The drowning syndrome halted.

While George was sleeping, I went upstairs to visit Colonel Scott whose back was broken. The Scotts had a sweet daughter with Down's syndrome, so Carol couldn't come. He was doing okay but also in great pain.

I would go to the Good Samaritan's home late at night and return early the next morning until it was clear George would make it. They made plans to send him by helicopter back to Fort Bragg and Womack Hospital. At that time, Womack did not have a great reputation.

I drove back to Fayetteville, and as I pulled into the driveway, my Tara was sitting on the porch with bleached yellow hair. Her natural blonde was gone! I burst into tears and verbally jumped on both girls. They didn't seem to know how serious their dad was injured. Cheryl said Tara had started to bleach it, and it was spotty so she helped her get it all one color. *Yuck!*

Two days after I got back, they released George to Womack. He had his battalion surgeon meet the helicopter and release him home, as he feared he might be mishandled, even killed in Womack. It scared me to death. I was not a nurse and was terrified he would need some emergency care.

We rolled pads from camping cots to put behind his back to keep him upright in bed. The shattered wrist had been set last, so it was in a cast. We would walk him into the den during the day, settle him on the couch, and suspend his arm by tying a cord to the upstairs railing and tying the sling to be above his heart. He was on pain medications several times a day, but still every breath was agony. We could now truthfully say the brigade and battalion commanders were both on drugs. As the days went by, he gained strength and insisted on walking outside. For the first time, I could jog faster than he could but not for long.

While he was still recuperating, the brigade held an annual social event at the Officers' Club. Colonel Scott and George insisted they felt well enough to go, if we only went for the meal. Carol Scott and I arrived with our wounded soldiers on one arm and a pillow in the other. Colonel Scott was wearing, under his uniform, what we jokingly called his Barbie doll armor. It was a plastic body cast in a lovely shade of pink to keep his back in the proper position as it healed. We slid the pillowcases over the backs of the chairs so the men could lean back against the soft pillows. They had both taken medication before arriving so were somewhat comfortable. We cut their meat and helped them eat the meal and by the time dessert was over and the dancing began, the pain medications were wearing off. We left while they could both depart with some semblance of military bearing.

George got off the drugs as fast as he could and within two months was running again.

General Trobaugh, the division commander, said when he reached George on the ground he heard a whispered, "Sir, may I still come up to be G-3?" George had been selected for that slot before the accident and was assured the spot was still his.

The battalion planned his farewell amid great secrecy. It was to be held at our home, so George could be more comfortable. The afternoon of the event, he was told to stay inside and away from all windows. Right! He was seen peeking many times during the afternoon. An Arkansas flag was hung from the upper front garage windows, a pen was hastily erected in the backyard holding several chickens, a piglet, and a little goat. George's office had been moved to the back corner of our fenced yard complete with desk, carpet, and pictures which hung on the fence.

A pseudo still was fashioned with a clever device dripping bourbon from a hidden bottle, hillbilly music permeated the neighborhood, boards on sawhorses formed tables for the potluck supper, and the tree from which he had fallen was cut down by the troops with a chunk reserved as a gift. His reserve chute handle and a ladder were against a big pine in the yard.

As a final touch, as each car load arrived, they threw a piece of junk in our front yard. We had a car bumper, old mattress springs, tires, two wheels, a car engine, bottles, cans, and bags of garbage all decorating the lawn. There are homes in Arkansas that look that way, but up to then not ours. The entire place was priceless. We absolutely loved it.

It took two days to dismantle it all. One of the men who helped with it all sat at our kitchen table and talked with me for a good long while.

He was found dead the next week, and I always wondered if I could have asked different questions or helped in any way with whatever problems he had. A loss in a military unit is like losing a family member, so we all had "what ifs."

The change of command was emotional because the family had become very tight.

George moved up to be Division G-3, so my coffee group changed to division headquarters.

Cheryl decided as a graduating senior she wanted to go to Atlanta with her best friend, Anne Marie, and work in retail rather than attend college. She planned to leave the night of graduation. She had originally wanted to go to a design school in New York, but we simply could not afford the cost. I drove the girls to Atlanta a few weeks before graduation to find a safe apartment close to public transportation. Our friend from Germany, Ilsa Chamberlain, offered to hire her at a large Atlanta department store but cautioned she would be folding sweaters and the like with only a high school education. We found a lovely controlled access apartment they could afford on the bus route.

Graduation night at Pine Forest was rowdy and rather wild. Local police lined the aisles as a precaution. Times had certainly changed!

The girls went home afterward, loaded their belongings in Anne Marie's car, and took off for the big city. We were really worried about them. Anne Marie's boyfriend showed up there shortly after their arrival, and it was only a few months before Ilsa called to say she had had to fire Cheryl for often not showing up for work or being late when she did.

Cheryl got a job at a restaurant which encouraged the girls to dress wildly. That fit right into Cheryl's idea of a fun job.

George had business in Atlanta and went by to check on her. He came home with tears in his eyes and found it difficult to describe her situation. She and two other waitresses shared a room. Clothes were piled everywhere, a cat with a litter of kittens had taken up residence in the only tub, and the entire place was a disaster.

We decided to offer her a used car if she would like to go to college. We called her and she announced the owner had offered her the managership of the newest restaurant in the chain. We offered our suggestion, and she said she did not want to be a waitress or in the restaurant business the rest of her life so would agree to college. We sent her a plane ticket to return the week of Christmas so she could get clothes and other needed items for college. She had been accepted at Appalachian University in Boone, North Carolina, and they would accept her at semester. All her clothes had mildewed and ruined in the leaky trunk of a friend's car, so she had very little.

My parents came for Christmas; and my older brother, Voland, and family were to arrive in a few days.

Tara and I drove to the airport in Fayetteville to get our prodigal daughter. She was a vision getting off the plane. She almost caused a total standstill in the airport. She was wearing tight bright floral pants, at one time new, riding boots whose sole was flapping, a satin shirt, a big black long coat with cigarette burns in the lapels, at least fifteen bracelets on each arm, dangling earrings, several cross necklaces, and topping it all off, a foot-high white Mohawk with close-cut black sides. We learned later it was blackened with shoe polish. How creative! We remembered who was beneath it all—our darling Cheryl—so we rushed up, grabbed her in a bear hug, and welcomed her home. We ignored the stares, gawks, and whispered comments all the way to the car where the Mohawk bent to fit.

When we got to the house, she went in to astound her grandparents. They both looked up not blinking twice, and Daddy said, "Hi, Cheryl, Merry Christmas!" And Mother pointed to the middle bracelet on one arm and said, "Oh look, I love that one. May I borrow it sometime?" Living through the seventies with my younger brother, Lyn, they were hardened to shocks.

For a last foray as a punk rocker, Cheryl and Tara went to the mall to shock and awe. They were not disappointed as she was definitely one of a kind. While there, however, Cheryl ran into her hairstylist who was aghast. She clearly explained that Cheryl's hair was so damaged another bleaching would break it off at the scalp! She gave Cheryl an emergency appointment to come get it fixed.

The next day, Voland arrived with his wife and two children. He had insisted his son, Jay, get a haircut before coming; and they were very well dressed and coifed.

When they saw Cheryl, it was hard not to laugh, but we did understand their reaction. Jay still recalls that day and regales Cheryl about her appearance and how mad he was he had to cut his hair.

The hairstylist cut her hair to cover the shaved sides, dyed it all black, and made her promise to take better care of it.

After Christmas, we bought her a used car, new clothes, and dorm room necessities. We packed up both cars, hers and ours, and drove up to Boone, North Carolina. While we were settling her in, her roommate and parents arrived. The girl took one look at Cheryl's black hair and Guns and Roses poster, paled, and we knew she would not last. She then moved out the first month.

Two months into the semester, Cheryl was at a party in a room on another floor of the dorm. She got into the elevator to retrieve something from her room when she was accosted at knife point and forced into her room. She deduced the young man was high on drugs so told him she would be right back; she had to tell her friends she would return shortly, or they would all come to her room looking for her. He somehow believed her, so she escaped and called the campus cops.

They arrested him, and she brought charges even though she was told by Appalacian the young man was on an athletic scholarship, as if that should make a difference. We were so proud of her for keeping her wits about her and surviving a possible serious outcome. She came home two days later for spring break and couldn't stop crying. It was a terrifying experience for her and a sobering one. She returned to school determined to finish college, no matter what.

George received word he was selected for the Army War College in Carlisle, Pennsylvania. We were all so excited for George and for us.

That spring, our builder, remember him, rose from the dust to astonish us. He claimed we owed him one thousand plus dollars in rent for the month before we closed the two years before.

At the formal "closing" on the house, the builder was specifically asked if any rent or other expenses were outstanding. "None of any kind" was the answer. We should have become suspicious when his lawyer had the wrong amount for the house from the building contract which would have overcharged us by ten thousand dollars.

I immediately called Daddy, who remember was on the Arkansas Supreme Court, to ask his advice. He said, "Sis, this is so blatantly wrong. You really don't even need a lawyer." We got one anyway. We listed the things that were never done, his assuring us we didn't owe anything for rent, his delay of closing, then panic to close, and his bringing prospective clients by to show the house. The lawyer agreed it was a slam dunk. The builder's wife had a curtain shop in a very-high-rent shopping area, had broken her leg, and was reportedly in financial difficulty with her store. We assumed that was the reason for the suit at this late date.

The court date rolled around, and we went prepared for justice. I had forgotten how small town southern justice worked until we were in that courtroom. Looking around, we saw his entire family there. His lawyer was the one who had "represented" the veteran (us). It was not ethical, and it was election year for the judge. Groan! After we all said our piece, the judge ruled we owed the builder rent but he had to add dirt to our yard, sod it, and fix the windows. We were astounded! When I called Daddy with the news, he said sometimes even good men make bad judges and such is the case here, I assume. I really wished I could vote there.

Someone had burned the builder's house to the ground a few years before we moved there, and to be honest we could sort of understand that kind of rage. He had put a lien on our house before the judgment, and we wanted to sell before leaving, so we went to the attorney who handled the school district's legal affairs. When I told him of our plight, he was as astounded as we were. He wrote a letter to the attorney who illegally took the stand for the builder. It just so happened that this attorney was head of the Ethics Committee of the North Carolina Bar Association.

The North Carolina Ethics Committee offered him a "deal he couldn't refuse." He could return the money, drop the claim, or be disbarred. It was only fifteen hundred dollars or so, but it was the principle of the deal that angered us, especially when the builder made his living building for military families. Several years later, the builder's attorney committed suicide. Ours was, no doubt, not the only illegal thing he had done.

To sell the house, we used our friend, Donna Lampkins, who was new to real estate.

The house sold in ten days, leaving us immensely relieved since other homes in the area had been on the market for a year or more. The extra room above the garage gave us the only five-bedroom home in the area.

15 | Carlisle Barracks, Pennsylvania
Army War College "Return to Carlisle"

WE WERE ASSIGNED quarters only one block and across the LeTort Creek from the Old Mill where we had lived years before. Not much had changed in Carlisle since we first lived there. The town itself was as quaint as ever with the new mall outside town spreading the shopping a bit further. The countryside in Pennsylvania was just beautiful with aging rock facades of farm homes nestled in green hills. Carlisle Barracks was a solid reminder of some of the brightest and darkest history. The Indian school cemetery was filled with children with English and Indian names, and much of the original buildings still stood although modernized.

Our quarters were a split level, so our very large corn plant would fit in the entrance if we could just get it there. George had found another old car to restore, so that proved to be the answer. Before leaving Fort Bragg, Tara decided her white French provincial canopy bed which she had always despised should be sold. Some people who owned a local used car lot came to see the house we were selling, and although they decided not to buy, they did strike a deal with George. He would give them the bedroom suite in exchange for the use of the flat bed hauler to take his old car up north. George was told the truck used a bit of oil but otherwise, it was just fine. We loaded that car and trailer with all our plants, tying the giant corn plant to the flat bed. Again, George looked like the original Oakie as he drove north. The car and plants were stashed with friends who were already in residence at Carlisle.

The flat bed and George returned after a two-day driving marathon and thirty quarts of oil that blew past worn-out valve guide seals to keep the old girl gliding instead of grinding to a halt.

The movers arrived in Carlisle to unload our "stuff," and thankfully we had only slight damage.

I bought even more curtains since, of course, all those we had wouldn't fit the windows in these quarters. The split level went down to a combination living room and dining room, laundry room, a short hall to the right past the washer/dryer to an eat-in kitchen. The front windows were at ground level. The previous residents had obviously trained one of many local squirrels to have meals with them. Our first day, we heard a knock on the window, and it was "Chatter," the squirrel, wondering when the next meal would be served. We would open the sliding glass window a crack so he could grab a nut, spin it to check for freshness, chatter thanks, and be off. Three of us thought it was adorable; George kept looking for a gun.

Upstairs were four bedrooms and two baths. Brack and Tara had a room each, George and I took the master, and the fourth we made into a den or guest bedroom. We used it for a computer room and bedroom for Cheryl when she was home from college.

After settling in, getting Brack registered in his new school, Tara and I went to the high school. Tara had taken auto mechanics at Pine Forest High School and really loved it. She was looking forward to taking year two. It never occurred to us it was strange to ask for that class, but the counselor assigned to her was aghast! He suggested she take home economics or typing or art. We suggested he sign her up for year two auto mechanics. He even brought the principal in to talk some sense into us but to no avail. They signed her up reluctantly, and she prepared for a difficult year in that class.

She had to have a one-piece work outfit for the class, so we bought a white one and dyed it pink. She was very well endowed, so it did nothing to hide her cute figure, but it didn't flaunt it either.

She also tried out for the field hockey team. When she went out on the field, they didn't have equipment for her. She was the only Carlisle

Barracks girl trying out. The "townies" as the locals were called had ways of weeding out the kids who were there only a year. The townies called the barracks kids "post toasties." Needless to say, she didn't make the team, never being allowed to even try out. As I told her, it was their loss as she was extremely good.

Many tears were shed those first few months as the auto mechanics boys stepped up their harassment. One day she found a dead rat in her locker, and it went downhill from there. She didn't' share much of this with us but endured with silence and a grim determination. By the end of the semester, several of the boys realized, not only did she know her way around an engine, could get her smaller hands in places they couldn't, and no amount of insult could run her out of the class, they accepted her and became friends. The rest of the class never came around. That class was not known for its group intelligence, so much of the ignorance was ignored. Her few friends would invite her to parties, and one of them was a sevnkagr. We had to hear it three times to understand it was a seven kegger beer party. She didn't go but was grateful to be invited.

The barracks kids tended to stick together more for survival than desire. That only made the division worse, but the school administration turned a blind eye, so it never got better.

Brackett on the other hand loved his school which was staffed by excellent teachers who made learning fun. For him, the year was a huge success.

Cheryl came home on breaks, and she and Tara would sign up at the commissary to bag groceries for tips. Barracks kids could work weekends and in the summer. They drew names every morning, so it was truly the luck of the draw who got to work and who didn't. On the days Cheryl made the draw she would make twenty to forty dollars in tips. Much to her disappointment, Tara's name was never drawn. It was a great safe way for the kids to earn some extra money.

Others of our friends were at Carlisle that year: Keith and Paige Kellogg, Buck and Maryann Kernan, Juan and Maria Chavez, all from the 82nd.

The war college class was broken down into work groups that changed at semester, thus allowing you to get to know your classmates. The study groups were for the war college classes, as well as, social groups.

It was always fun to get together for cookouts, baseball games, or other gatherings.

I worked out several nights a week with a Isshin-Ryu dojo run by Master William Washington Roku Dan. He was a large black man who had an amazing talent for teaching children. Although Isshin-Ryu was a different style than the Tae Kwon Do I had practiced; it was a great work out. As I learned the katas, I was asked to help teach the new ones. What a great feeling to help little ones, especially the girls, learn to protect themselves and get a great work out at the same time.

I left there with a second-degree black belt, Ni dan.

The Officers' Wives' Club was, of course, alive and well. The one event they sponsored that was a great memory was the house tour. Everyone on the tour obviously had spent weeks getting their houses just so. We went from lovely house to lovely house traipsing though admiring and taking notes. There was one house on the tour that was opened by the resident in her bathrobe, hair in curlers, no makeup, who exclaimed, "Oh no, is this the week?" We trooped through her house, past the toilet paper trailing down the stairs from the upstairs bath, into the living room. An open newspaper lay on the coffee table with earrings and two half empty wine glasses on top. Shoes were discarded under the table, and a jacket hung over a chair back. The dining room table hadn't been cleared from the breakfast meal. The kitchen sink was full, flour from biscuits covered one counter complete with cutter and dough remnants, and every other surface was covered with the mess of breakfast preparation. As we went upstairs, laughing all the way, we discovered every bedroom a mess. My personal favorite was her son's bedroom where he had obviously stepped out of his underwear and jeans the night before and left them on the floor by his bed. It was priceless! It must have taken days to set it all up and not mess it up with her children's daily activities. I filed that idea, and we reenacted it years later on another post. Military wives are so creative.

The war college for the first time offered a year-long facilitator class for spouses of students. Major Schoonover was going to lead a class in facilitation which would certify the students at the end of the year. I signed up with about ten other wives. They brought in experts from all over the country, and we got to practice with various groups. Another wife and I went to DC and facilitated a workshop for spouses of Reserve and National Guard Commanders. It was a great experience and added to our knowledge of facilitation and the problems of spouses of the Reserves and National Guard.

At the end of every year, the war college students have a Shipwreck party. Work groups dress up as a group, vying for prizes and have a hilarious evening.

Our work group decided to go as shipmates on the Titanic. We made everyone white long sleeveless T-shirts and navy knee-length pants to represent old bathing suits. We had towels with Titanic written on them, and the girls wore headbands.

Another group went as a giant starfish. The costumes were very creative. The long trestle tables had gold fish in bowls as centerpieces. By the end of the night, a few who had had a few too many ate some of the goldfish leaving a few centerpieces only a bowl minus fish.

At the end of Tara's junior year, she was invited to the Junior-Senior prom and knew just what she wanted to wear. I found a pattern and made her a simple long white satin dress. The top we covered with black lace, and I added faux buttons down the entire back to the top of the split at her knees. We rented a black tux jacket she wore over it. Mother and Daddy were visiting, so Mother made her a white satin covered with black lace pocket handkerchief. It was just perfect.

We ran into old friends, Pete and Joan Bondi. Pete was a rear admiral working in Mechanicsburg, and Joan invited me to join their Bible study group. I was thrilled so went once a week and really enjoyed, not only the class, but meeting the navy wives.

The brigade commander list came out, and to George's absolute delight he was on it, and we were headed back to the 82nd. He grinned for a month!

We had buried Brackett's hamster in a wooden box under a giant oak tree in the backyard, so it was time to get a new pet. Our love of collies demanded we not look at any other breed. We found a breeder and went out to see the litter. We picked out our Windy and brought her home. She was a love. The wind was howling when we came home with her; and although Brack wanted to name her Cozy, we outvoted him, and she became Windy. Her registered name was Chertabra's LeTort for her owners and the creek behind the house. As with all the others, she was instantly a dearly loved part of our family.

We cleaned our own quarters again, wearing nails down to the skin but saving big bucks. I was deciding it might not be worth the savings.

The packers came again, and we once more piled suitcases, dog, kids, and us into the car.

16 | Fort Bragg, North Carolina
Brigade Command "Hooah x Four"

HERE WE WERE again, moving into quarters at Fort Bragg. This time we would be living in the huge (to us) quarters just a block off the main post parade field.

Tara would go to EE Smith Senior High School on the other side of Fayetteville. The formerly all-black high school was integrated by bussing many white Fort Bragg high school students although two other high schools were much closer. It was an opportunity for Tara to experience what it was like to be a true minority. That experience would serve her well when we lived in Hawaii. The social experience was nonexistent as the nonmilitary black students were exclusive in their gatherings on their side of town. She did have two dear friends who were both black, and we told them they were the Oreo trio. Their friendship has lasted for years.

Brackett was enrolled in the on post middle school Albrighton. He had an excellent principal and some great friends. He learned to golf and was on a soccer team. His real passion seemed to be skateboard.

We settled in and jumped into brigade life after a change of command on the main post parade field. George took over from Mike Steele. It was so comforting to take over from old friends who were great at what they do.

The brigade commander and wives were the following: First Battalion was Randy Medlock whose wife was in DC, Second Battalion was Ed and Cindy Kersey, and Third Battalion was Boone and Sharon Bartholomews. What a delight they were! Sharon and Boone were both physically attractive, tall, and very capable. Sharon was on top of things and great fun. Ed Kersey had movie star good looks and Cindy was cute as could be, with a bubbly warm personality, and dearly loved by everyone in their unit. Randy Medlock left shortly after we arrived, replaced by Bob and Pixie Killibrew. Bob, a published author was very professor-like, but fun; and Pixie, a high school math teacher was never seen, even in sweats, without her pearls. They were both fantastic.

We started the usual brigade events we had used for years as a camaraderie builder.

We also had top ten events every month, taking turns hosting them.

The Division Top Ten had a party we remember. A hay wagon pulled by a tractor and came through the housing area picking up everyone, continuing on slowly through the housing areas caroling. It was so much fun, and it really didn't matter only a few in the group could sing. We suggested we carol for our battalion commanders and caught at least two totally off guard.

The brigade birthday parties held for each battalion commander and wife were decided on by the rest of the group. Some of them really stood out. When Ed Kersey's birthday rolled around, he decided to go hunting instead. Cindy was a great army wife, and we all felt it was thoughtless of Ed to leave her knowing we'd throw a party. So we threw him a mock party. We spent most of the afternoon decorating their home with leftovers from whatever party anyone had been to recently. We had just celebrated a child's birthday so took crumbled streamers and the leftover birthday cake. We ate all but one piece of the leftover cake, so it was obvious a large cake had been there. Balloons were left floating on the floor and gift wrap was everywhere. We left a large unwrapped box with a note stating, "We opened this for you, and it was just my size. I love it! Thanks!" We took empty wine bottles over and put dirty paper plates and plastic cups in a large garbage bag. We waited for him to come back to no avail, so we went home to await Cindy's call. He came home about 9:00 p.m., so George and I went over to wish him a belated birthday and rave about how fun his party had been. He wasn't sure it wasn't true until sometime later when someone spilled the beans. He did get a much smaller party later.

When the Killebrews came on board, Pixie's birthday party was held at our house where they had been invited for dinner. When the Killebrews walked in the door, Pixie roared with surprised delight, we think. We were all sitting in the living room with white mop wigs styled like Pixies prematurely white pageboy and a string of very large styrofoam pearls. After dinner we all moved outside for games, ice cream, and cake. It was a success.

During this party, I received a call from a young wife, Lee Ann Ramsdell, who was in tears. She was one of the young wives George called my "other daughters." It seems she had an ultrasound earlier that day, and the doctor told her with no preparation that she would be medivaced to Walter Reed in DC to terminate her pregnancy. He told her she had twins with no heads. She was so stunned she just sat there. When she called the unit to have them get her husband, Gary, in from the field, he came in demanding the doctor X-ray. The doctor said it was too dangerous. Gary said, "If you are terminating, what difference will it make?" They reluctantly x-rayed to discover there was one healthy baby with a head.

They simply couldn't believe it. Womack Army Hospital had struck again.

I loved going by Pixie's for a brief visit over tea. They were both delightful. Pixie told her young wives, "I'm not your mother, so I won't treat you like I am, but we can be friends, if you want.

Bob's birthday was another themed event. His brigade had been told by the division commander to paint all the green on post street signs brown. There was much grousing about real battle proven paratroopers being used as common maintenance help so we gave Bob a *brown* birthday party at a local fish house. We covered their tables with brown packaging paper, we all dressed in brown shirts, gave Bob gifts pertaining to painting and brown, had chocolate ice cream, and chocolate cake with fudge frosting. He said he wondered why in the world Pixie had on his OD T-shirt under her shirt.

One of the Top Ten parties was Italian—we had grapes in a tub on the front porch for guests to stomp if they wanted, and everyone came in costume. Cindy came as a table with her head through the red and white checked table cloth, a candle dipped wine bottle centerpiece on her head, and a place setting glued to the side of the cloth. Ken La Plante, the S-3, and wife, Norma, came as gondoliers; and others just came in Italy's colors. A few actually stomped the grapes for photo opportunities.

The most memorable birthday party was for Lynn Moore who was born on leap year. We determined he was really only ten so had a surprise McDonald's party for him. We booked a birthday party, then all gathered at the nearby McDonald's with Dawn in charge of getting him there. As they drove in, he looked in the window to see the Top Ten waving at him. He was in sweats thus totally embarrassed, but was a great sport. They came in, everyone received their Happy Meal, and a cute very young high school worker in charge of our booked party totally lost control.

At one point, Ken LaPlante was sliding his straw up and down making an irritating squeaking noise. Our hostess looked him in the eye and said, "Mr. Straw doesn't like to sing!" All the men ordered more hamburgers as the Happy Meal just wasn't enough. We watched as Lynn opened his gag gifts. Everyone had tiny water pistols as party favors which was a huge mistake. We were politely asked to leave when the indoor water fight got totally out of control. It continued into the parking lot with everyone going home at least damp if not soaking wet, laughing till our sides hurt.

The most infamous party was a Top Ten we hosted in October. We had a Harley Rally with everyone required to dress as bikers. I went to the local Harley dealer to reconnoiter and pick up some prizes. I explained we were having a rally. It was like the commercial where silence occurs and all heads lean in your direction. Realizing my mistake, I clarified it was a private rally. Not only did I get some neat prizes but came home with what could only be costume inspiration.

George and I dressed the part, welcomed the brigade bikers, and divided them into gangs. Each gang named themselves and were given a pumpkin which was the head of their lost gang member. They had a list of parts they were to go around the neighborhood begging for their comrade. They needed eyes, hair, ears, nose, mouth (teeth were optional), and sunglasses. Prizes were given for fastest reconstruction, best-looking lost member, meanest, etc.

What we forgot to do was notify the neighbors we were sending biker gangs out into the neighborhood to knock on doors at night. We received a frantic call from another brigade commander and wife who lived across the street. They had gone out for the evening, leaving a babysitter. The sitter had called hysterical about scary people at the door. We had not intended to terrify anyone, but the gangs all looked wicked good!

The High Throttle gang came back first with their begged and borrowed trove and got to work putting spaghetti on for hair. They had gotten one family at dinner before the sauce was added. Two hard-cooked eggs were placed in carved eye sockets, a potato nose, corn teeth, apricot ears; and someone's extremely attractive sunglasses made him look fearsome. The other gangs were equally successful. The new gang members joined us for BBQ and all the fixings.

We decided it would be a great idea if I taught again. The extra money would truly be helpful especially with Cheryl in college and Tara about to graduate.

The great vice principal for whom I had worked before was the principal at Cape Fear High School, so I interviewed for a home economics position and was hired. It was a forty-minute drive across town, but it did give me time to change hats from mom and brigade commander's wife to teacher and back again.

I had really interesting classes. Child development and interior design were two. The design class was composed of about twelve senior boys and girls.

We had bought Jack Hamilton's Fiat Spider which I drove back and forth. On days we went on field trips, I took our old station wagon that hated me. It never stopped in the middle of intersections when it was loaded with kids, but would if I was alone or the girls were driving. The back window wouldn't roll all the way up, and the front windshield would fog up. On one field trip, it was raining cats and dogs. We were going to a manufactured home dealer and on to post to see three different décor styles. One of the boys sat in the right front seat, wiping the fog from the inside front window so I could see, and three boys were in the far backseats keeping a towel stuffed in the rear window crack to keep the back half dry. The girls were crowded in the other seats. Our house was eclectic, the second house with no children was ultra modern, and all in white, red, and black. Even the refrigerator had been replaced with their black one, and the kitchen and pantry blinds were red. The other home we visited was very Victorian, so the class got the idea how the same space could look totally different using different decorating styles. One of the students' dad invited us to check out their very rustic home, so we got to see much variety. Their end-of-year project was to design a home with no holds barred, so to speak. The designs were amazing as their imagination ran rampant.

George's XO (Executive Officer) at one point was Karl Johnson whose wife, Diane, was manager of the area Paella window dealership. She worked long hours but still managed to be at all evening and weekend events. She was the quintessential working army wife who had a career and was willing to be active in army family events. I admired her greatly for her willingness to support, as well as, having good common sense and great fun to boot.

Shortly after moving into our quarters, we noticed the area around the back steps was always muddy after a rain, so I decided to dig up a small area and lay large concrete block pavers to give us a patio area to control the mud. Every so often, I'd hit something metal with the shovel. I dug up one horse shoe after another. After checking with post housing we discovered the livery stable and blacksmith had been housed in the area of our house.

The engineer, Bob Flowers, and his family lived directly behind us with three of the cutest tow-headed boys. They had lived near us in Yadkin North when we were previously stationed at Bragg. We surmised their more recently built house was over the site of the stables themselves. All older army posts hold so much history, and some like that tidbit was all but lost. We left plenty of horse and mule shoes buried to be discovered by another family years in the future.

There were obligatory things we wives were expected to do. The thrift shop was one of them. Items were consigned there, and the consigners would receive a part of the sale price. The rest went to the thrift shop to be doled out to needs in the army community. Another benefit was giving, especially young families, a place to purchase all kinds of items at bargain basement prices. I loved working the consignment table because we got first dibs on items. It was really fun to work there after we arrived, but the thought of our brigade having to work a certain day was not one of our favorite things. Fortunately some loved it, but others hated it so I tried not to make anyone feel they had to go. Often I'd bribe them with lunch at McDonald's or the Golf Club House, if they would sign up. It worked for us to let the FSG (family support group) work our day as it gave us more ladies to volunteer and was one more event to do together.

There were often incredible finds but more often as a consigner, we tried to keep a straight face at some of the more bizarre items. The bouquet of faded crocheted flowers and the lightbulb salt-and-pepper shakers were some of my favorites.

When a close bond is formed within a unit, they become your family. This was so helpful when hardships or disaster strikes. In March of 1988, the brigade was first in line for deployment and were called to go to Honduras, as a show of force to deter the Communist dictator, Daniel Ortega, in Nicaragua from sending his army across the border into Honduras, a US ally.

George and his artillery commander, plus members of the staff, were attempting to cross the mountains via helicopter when the engine literally ran out of fuel. The pilot saw a semiflat protrusion on a mountain and headed for it.

The pilot attempted to perform an "auto rotation" where the spinning blades are stopped just at treetop level, easing the plane to the ground. The pilot misjudged the approach and hit hard. Very hard. The plane literally flew apart, blowing away the tail section, skids, cockpit, glass, seats, doors, and occupants. The fuselage came to rest upside-down but did not catch fire.

They said it was popping and crackling and not knowing how much gas was in it, they scrambled for safety. As they checked each other out determining injuries, they realized George wasn't with them. Chuck Otterstet, with the help of CSM McClamore, who had chest and rib injuries, went back for him. He was suspended upside down in his harness bleeding copiously. They at first thought he was dead but released him and got him out thinking the helicopter was going to blow up any minute.

When George came to, he had lost current memory, and thought he was in Vietnam. It no doubt seemed like déjà vu after the three helicopters were shot down and another crashed with him in Vietnam. He regained memory in about one hour.

They were rescued, and most were medivaced back to Fort Bragg. George refused to return early, so the brigade surgeon kept a close watch, especially since it was a head injury.

I got the call later that day and was interviewed by a national TV newscaster. George's driver had a broken back; Marshall Reed broke his leg, Larry Gottardi had a broken ankle, and the pilot had facial injuries and lost teeth besides CSM McClemore's crushed chest and rib injuries. Until all the families were notified, I had to pretend we didn't know details. I was worried sick about George but had to act like I knew nothing. It was one of the hardest interviews I've ever done. I called the wives involved and finally got them all. Larry's wife was an airline stewardess out of DC thus was the hardest to contact. I went to the hospital to see if anyone needed anything. It turned out the pilot had run out of gas as he misread his gas gauge. All the men in the wreck commended him on at least hitting the only accessible area on all the mountains in sight. Not only that, ironically the running out of gas that caused the crash also spared them from burning to death. I do believe God has angels everywhere.

To this day, they all refuse to fly in a helicopter with George. I told them, "If you have to get in one with him at least you know you will survive."

The troops came back, joking they had been on Spring Break of '88.

While they were gone, I decided to check the effectiveness of the rear detachment. Someone was always left behind to staff the office and be available for families. I had gotten tons of phone calls from distressed wives, so I felt maybe they weren't getting the help they needed from the office.

I called with a faked hysterical request and got no help. The XO's wife and I drove over there at midnight to give them a personal chance to rectify the earlier mistake. The young man on duty had a notebook with numbers to call for help on any number of issues. We had a long chat about the importance of helping everyone who called no matter how stupid it may sound to him. That visit was critical in the future decisions on who was left as rear detachment. It had to be someone with a warm heart, calm, and knowledgeable about sources of help for families. We had developed a notebook for the rear detachment with helpful numbers and contacts for all kinds of possible situations.

Those first years of the official family support group formations were a constant learning experience.

Tara had decided she wanted to go to culinary school and had checked around. I encouraged her to apply at CIA (Culinary Institute of America) first as we felt it was the best in the USA and the costs were comparable. She had to first work six months in a restaurant that was not fast food. That was a great idea to preclude students coming in with preconceived ideas of a glamour job. She worked in a restaurant in the local mall and loved it. They gave her a glowing recommendation which she sent with her application. When she was accepted, she was elated. George took her up to New York for orientation. He came back so totally impressed with the organization, staff, and imposing edifice. She would spend the next two years in classes, working in CIA's five restaurants open to the public, with a semester in externship under a chef in a starred restaurant somewhere in the world. She loved every minute and made extra money recycling cans, bottles, and working parties for which CIA sent wait staff when requested. She made close friends who all worked hard.

Cheryl, meanwhile, was attending Appalachian State University in Boone, North Carolina, and working as a waitress for extra money. She came home for holidays, and we would go up to visit on occasion. She had several apartments during this time. One was in an old house where rooms were rented out. The living room was a common area. We met some of the renters, and one was especially concerning. He was an older gentleman whose room was used not only to sleep but housed his candle-making supplies. Melted wax was everywhere. The candles were very creative, but we had nightmares of the old wood going up in flames.

Another apartment was shared with her good friend, Chris, and was above a bakery on the main street. Our job when we visited was to take her grocery shopping because the fridge was usually full of gallons of wine. We think they were party central for the other apartments. She made her grades as an English major, so we didn't have grounds for many complaints.

At the end of two years as brigade commander, General Johnson selected George to be the chief of staff of the 82nd. For the chief of staff's wife, there was a two-page typed job description. She didn't *have* to do it, but someone did.

At the same time I was told by my principal that he was considering me as the new head of the home economics department.

The two other home economics teachers had been there a long time, and it didn't take a brilliant mind to see how they would take such a decision.

General Johnson's wife, Edna, was an amazing lady. One of their children was autistic. Jeff was a good-looking tall young man who looked perfectly normal but had the reactions of a young boy. His hearing was acute, so Edna's voice was very soft from long practice.

Edna was soft-spoken, rarely upset, was at all major events, and an all-around amazing woman.

To be able to work under her tutelage was an opportunity I just couldn't pass up, so I quit my teaching job at the end of the school year and signed on for that typed two pages of duties.

One of those duties was leading the monthly meeting of all commanders' wives and the CSM wife in the division.

In mid-December of 1989, Tara and Cheryl were home for Christmas break. We were loading the big old station wagon with Tara's belongings to outfit an apartment for her to live in while she did her externship at the Hotel Thayer at West Point. She had rented a small three-room apartment in Cornwall on the Hudson and would drive the Honda Accord back and forth over Storm King Mountain. It was dark as we were putting the last suitcase in so we could get an early start the next day. Everyone was excited about going back to the West Point area if even for a day or two.

Out of the darkness, a tall figure emerged. It was General Jim Johnson. After a few words of greeting, he and George went off to the side for an obviously deep discussion. I thought, *Oh, great! Not again and not now.* Of course, it was again, and it was now. General Johnson left as he had come and George said, "Y'all are going to have to go without me. Something has come up."

That something was Panama and General Noriega. We wouldn't know that until we were on the return trip but as always in the 82nd, we just kept on keeping on.

The next morning, we drove north, one person short, taking turns driving and leading. Our first stop was the IKEA store in Dale City, Virginia, south of DC, to select and load up an apartment of basic furniture. Most of it came in cartons, so we folded down the backseat of the station wagon and piled it to the headliner. The platform bed went on the roof rack tied with enough twine to hold a herd of horses.

We hit the Jersey turnpike and tried to stay close as it was getting dark, and we were unfamiliar with the roads. The gas tank on the Honda was smaller than the station wagon, so when it was low on gas, whoever was driving it took the lead. We rolled into Cornwall on the Hudson late that night and unpacked a few small items before finding a motel for the night.

The next day, we unpacked all the boxes, put together furniture, and generally got the apartment livable.

That night we went to a great little Italian restaurant in Highland Falls outside the West Point gates, still not knowing what George was doing.

We spent two days getting Tara settled, and then left for home, leaving the Honda for her.

On the trip back, we listened to the radio and learned the 82nd had invaded Panama, intent on ousting Noriega. *That's* where they were!

When we returned to Fort Bragg, we discovered the assistant division commanders (ADCs) were all elsewhere, so George had to stay back as rear detachment. He was frothing at the mouth to go, but there was no one to leave behind in charge. We weren't there, but I would not have been surprised to learn he begged and pleaded, but to no avail.

Cheryl went back to college, and we went on with life.

A sensitive situation occurred while the men were in Panama. Several of the young wives had, against orders, communicated by phone with their husbands and were discussing details of the mission. With the surveillance techniques of our enemies so readily effective, the results could have been disastrous. The ladies were visited by me and a meeting set up with Edna. One of the women was Edna's daughter-in-law, and another was a chaplain's wife. Edna explained very clearly the importance of keeping information about the division private to help keep the men safe. She told them what harm their gossip could have caused. They understood and apologized. General Johnson took care of the loose lips on his end.

The family support groups were alive and well. Some were better than others, of course, but at least all were functioning.

I had a great opportunity to go to DC and facilitate the Army Family Action Plan Conference. Then it convened once a year to discuss issues which arose from the soldiers and families worldwide. The issues chosen as the most important were sent to a council to sort and send them to Congress or "in-house" resolution. The main issues that rose to the top were the ones discussed in issue groups lead by a facilitator, an assistant, a recorder, and a typist.

Our group discussed housing and sent our recommendations forward. In that group was a young woman from Hawaii, Cathy Gardner. She was a great addition to the group, and we hit if off immediately. Often in the army, we meet people we would never have run into otherwise who become good friends. Cathy (Cat) was one of those. Cat and Steve Gardner had two children, Eric and Kristy.

Kristy had been born with spina bifida, and the doctor was surprised when Steve insisted on riding in the helicopter to medevac the tiny infant. The doctor explained many parents considered it unnecessary. In the years that followed, she would undergo multiple surgeries on her back, legs, and spinal cord. When I met her, she was active in all sorts of school activities, bubbly, smart, and the cutest little blonde. Cat, Steve, and Eric had treated her as perfectly normal, so she responded in kind.

The army, like any community, is full of amazing human interest stories. The difference is usually the army stories from the home front are about amazing wives and children. In our case, the men were busy protecting our way of life, and we were all busy holding the home together and keeping the home fires burning.

I talked to my parents at least once a week, but on one fateful day Daddy called. I was busy putting final touches on the table set for the staff and wives. They were expected for dinner at six thirty. Daddy told me Mom had been taken to the hospital in Little Rock. She had fallen down the steps at the lake house in Clinton and mashed her nose. Her comment had been, thank heavens she didn't break the mason jar of fresh flowers she was taking to a sick friend. She went to the doctor because she was feeling so weak. Dr. Krishna Reddy took a blood sample, told Daddy to stop by home to pack her bag as he arranged for Dr. Fernade Padilla in Little Rock to meet her at the hospital. Her red blood count was so low he couldn't believe she was walking. Dr. Padilla was a hematologist, internist, and an oncologist. A brilliant doctor who's no-nonsense manner was to become much appreciated by us all. I cancelled the dinner and packed.

She was diagnosed with aplastic anemia. I had never heard of it but started researching immediately. A few years before, it had been one hundred percent fatal but new treatments were sometimes successful. She was deemed too old for a bone marrow transplant, but Dr. Padilla had heard of a new experimental serum from Switzerland. It was ten thousand dollars a shot, so he sat Daddy down and told him the options. Daddy said, "Get it!"

Aplastic anemia, as it was explained to me, is where the bone marrow slowly quits producing red blood cells and instead produces fat in those cells. I could only sit in her hospital room, read and talk to her, go home to cook dinner for Daddy, then we'd go back to the hospital. I stayed a week until I was sure Daddy could handle it. My older brother, Voland, and younger brother, Lyn, both came; and each went with Daddy to pick out grave sites and pay for funerals for both of them. We were all fearful she would never leave the hospital.

I lined up relatives to come for a week each to help. Lyn's girlfriend, Bettie, came a week several times; Daddy's sister, Earnestine Roberts, a week, Mother's sister, Polly White, a week; I returned for a week; and on it went. Mother had over one hundred blood transfusions and was in and out of the hospital multiple times. At one point when she was home, Judge Kaye Matthews and his wife, Jerrie, whom Mom had taught years before came by to visit. Daddy had been trying to talk Mother into going to the hospital for two days with her adamantly refusing saying she would be fine.

Jerrie took one look at her bloating purple body and called an ambulance. Then she called me. It was back to Little Rock on the next plane.

It was about this time that Daddy noticed he had trouble turning his head, and he was on what he called his candy diet. He had lost weight, so candy was just fine. I drove him back and forth to the hospital to see Mother and to the doctor to check his neck. The cancer had returned and was in his bones. He chose radiation for his neck, so we started the radiation treatments. If he even mentioned he liked something, I tried to make it. He reminisced about a sweet biscuit cooked in cream that Grandma Jones used to make, so for three mornings I made it till we got it right. If he wanted bacon and eggs, he got it.

The serum slowly worked for Mother, and combined with the blood transfusions, she gradually came back to us. I truly believe knowing how much Daddy needed her helped in her survival. She slowly improved, and Daddy held his own.

After the close of the Panama invasion, the 82nd troopers returned to Ft. Bragg in the traditional manner: they jumped into Bragg by parachute.

After the troopers landed and were forming by unit, General Foss turned to George and said, "I'd like you to be my executive officer. I have the executive travel with me as well as manage the office." Stunned, George mumbled something about being needed in the division. General Foss replied, "Okay, just think it over and let me know."

Although four-star generals may certainly select their personal staff, the usual process is a detailed screening and series of interviews boiling the slate down to two or three. General Foss knew George personally from his division command days when George was the 82nd's G-3.

George later casually mentioned the offer to General Jim Johnson, the 82nd commander, adding that he had told General Foss he is needed at Bragg.

General Johnson said, "What, what?" You don't say no to a four-star's personal invitation! Do you realize what a great honor that would be? You must accept! It's the army way. Period."

George accepted and although sad to leave the 82nd was secretly very excited to work personally with General Foss. His wife, Gloria, was another army wife most of us strove to emulate, so I too was delighted.

Fortress Monroe (so named as it contained a moated inner fortification that qualified it as a "fortress") was to be our new home.

When George turned over the brigade to Jack Nix, the brigade commanders' wives gave me a farewell. I was told to wear red, my favorite color. Mother and Daddy had managed to come for the change of command, so Mother was going with me to the dinner. She never wore black but insisted on wearing a black outfit I had never seen.

Abe Turner was a charming major who stood well over six feet. He drove up to the house to pick us up in a big car wearing a chauffeur's hat. In the backseat where he seated us, there was a bottle of champagne on ice and two wine glasses. It was a hoot! Mother, who rarely drank anything alcoholic, lifted her glass with mine in a toast to our driver. He drove around the neighborhood for a good ten minutes constantly turning over a homemade mileage meter. We were headed to the club two blocks from our house, so when he finally pulled into the O' Club drive I owed him ten thousand dollars for the ride. He took my rain check.

The room for the farewell was decorated in black and white. I was the only color in it. Everyone there wore black and white. The girls had borrowed the back drops from a local theater from the play *New York, New York*. It was awesome.

After dinner, the variety show began. The commanders, CSM, and staff wives were all dressed in black-and-white costumes and put on a variety show complete with reworded songs and dances to put Broadway to shame. It was overwhelmingly special and a memory I will always treasure.

As they did their numbers, I flashed back with each of them. Pixie and Bob Killebrew. I remembered tea in Pixie's living room, watching wildlife in their backyard. I remembered walking into Pixie's classroom in Pine Forest High School on her birthday dressed as the movie's version of a hillbilly. We had cleared it with the staff for her last class. We had blacked our teeth, ratted the hair, and dressed the part. We took her a cake and told her class we were her sisters "comin' to brang her a cake Momma done made. Since she couldn't git home, Momma sent usens to brang it to her." We hugged her and told her how much we jest loved her. She didn't bat an eye! She didn't deny nor confirm. The second the bell rang, the room emptied, and she grinned big and said, "Sisters, let's eat the cake."

In Second Battalion, Kim and Harry Axom had taken over from the Kerseys. Big tall Harry and Kim who's Daddy had been the corps commander years before were a seasoned military couple. Kim worried about her group and was a great addition to ours.

Dawn Lake Moore and Lynne Moore: I remembered several things about Dawn. She was a new army wife but had been in the army herself. After her first coffee, she called upset that she had an agenda, and two of the girls just stood up and walked out! She was mystified and irritated. After a few questions, it was mentioned that they were new moms who were breast-feeding. The wives are not in the army so didn't have to sit through an hour meeting, especially when babies needed nursing. Usually, the coffees were an hour long including snacks and visiting. She apologized to the girls and marked that one up.

Lynne had a twelve-year-old daughter who, typical of that age, was not pleased to have a stepmom. I thought Dawn handled her very well, even at one point rowing her out to the middle of their lake and setting down some rules.

She called me one afternoon very upset that she had dropped a teapot with tea at a formal tea the battalion sponsored that afternoon. The handle had broken off. I was usually an "up" kind of person, but the weight of multiple responsibilities literally had me depressed for the first time in my life. I simply couldn't have gone to the tea, or I would have cried all afternoon. Before I had always thought those with depression could just pick themselves up, dust off, and get on with it. This depressed feeling I had would not go away. That afternoon as the tea began, I was in the basement in front of the washer, sitting on a pile of dirty clothes, crying as if I'd lost my best friend. When I shared that with her, she said it meant a lot that I knew how she felt. That bout of depression didn't last long but was long enough to give me an understanding of those who suffer this malady. It was very helpful to be able to say honestly, "I know just how you feel."

Dawn and I learned from each other. She was so talented in so many areas that we felt blessed to have her.

They had an artist paint our quarters and presented it as a farewell gift. It is always hard to leave a group who has become family, but I always took them with me in my heart, hoping to be with at least some of them at another post.

17 | Fort Monroe, Virginia
"A Moat, Ghosts, and Grave Stones"

FORT MONROE IS a semi-island next to Hampton and across the bay from Virginia Beach. When Robert E. Lee was an engineer lieutenant, he helped build the moat that surrounds the inner fort. Many large quarters, barracks, and even the cell where Jefferson Davis was held after the Civil War were "inside the moat."

We were assigned one of the first duplexes on the entrance street, so were not inside the moat.

George's mother came up to move with us since George had to go ahead of us. We packed the dog, Cheryl's cat we inherited, Brackett, Mother Crocker, and me with everything but the kitchen sink in the station wagon. We weren't a hundred miles north till the cat Serra clawed his way out of his makeshift cage and was climbing all over everything. I pulled over, grabbed the terrified cat, and put him in the dog carrier with the dog. There was much growling, hissing, and posturing for the first hours. After that they settled down, and several hours later we rolled into Fort Monroe.

The house was huge. They were all on the historic register and were from a different era. The large entrance hall had a pressed tin ceiling above the winding staircase to the next floor. A small bath had later been tucked under the stairs. To the right was a library with floor-to-ceiling shelves and to the left a living room with a fireplace. Large sliding wall doors could close off these rooms. A large dining room also with a fireplace was next and featured a door to the screened porch and a radiator heater with bread warm riser built in. The butler's pantry and kitchen were in the back. A back stairway for use by the staff, in this case us, continued to the attic.

The second floor had two bedrooms with fireplaces, two without, and two baths. The attic had two finished rooms, a bath, and very old floors that I know could have told some stories.

Brackett chose the attic bedroom where we received permission to put up his water bed. We were a bit worried about floors that old.

We took the second floor master bedroom with bath and used quartermaster furniture to outfit the other bedrooms.

Brackett attended Phoebus High School, the town right outside post, where he played soccer. He also played on the local team, so our weekends were spent in lawn chairs cheering on our favorite player.

Tara was still at CIA and Cheryl at Appalachian University.

A few days after George's orders for Fort Monroe were cut, Desert Storm was announced. General Foss's aide had just come from a Ranger Battalion, so the three of them could not believe a war was occurring without them. We wives offered to shoot at them when they walked home to make them feel better. We just got scowls.

As it turned out, the 82nd trained incredibly hard only to be given a secondary mission to the armored units. It was a great waste of war fighters.

It was so odd not to have a thousand things to do, but Mother and Daddy's health were a constant concern. I went home for a week shortly after we settled in. The fort's sea wall was a great place to run, so George and I ran together every weekend and by myself during the week.

On one trip back to Little Rock, Lyn was there. Daddy was so obviously in agony that we questioned him regarding his medication. He told us he had asked his doctor, not Dr. Padilla unfortunately, to make sure he didn't have to suffer the pain. He obviously wasn't getting enough morphine. Lyn and I had called the doctor's office to be told repeatedly he was not in. We drove over there and found only two office staff who would just say the doctor was out. In desperation I spoke to Dr. Padilla about it, and he called Daddy's doctor who it turned out he had taught in medical school. In his no-nonsense way, he asked cryptically when told the doctor wasn't in, "Where is he, on safari, *again*?" He asked her to have the absent doctor call him about his patient.

Daddy did get more morphine. I was there again for a week in late February and discovered Daddy, the judge, the attorney, didn't have a will and Mother didn't' have a power of attorney. I called Judge Kaye Matthews who most graciously was there the next afternoon with his secretary. They sat by Daddy's bed and had him sign the power of attorney and a handwritten will Daddy had written earlier but not notarized. He had distributed property titles to the three of us years before with the understanding we were to take care of Mother. The next day he couldn't lift a pen.

The next night, Mother called me to help. I had told Daddy some of the story of Lonesome Dove which had recently broadcast on television. As he was so much like the Gus McCray character, I knew he would love it.

Daddy had managed to get out of bed, walk to the next room, and had fallen. He hurt everywhere, so to touch him caused him great agony. We put an ironing board in front of him for him to pull himself up. I asked what he was doing and in his morphine-fogged mind said, "Why, sis, I was taking the herd to Montana." I told him, "Of course, and all of them are safely penned, so it is time for bed." He agreed he was really tired. Riding the herd will do that to you! We got him back to bed where he fell instantly asleep, hopefully dreaming of a successful cattle drive.

When I left two days later, I knew I'd not see him alive again. I gently hugged and kissed him goodbye, hugged my brave little mother, and cried all the way back home.

Uncle Creo, Daddy's brother, came to stay. He and Mother had put a hospital bed in the living room and were by his side when he left us. The world was lessened by his demise.

We all came back for the funeral which had been so fortunately prepaid and arranged thinking it would be for Mother.

Brackett's first soccer match occurred the week Daddy died, so he missed it and was deleted from the team. Cruelty!

Aunts, uncles, cousins, brothers, and families were all there. The funeral was such a tribute to a great man with people sharing stories we had never heard of his generosity and wisdom.

Many amusing stories brought laughter through the tears. George had loved him too and was my rock. He and the children left after the funeral, but I stayed another week to help Mother. She was in tears most of the time.

She was scheduled for yet another blood transfusion a few days after the funeral. At the appointed time, I took her to the transfusion area at St. Vincent Hospital. They had about ten beds in a row with transfusions going in each. Mother was put in a bed at the end of the row. I had a book but had planned to walk across the street to window shop at a mall. For some reason, I decided not do that but read instead. Pulling up a chair next to Mom, I started to read. Every few minutes I'd look up to see her smiling at me or resting. After a few minutes on the IV, she had a strange look in her eyes; and when asked what was wrong, she couldn't answer. I yelled at the nurse on duty who came immediately, removed the IV, and sent an urgent call to Dr. Padilla, who's office was across the drive. They shooed me out, and all I could do was lean weakly against the hall wall and have an urgent conversation with God. I reminded him that he promised he would not give us more than we could bear, and losing two parents within a week of each other was way more than I could bear. He obviously heard me because Mother recovered quickly once the offending blood was removed. Dr. Padilla would be heard ranting and raving at the nurses for not keeping a closer watch. If I hadn't been there, they would not have noticed her distress till it was too late. We returned home more shaken than ever. It was almost the last transfusion she would have till she broke her hip at ninety-nine years old and underwent surgery.

She would join Daddy at 101 years old and bless more lives by her presence than one can count.

I went back to my family, knowing the home health nurses would keep her going and her many friends would drop in often. She even volunteered for the home health nurses by making calls to ease their workload.

Thanksgiving eve, Tara and her CIA classmate, Kim Bouchei Rivera, drove down from New York to prepare a turkey dinner for us all. They arrived at about 2:00 a.m. so slept in more than they planned. They were exhausted. They had printed menus and had brought some things, but I had also shopped with their list.

They cooked all day. Every pot and pan was used, so I borrowed from my neighbor.

The meal was finally ready and worth the wait. It was so good we moaned through course after course. Absolutely delicious as well as gorgeous!

Tara graduated from CIA in January 1991. Cheryl came home, and we drove up to Hyde Park, New York, together. The day of graduation was a snowy wonderland. It was an amazing celebration. We had a tour of the facility which was awe-inspiring to this old home economics major. The seating for graduation was a large room with long linen covered tables set for lunch. Students prepared and served a multicourse meal complete with appropriate wines to each of the graduates and their families. Every bite was perfectly prepared, the long tables perfectly set, and the excitement was palatable.

The graduation speech was given by a famous chef, and each graduate was called to the stage, and their neck was draped with a CIA medallion on a ribbon and awarded a graduation diploma. They also received an associate's degree from the state of New York. They all joked afterward how expensive the medallions were.

We packed up our youngest daughter for the long drive back to Fort Monroe.

It took her about two days to get a job at two different restaurants. The CIA credentials were like using a magic key in the restaurant business. I don't think they ever graduate mediocre chefs. She could walk right out the front gate to one restaurant that was on the water while the other was farther away. She learned a lot about seafood at both locations.

Brackett was having a fun playing intramural soccer with a military youth group team. If we didn't get there when it started, we'd miss one of his goals. He would appear to be just standing there, then suddenly rip down the field and kick it in! The girls would kid him about his cute legs, and I told him he got them from his dad.

Behind our house was a harbor with sailboats at anchor. The clanging of the rigging in the wind was like music.

An old movie theater was a block away; so on most weekends, if it was a movie we wanted to see, I'd pop popcorn, we'd grab cold drinks, and walk down.

There was so much to do in the area we never had to look far for something fun and different.

As with many old military posts, ghost stories abound. Our duplex supposedly had one in the basement on the other side. Chaplain Gaylord Hatler and his wife, Diana, lived there; but Gay was in Iraq, so it was just Diana and their sheltie. The dog refused to go into her basement and the one time I was down there, it was very cold and the hairs on my arms stood up. I left as soon as possible!

I didn't think our side had one, but Brackett had just gotten to bed in his attic bedroom one night when he looked up to see a bluish white man over six feet tall with chains around his waist and wrists standing at the foot of his bed. He thought, *Oh, shit* and pulled the cover over his head, peeked back over the covers, and the guy was still there. He dove under again, waiting a few minutes which seemed like an hour, peeked again to find the room empty. He finally went to sleep. The rest of us never saw one.

There were stories from perfectly sane people of pets barking and meowing to come in when they had already been let in and the doors locked. The doors were still locked, but the pets were outside.

Furniture was constantly moved in another house, and one inside the moat had a ghostly housekeeper who walked through doors with a stack of linens only to disappear into a closet.

George's mother on one visit was curious about the white marble stepping stones along the front of our house. They had almost sunk underground over the years. With much effort and much digging, she unearthed the first one. Part of the underside of it had letters chiseled off, but it was obviously part of a Confederate States of America (CSA) tombstone! We were all in the game now and dug them all up. Everyone was part of a tombstone at least four inches thick. We checked with the museum on post and were told the old cemetery had many tombstones that were broken, vandalized, or otherwise damaged. They replaced them and used the old ones as erosion control. A much earlier occupant had obviously used some as stepping stones. A month or so after, we reset them above ground; a tour bus stopped in front of the house, and I just wondered what story they were telling.

Our home was on the historic home tour that year, and it was fun to spruce it up for the public to walk through. It was a fine example of architecture of that period.

Soon after our arrival, I took Brackett to Virginia Beach to a surf shop where he found a used surfboard and was thrilled to death. He tried surfing thinking it looked *so* easy on TV. It wasn't, but he tried repeatedly anyway. The surf did lack something there.

Gloria Foss was very creative and offered to share her method of making angels from twist paper. Several of us met at her home and had a grand time forming our own. Mine never looked as professional as hers, but it was fun to try. She and I had a booth at the local craft fair that year and did fairly well.

The Chamberlain Hotel was on Fort Monroe but was privately owned. It was a grand old girl, and many parties were held there. It was on the bay with a swimming pool between the water and hotel. One night, Brackett had a friend over to spend the night. George had gone with General Foss on a trip, so it was just the four of us. Tara was asleep after a very long day on her feet. I went up to the attic to tell the boys good-night as it was after midnight. There was no response to my good-nights, so I checked. No boys. Right! I settled in on the back stairs which had a small window overlooking the fire escape that ended at Brackett's bathroom window. Obviously, that was the route of escape and would be the route of return.

Soon after 1:00 a.m., I heard muffled giggles and elbow jabbing. They were soaking wet and climbing the ladder to the third floor but not as fast as I climbed the stairs. As they crawled in the window, they were greeted with a low, "Well, did you have a good time?" They almost fell out the window. I was really scared they had been swimming in the bay at night with the sharks. After the inquisition, they admitted they had snuck into the Chamberlain Hotel pool and been swimming for a good hour.

George was selected for general officer and a command in Hawaii. He was to be the commander of Special Operations Command Pacific or SOCPAC. I was so proud of him and so happy so many family members could come to his promotion ceremony: his mother, Uncle Jeff Ellis, Aunt Francis Ellis, Cousin Jeff, and Helen Harvell from DC, as well as, our children. He was promoted by General Foss near the gazebo on the bay with a small reception at the Chamberlain afterward. Our idyllic year with no troop families to worry about had ended.

The house was invaded by packers again, and we were off!

Vonda and Donna Parker

Vonda and Maureen McNeil

Teaching and Linda Sheriff

Brackett with Windy at Fort Bragg Brigade Command

George's helicopter crashed in Honduras

George and Vonda at Halloween Harley Rally for the Brigade team.

Farewell Follies: Dawn Moore, Pixie Killebrew and back up chorus

Brigade Farewell: Sue Steiner, Linda Sheriff, Elva Scholes,
Edna Johnson, Lorea Jones and Vonda

82nd Abn 1st Bde. Farewell quilt wives made. Vonda and mother.

82nd Abn 1st Bde Command Wives. Elizabeth and Pixie
Killebrew, Vonda, Kim Axom, Dawn Moore

Pre gala gathering of command team. Ed and Cindy Kersey, Lynn and Dawn Lake Moore, Ken and Norma La Plant, George and Vonda, Bob and Pixie Killebrew

18 | Fort Shafter, Hawaii
"Paradise"

WE HAD TO decide how to get all the vehicles where they needed to be. We decided to ship the Fiat first since it would take longer from the east coast, we'd drive the Honda and Explorer to North Carolina, dropping the Honda in Boone for Cheryl to use and continuing on to California. George would leave us at base housing in San Francisco and drive the Explorer to San Diego where the next navy ship would take it to Hawaii.

My cousin, Dr. Alan White, and wife, Carolee, had agreed to keep our collie while we were in Hawaii because Hawaii had a six-month quarantine policy. Many animals had sickened and died during the long seclusion. It, of course, was ludicrous to keep animals that long supposedly for rabies control but in reality for the green backs. It was later shortened considerably. Alan was an equestrian vet, lived on a ranch, and was very dear to us. Windy would be in collie heaven with them.

Tara, Brack, and I had dinner with them in San Francisco near the wharf which was our first experience there. We had a great evening getting reacquainted.

George met us at the airport the next morning, and we boarded the plane for Honolulu.

We were met at the Honolulu Airport by the chief of staff and deputy.

The deputy was Shannon McCrary and his wife, Mary Pat. They were to become very good friends.

Our quarters on Palm Circle wouldn't be ready for several weeks, so for a few days we were housed in transit quarters on the navy base. We noticed quarters up the street had the name Bondi. What a thrill to find my friend, Joan, a block away. Again, I joined the navy wives in Bible study.

After a few days, we were moved to another house on base then to a suite, of sorts, at the Outrigger Reef Hotel on Waikiki. "What a bummer," the kids and I said with wide grins. We were ecstatic. George was horrified. He would have to go to work in fatigues every day. We thought of it as a minor inconvenience.

The one tiny bedroom was ours, Brack was on the pullout living room couch, and Tara the double bed in the living room.

The three of us began exploring the island. We had rented a car until the Fiat arrived, but George took that to get to Camp Smith and his office. We walked to the zoo, the aquarium, the tourist shops, tried all the shave ice stands, and spent hours snorkeling in the usually clear waters of the Pacific. We found watches, room keys, car keys, and all sorts of other long lost items on the floor of the ocean.

One morning while getting ready to go to work, George came into the bedroom where I was making up the bed. His face was red as he spat out, "What is *that*?" He said this while gesturing to the dining room.

I just couldn't imagine but went with him and had to hide a grin as he gestured wildly at our Tara. The sheet had ridden up her leg during the night exposing her leg. Her birthday tattoo of a multicolored dragon was prominently displayed. She had never mentioned it to him, knowing his reaction, and she was not mistaken about the reaction. She was shaken awake and asked to explain. She had gotten it in New York on her twenty-first birthday but had worn shorts over her bathing suit when he was with us. I had known, of course, but at twenty-one it seemed to me, it was her call. He quickly calmed down but just shook his head for days. Afterward she was free to wear her suits minus the shorts.

We ate plenty of TV dinners since we had a microwave, sink, and a coffeepot. It was cereal for breakfast, sandwich for lunch, and nuked something for supper. The cost was prohibitive to eat out much.

We checked out a scuba shop that offered a trial dive. One early morning, the three of us headed out with a wild-looking young man who had a glint in his eyes. He suited us up, gave us a ten-minute class on how to dive, and in we went. It was later he told us it was Shark's Cove. It didn't matter because we were hooked.

We signed up to take lessons at another shop. Tara and Brack went on the ocean dives first while I waited. We told about our practice dive which included caves and the instructor said, "Oh no! That was Mad Bart! You do caves in advanced classes." We had two days in the pool and the rest in the open ocean. What a scary fascinating sport. To be thirty-five feet under water with fish swimming close enough to touch, trying to keep from touching coral, breathe correctly, and keep track of your class was exhilarating.

After a few weeks, Tara went on a job hunt and registered at Honolulu Community College for her two years of basic courses before transferring to the University of Hawaii.

She got a job almost immediately at the Waikiki Seafood and Pasta Company.

Brackett registered at Moana Loa High School which had a lot of army and navy kids, but mostly Japanese.

We were amazed at the numbers of Japanese on the island. We were to learn that every hotel but the army's Hale Koa was owned by Japanese or other foreigners. A majority of the Japanese families had been there for several generations so thought of themselves as Hawaiian, as indeed they were but many had retained pure Japanese bloodlines.

The cuisine had a heavy Asian influence with very few Hawaiian twists, and the English language had morphed into pidgin. For example, pau means finished and other words were slurred more than my native south. It took a while to understand the locals, but it wasn't long before we all had it down.

We finally got the Fiat but since it was a two-seater, it limited its use. George took it to work, and we used the rental. One weekend, George and I drove over the Pali in the Fiat to the North Shore to sightsee. As George started to shift the shifter, he lifted it up in his hand. We were rolling down the highway with no shift shaft. He stuck it back in, and I held it in place.

We headed back home going over the mountain in second gear! Our "Fix it again, Tony" car spent a lot of time in the European car shop on Sand Island.

The day we signed for quarters was a big one for us. Living on the beach in a hotel had its benefits but was growing old.

We were given Quarters Three on historic Palm Circle at Fort Shafter. The parade field in front of the houses was circled with Royal Palms. It was truly beautiful. Ours was the first house on the circle, so we had a large side yard and a garage plus parking slab across the alley from the house. The front and side porches had glass-louvered windows and screens. The quarters had no air-conditioning at all which we rarely needed with the trade winds, but all closets had a heated pipe to keep things from molding with the high humidity.

The quarters had a large front second-floor bedroom with bath. There were two other bedrooms on the second floor. Brackett took the basement bedroom with early gas-station-type bathroom, and Tara took the back first floor bedroom and bath separated from the main house but connected by a side porch. The second floor bathroom for the guest rooms had two doors. One opened from the hall and the second from the back stairway. That stairway started in the basement by Brackett's room and appeared to have been outside at one time. The large kitchen was separated from the house by that stairway. A huge bougainvillea grew across the kitchen window giving one a sense of being in a garden.

Mango trees were everywhere, so we had their fruit every morning. It wasn't until my hands and mouth broke out with what appeared to be poison ivy did we learn the close relationship between poison ivy and mangos. I was more careful peeling and eating after that.

There was a swimming pool across the parade field, so after we found Brack a used car to go to and from school and George bought Tara a motorcycle which she learned to ride one afternoon in the yard, I started swimming every morning. The lifeguards were very friendly and helpful by correcting my stroke, as well as, encouraging my efforts. We became friends as we visited every day.

After several months, the phone rang at the pool and one of the lifeguards said with a question in her voice, "Is there a Ms. Crocker here?"

I said, "Oh, that's me." They instantly changed demeanor, and I could see the glass wall coming down. "Oh come on, girls," I chided. "It's just me! We've been friends for months." They said, "We didn't know you were a general's wife." "So?" I asked. "He's not swimming, I am! He's a general, I'm not." We never did get back to the easygoing friendship, and it was really sad.

The wives in the unit were just awesome. It was a purple unit meaning the men were from all branches of the service. Navy Seals, Army Special Forces, Air Force Special Operations, and Marines were all together in this unit.

Once more we started by forging a military family out of individuals. When the men left on missions all over the Pacific, we had dinner and a movie night or our favorite pool party. I'd fill a plastic kiddie pool with ice for beer, wine, and cold drinks; and we'd have a potluck. When the men were home, we'd have the usual Halloween costume party. One of our favorite couples was Karin and Vladimir Sobichevski (Soby). Karin was gorgeous. She never had a dark hair out of place; her clothes fit perfectly as she had worked at a well-known designer shop and had her clothing tailored, so she appeared as a fashion plate. For at least thirty minutes, no one recognized her. She came as a bag lady wearing a green garbage bag tied at the neck, carrying another one with her glorious hair ratted out in all directions and dirt on her face which was devoid of all makeup. She won the prize!

Everyone was ready to help another, so it was truly a tight-knit group. We were also rather on the fringes of other groups so didn't fit with any of them.

George worked for Admiral Larson, so we were included in many of their events and also going to conferences with them.

One conference was in Alaska where I had never been. We flew up with the Larsons in his plane. The only window was in the bathroom. I spent so much time in there the pilot finally asked me to come up and look out their windows. Magnificent! Alaska is all about awe. George succumbed to my begging and at 11:00 p.m., which was as light as four, he took me around the airfield looking for moose. We saw several including one momma with her calf standing right beside the road. At a dinner we attended in a lake side lodge, the caterer told us the weekend before at a wedding reception a black bear came uninvited. Everyone fled into the lodge and watched in horror as the bear slowly ate his way down the buffet table ending with the wedding cake. We really wanted to see a bear! We experienced the phenomenon of being wide awake and filled with energy late at night because the sun never sets in the summer. Of course, the winter is the opposite. Our windows had blackout shades to help us sleep, thank goodness.

Joan Bondi and I had been meeting for Bible study with the navy wives when we decided to take the Precepts Bible Study course. It was a very intense few days of classes teaching us how to teach the precepts method of study. It is a very in-depth method of study requiring many hours per lesson.

I did some substitute teachings at various schools as the pay was very good and for the most part, the kids were fine. I had substituted at Moana Loa High School a few times but was very surprised to get a call from the principal asking if I would like an interview as a full-time substitute in home economics for the rest of the year. I really didn't want to work that much as the families and our children kept me really busy. I did go for the interview and was asked if I thought the pidgin English spoken by the kids would be a problem. I told her, if they could handle my southern accent, pidgin would be no problem. I got the job.

The next day on a preliminary walk through of the Home Economics Department, I didn't recognize anything they were cooking. Oh, boy! This was going to be a bigger challenge than it first appeared.

The other two home economics teachers were great. They even offered to give me lesson plans, but as I had done this before, I made my own. For the first few weeks, I was very grateful for any guidance they could give.

They were both Japanese, so I settled in to learn how to cook in a whole new way. They had recipes printed for me and were only a door away. Whoever had been there before had not had time to thoroughly clean the room I was to use, so the students and I did it slowly and methodically. All the students were respectful, but had the constant call of the ocean on their mind. The classes were divided into Monday, Wednesday, Friday, and Tuesday, Thursday classes, not unlike college. I was delighted as the longer classes were so much easier to teach. They had morning snack break, lunch, then were out by 2:00 p.m. I had a beach bag packed in the back of the Fiat, and Brack had his boogie board or surf board in his car. After school, we'd head out. We spent many hours at the beach, me reading, swimming, reading, swimming, and him riding the waves with his pals. What a life!

George's secretary, Marion, was a treasure. When our first of many guests came to visit, she got us reservations on the admiral's launch to tour Pearl Harbor. It was fascinating, humbling, and brought history alive as we wove through ships, toward the Arizona and motored past some of the fleet. As we passed the first ship in port, a series of whistles were heard, and navy personnel lined up along the ships railing at attention saluting. I asked George why they were doing that, and he said quietly, "My flag is flying." I had noticed the one-star flag in the front of the boat but didn't compute it meant more than George was on board. It meant that and that the sailors were saluting him. I was impressed. I guess everyone on board knew that custom already or didn't care because no one asked the tour guide.

About this time, Tara came home from school one day and said she had met a really nice young man. He was from America Samoa and had sat next to her waiting on the bus. He had asked her if she was waiting on her boyfriend. She had answered, "No, are you?" Thinking he would be offended, brushed off, and leave her alone, but it didn't phase Saivatia one bit.

He continued the acquaintance; they began dating, and finally he came by the house to meet us. He was a very courteous, very shy young man whom we instantly liked.

They dated two years, fell in love, and decided to get married. Tia came to ask for our permission. They both understood the great differences in the cultures in which each had grown up so really took their time. Tara took Samoan in college, and Tia worked on his English. We gave our permission, but Tia's family in Samoa needed to give their approval, as well. They planned to go visit during spring break. Tara wanted to take a gift to Tia's mother, Mesepa, so she decided a king-size Hawaiian-style quilt would be perfect.

We had an unused room downstairs in which we "jury rigged" a quilting frame, selected a Hawaiian bread fruit design in green on white background, and set to work on the entrance hall floor. The bread fruit design was cut and appliquéd on the white background, strung on the hanging quilting frame, and hand quilted in rows out from the design. It took months; and anyone who dropped by for a visit got dragged downstairs, given a needle, and begged to quilt! Even Tia got commandeered into adding some stitches, begging us not to tell anyone. The proof was in the blood he left on the lining. None of the stitches were perfect, but when it was finished at two in the morning they were to fly to Samoa, we were all amazed at what we had accomplished. It was lovely.

Tia's mother loved it by all accounts. Tara met Tia's six brothers and two sisters and toured the island. When she returned, she had grease under her fingernails. We asked about that as it was very unusual for her. It seems one of the brothers' alternators was having problems, and she had been fixing it when they had to dash to the airport to catch the plane home. She had been approved.

They announced plans to marry the following summer.

Meanwhile, our home had become the Crocker Hotel for all who had ever wanted to visit Hawaii. I became a very apt island guide and could tailor a tour depending on interest.

George's mother sent her friend to stay. She was a stranger who turned out to be a delightful guest. Another army friend, Herb Lloyd, called to say his son, Mark, was coming through. We insisted he stay with us and found him charming.

My mother and younger brother came. We rented the VIP guesthouse on Bellows Air Force Base, next door and over the hill from Shirley Temple's estate. A large Jacuzzi was on the patio overlooking the Pacific, and Mother had her first spa experience. We almost couldn't get her out of it.

George's aunt Francis, Uncle Jeff, cousin, her husband, and mother-in-law came. So did Hurricane Iniki. We had a room for everyone but Jeffrey's mother-in-law, so we set up the butler's pantry with curtained doors and a cot. She was such a good sport, always looking for the butler.

Iniki was headed straight for us, and we were all sound asleep. Alarms went off, and the phone rang, warning us. George and I got up, dressed, and woke all the guests. George went to the post exchange gas station to gas up and buy water and multiple rolls of masking tape. When he returned, we doled out the tape, gave everyone a room, and had them tape every window. We got a call from the mainland from a friend asking us to check on his family and give refuge if necessary. We assured him we would and started trying to reach her. She was a high school principal and was found busy setting the school up as a refuge, so all was well!

The hurricane veered toward Kauai, bringing devastation to that beautiful island, but Oahu got its share. We were on high ground so only had broken branches, flying palm fronds, and battering rain. Tara's restaurant's storage rooms were flooded, fish swam in the lobby of the Outrigger Reef, and water damage on the shore was devastating. The beach at Barber's Point literally disappeared. The farther west one went, the worse it became. The Samoan community on the western end of the island was devastated.

Uncle Jeff, Aunt Francis, and Jeffery's crew will never forget that visit.

Old friends from college came by while in town for conventions and Charlie Boyce, George's oldest friend in life, with his wife, Arden, came to town. They were a joy to host. Arden who was an outstanding artist took tons of pictures while they were there. She later painted from them giving us two paintings. Her use of light was outstanding, reminding us of Renoir.

My older brother, Captain Jim (Voland) Jones, who was the naval attaché in Kuala Lumpur, Malaysia, was even in Hawaii one day and had time to visit. That was a marvelous treat.

The Dallas Cowboys were to play in the Aloha Bowl; and we debated calling my high school and college classmate, Jerry Jones, and asking them over for a BBQ but didn't want it to appear we were angling for tickets or future favors! I'm sure he gets more than his share of that. In retrospect we probably should have since surely he would see it for what it was: a kindness to an old friend.

One of the most embarrassing visits was from our best man, Tom "Wish" Beasley. He was CEO and founder of Corrections Corporation of America (CCA) and had a meeting of his worldwide board in Hawaii. He asked us to dinner, but since George was gone he asked me. George was delighted one of us could visit with Wish.

I invited them to the house first for a drink and pupus. We were sitting on the front lanai when the house alarm went off. I raced to the back but no intruder. In three minutes the MPs were at the door, and there I am with several men, George gone, babbling as one is won't do, about how this is the best man at our wedding, men here for meeting, dinner, blah, blah, blah. They just grinned bigger saying, "Yes, ma'am." I was thinking they were thinking, "*Sure!*"

The second they got the alarm off, we were off to the restaurant before I dug the hole deeper.

Cheryl called us to tell us she was totally in love with a young man, and they were getting married! We had never met him, and she had a year to go before graduating from Appalachian State University. She had found the perfect dress at an antique clothing store.

We suggested they come to Hawaii to marry since we all couldn't come to North Carolina. Tara agreed to do the reception at our home. We were only inviting those who had known her in other places.

Cheryl and Todd were excited at the offer and agreed. We sent tickets and were told Todd's mother was to arrive the day after they did. She would stay with us. George's mother insisted on coming as we knew she would.

We met them at the plane. Our Cheryl was lovely, but her young man was a different story. We had learned through the years when to gasp and when to bite our tongues till they bled. He was very thin, with long stringy dark hair and earrings, in a word, a throwback sixties' hippie. If Tara's tattoo hadn't caused George to have a coronary, I was afraid this would. I kept thinking, "Oh, Cheryl" and then, "He probably is a sweetheart." We continued to bite our tongues until they bled.

Todd's sweet mother arrived the next day, and the event was set.

The night before the wedding, Todd's mother ordered pizza for the rehearsal dinner. George's mother kept muttering about the cheapness of it, but honestly, it was perfect for us all.

We had rented the gazebo up the street by the parade field, flower baskets on pedestals, folding chairs for guests, and a carpet for the bride. Our dear friend, Chaplain Mike Tarvin, officiated.

She dressed at home and was just lovely in an antique lace dress that hugged her figure. She had a flower haku encircling her head. She waited at our friend's house next to the gazebo for the ceremony to start.

She walked out carrying local flowers. We shed a few tears as she was a beautiful bride. The ceremony was very sweet and short. Afterward, we took the baskets to the house as everyone walked back to our quarters. Tara had done a superb job preparing all the food.

We had ordered a limo to take them to the Hale Koa for a three-day honeymoon, all paid for by us.

The next day, we took Todd's mother to the plane, and two days later the newlyweds flew off to their new life together in Boone, North Carolina, and hopefully for Cheryl to finish college.

Shopping in Hawaii was either touristy or local but all very expensive. The answer for most of us was the flea market at the Aloha Stadium. It was open Wednesday, Saturday, and Sunday, when there wasn't a big football game. Three or four rows of vendors encircled the stadium. Parking was one dollar fifty when we were there. One could find everything from food, fabric, luggage, clothing, electronics, art, crafts, and everything in between, all brand-new. Pirated or rip-off designer everything was in abundance. I even had my favorite vendors and loved getting an ice-cold coconut plucked from a bucket of ice water, the top loped off with a machete, and presented with a straw. On a hot summer day, it was the best.

Brackett was selected for the soccer team at Moana Loa High School. This was no surprise to us since he had played so well in Virginia. He and another boy were the only two haloes or white boys on the team. They rarely played. Both were big strong boys who had played lots of great soccer in the past. They were only allowed to play the last few seconds of a game if the team was ahead. Of course, their teammates, who never played with them, rarely passed the ball their way. The Japanese players were all short and small, so we were amazed the coaches weren't utilizing our big guys. He did use them to pick up all the soccer balls after the games and haul them back to the field house.

Now, all of my children had had an opportunity to know how it felt to be a minority. This was an excellent life lesson but frustrating as we all get out to watch your child's talent lie dormant.

The second year, Brack quit the team and competed in boogie board contests, winning trophies in that.

While I taught there, I had each teacher leave me a note at the end of each week describing Brack's class work. It was most helpful to keep him on track in such a laid-back environment. Should he mess up, there was no car for a week.

When it was time for us to leave Hawaii, George received orders for Panama to be the commander of United States Army South and a second star, I must admit my heels were embedded in the cement. It would not have been proper to kick, scream, and sit down at the airport; but I really wanted to.

We had the Explorer windows tinted a dark hue for security. It was too dark for Hawaii legal limits but fine for putting on the boat for Panama.

I was so happy for George and this marvelous opportunity, but I did love it in Hawaii, and I would leave Tara and Tia there planning the wedding. I did get to help her pick out the wedding dress. It was being altered with a piece added to cover cleavage. She and her friend, Kim, would make all the flower bouquets and get invitations, napkins, favor boxes, etc. I just left money knowing it would be perfect.

Meanwhile, Cheryl's graduation drew near, so I planned to fly to Little Rock, pick up both mothers; and we three would fly to North Carolina, rent a car, and head to Boone in the mountains. I had ordered leis to be shipped to arrive the morning of graduation.

I learned a very good lesson on that trip, never to let my precious mother be alone with George's mother. For someone who could be so fun and kind, she could turn in a heartbeat and a vicious tongue would lash like a whip. She did that to Mom repeatedly on that trip. My mother was valiantly self-sufficient, but after her battle with aplastic anemia she was weak as a kitten. She tried to do as she always had done, but her energy reserves were very low. I helped her roll her bag at one point, and George's mother in a very superior voice announced she just wouldn't travel if she couldn't pull her own weight. I wanted to trip her but restrained myself, learning from mother who ignored the comment and went on her sweet gracious way. The snipping continued nonstop and so did the ignoring.

Cheryl was so thrilled to get that BA in English, and we were so proud of her. The leis finally arrived, and we each wore one to put over Cheryl's head after graduation. George's mother announced that would be fine, but she wanted hers back after Cheryl wore it a while. Cheryl gave it to her, but she was the only one other than Cheryl who wore one.

We paid for four years of college. It was our deal for all three kids, and they paid for anything more. Cheryl had wasted hours her first few semesters but got smart, buckled down, and worked for her classes the last two years. She waited tables and shared very amusing stories of her customers. After the ceremony, we spent the evening with Cheryl and Todd. They prepared BBQ outside, and Cheryl had earlier made the side dishes. It was a milestone for her that we were delighted to share.

Back in Hawaii, we enjoyed a tear-filled farewell from the unit, and each lady gave me a silk flower that best represented them. I was so touched and loved each dearly. The arrangement of those flowers has been redone several times, but I still have all of them.

Just before we left, we bought a large classic pool table and had it delivered in the boxes. It was shipped the same way to Panama. Brackett was really looking forward to putting it to use in our new quarters.

When the day of departure arrived, most of the command came to the airport to see us off. We had so many leis around our necks we could hardly breathe. Brackett's friends were there en masse forming another emotional group. Our Tara and Tia were there sending us many love you and miss you, tears, and waves. George got on one plane to Panama, and Brackett and I got on another to head to Arkansas for a week or so of family time before beginning another overseas assignment.

I cried most of the way to the mainland. I know the other passengers were thinking, "She must have really had a great vacation." Brackett was subdued as well, missing all his pals and concerned about starting his senior year in another country.

George had called to say everyone in the new command wondered where I was, but he explained we were scheduled to join him shortly.

Brack and I loaded with luggage and a crated Windy—Cousin Alan shipped her to us in Arkansas—then headed out yet again.

When your parents age, you just hate to leave them, knowing they would have benefited from you living closer. Mother was a trooper, but we were really going to miss each other, and I worried about her.

19 | Fort Amador, Panama
"A Third World Adventure"

BRACK AND I were upgraded to first class from Little Rock to Florida for his first taste of that mode of travel. He announced he never wanted to ride in the cattle car section again. I said, "Me, either!" Good luck! We transferred in Florida and arrived in Panama City, Panama. We were met by George and several other people, five of whom were his security detail. It would be a whole new experience! We were whisked through customs by side doors.

We drove by our seven-thousand-two-hundred-square-foot quarters, and it looked like a hotel. There were bars on the windows, a long canopy over the front steps from the front door to the sidewalk flanked by American and Panamanian flags. There was a side porch overlooking a large patio and the Bay of Panama. Ships could be seen lining up to enter the canal. It was gorgeous.

George's head of security was Sergeant Vasquez. He was a wonderful man whose duty was to keep George alive. I was so grateful all five of the men would be with him everywhere. He had two armored cars at his disposal. One was an older Mercedes level four hard car sedan and the other a huge Chevy Suburban.

We moved in and got Brackett registered at Balboa High School, his third school in four years.

So much had changed since my 1966 visit that it was unrecognizable. Thanks to Jimmy Carter, much of what had been the Canal Zone had reverted to Panamanian government, and the jungle had reclaimed it. It would be hard to find where beautiful housing areas once stood. All had been looted of everything useable, leaving rubble or nothing at all.

The rooms in the quarters were very large. The entrance hall featured a guest bedroom with a special communications package and bath to the right. A large formal dining room lay straight ahead next to a large kitchen to the right and a family dining room to the left.

Immediately to the left of the entrance was what we called a, "meet-and-greet" or reception room, a bath tucked in, and through the meet-and-greet room to a huge living room. The living room opened to the reception room, family dining room, and out onto a lovely covered terrace. Outside curving stairs led down to a very large patio. Beyond the grounds, the Bay of Panama gleamed in the sun as ships lined up on the horizon to enter the Panama Canal.

Two stairways led upstairs. The back stairs from the back door in the kitchen opened into a small bedroom then a pantry opening into a huge family room. Another bed and bath were on the right at the top of the front stairs. Brackett took that one. On the other side of the family room were two guest bedrooms and an enormous master bedroom and bath. The latter was situated over the formal living room so also had a panoramic view of the bay and ships. Quartermaster wicker and cane furniture filled a lot of the larger areas, and there was a baby grand piano in the family dining room.

The piano was used by us at every formal dinner for dinner music. It was really special to have live music on those occasions. Our Ludwig piano had been sold in Virginia since only Cheryl played.

The pool table was set up in the upstairs family room with plenty of room to have a TV watching area and a card table area for games.

Our bedroom dwarfed the king-size bed and swallowed the large accent pieces like the chests of drawers and dresser. We designated areas by area rugs: one seating area at the foot of the bed, another on one side of the bed, and a desk on the other.

The basement was very interesting. To get to it one went down the outside kitchen steps through a large locked wrought iron gate and into the rather dank, dim interior under the entire house.

One small room had a locked steel door with an outer door of lockable wrought iron. It was air-conditioned and housed the liquor and wine for the quarters.

It had been years since most army officers offered anything but beer and wine, but in foreign countries one followed the local customs. In Panama and Latin America, hard liquor was the norm.

The washer and dryer were in one area, three rooms, two of them air-conditioned and a very narrow garage completed the areas off the large center space. All the windows were barred to keep out intruders. We stored our out-of-season things such as Christmas decorations in the air-conditioned rooms to preclude mildew in the humid conditions.

Windy loved living in the air-conditioned house and really hated going out in the sticky humidity for business purposes.

Brack was to begin his senior high school year at Balboa High School which was run by the Department of Defense. We registered him and discovered he was qualified to graduate at semester. He was determined to do that since he knew no one and had absolutely no ties to the school. One of the worst side effects of military life is the constant moving especially of high school students. All three of our children went to two or three high schools during those years.

Most states require their state's history for graduation. There are many horror stories of military children not graduating with their class till they complete the state history requirement. There is a concentrated effort now to get states to make exceptions, especially for military students moving into a school district on their senior year.

Not only do requirements for graduation differ from state to state but athletes have a very difficult time being accepted on a team as a total unknown. Many creative parents have sent videos to the new school ahead of a move, especially when teams are selected the year before. I know of two talented young girls who became cheerleaders at the new school before anyone had met them simply because the parents were proactive in sending a tryout video.

The first few weeks we were in Panama, I received a phone call from

Moana Loa High School asking if I could reconsider the failing grade I had given a young lady who was a senior. First, she had come to two classes all semester, and I would not be able to tell you what she looked like. Second, I had offered her an opportunity to make up for everything she had missed even though she had no viable reason for her absences. She declined, so I had failed her.

I assured the caller, I could not nor would I consider such a request and explained the above two points. I did say if the principal wanted to do that it would be her call, but it would be over my objections. We never heard the decision, but I would guess the girl graduated. I also assumed the principal would not have forged my name but used her own.

General George Joulwan, the CINC South commander, was George's boss and his wife, Karen, was, I suppose, mine. She was a great role model in many ways and another strong woman. I never had to guess what her agenda was because she was clear in her opinions but open to others. I found her fair in all things and a strong guide, if the way was murky.

We discovered we were both home economics majors which explained how she wore such beautifully tailored clothes. She made most of her things which I no longer did, but I truly admired her talent.

They lived in quarters one in Quarry Heights which to my knowledge had always housed the head CINC South. It was a lovely rambling house with guest quarters attached for VIP guests. It was always fun to see what had been collected from all over the world, and their home did not disappoint. Interesting items were everywhere.

Living in another country brings its surprises and dining out was a big one in Panama.

One night we were taking an official military visitor out to eat at a local restaurant. The hard car pulled up to the front door with the tail vehicle right behind us. I noticed an armed guard at the door and asked Sergeant Vasquez about him. "This is a two-shotgun restaurant. The other guard is inside," he explained. George further explained that they had gone to a one-shotgun restaurant in the past, but it was inevitably robbed, so to keep everyone safe we now only frequented two-shotgun establishments.

We were seated with our guest at one table. The security team, minus one who stayed to guard the vehicles, was seated at another table as if we were separate parties. It was very cloak and dagger, but very plausible to the casual observer.

The security team told me of an incident at a one-shotgun restaurant where gunmen overpowered the one guard, held all the diners at gun point until they stripped them of all their jewels and valuables and then their clothes. I'm sure it was not a pretty sight.

George's deputy was Brigadier General Jim Wilson. He and his wife, Sam, were very helpful getting us acclimated and knowledgeable about the country.

They had a beautiful lab named Boomer. He was a champion dog who found our collie, Windy, most attractive. The feeling was mutual which was very helpful living so close.

As a two-star general in a command position, George could have a junior and senior aide. The local temporary junior aide had been around a while, but his ethics or lack thereof concerned us so the hunt was on. Department of the army had a list of possible aides. We interviewed two who were quite frankly not acceptable, at least to us. It was George's decision, but since the junior aide was in the house most of the time, my feedback was accepted. His or her duties included: keeping uniforms ready (Yea!), the public areas of the house presentable (Yea! Yea!), cooking when needed, and generally keeping track of items for George.

After the two absolute *NOs*, George called in Command Sergeant Major (CSM) Irtenkauf and asked him to send over the very best men in Panama's mess halls. Sergeant Corey Smallwood came over for the interview and was accepted without reservations. He would go to school for aides to learn the basics but George and the senior aide guided him about the military side, and he and I had daily conversations about food prep, recipes, etc. He was absolutely solid gold. His wife, Gwen, was another treasure.

After we got to know them better, we discovered Gwen was from Arkansas, our home state, and Corey had played football for a college in Arkansas. They had met at college, gotten married, and now were starting a family as well as becoming part of ours.

Corey made the little bedroom above the kitchen his office and settled in.

I ran most mornings before dawn with Sam and our next-door neighbor, Pat Downey, out to the Panamanian police academy at the end of the causeway. We'd pass one of Noriega's getaway houses as we ran the length of the causeway. It was known as his voodoo house, as he kept a pagan alter in the living room and a self-acclaimed witch in residence.

After a few months, I began walking later in the morning with a new acquaintance, Wanda Holt. Her husband, Bob, was the ROTC instructor at Balboa High School, but they lived down the street.

On occasion you will meet someone who is an instant friend; Wanda was just that. We had similar views, beliefs, and our children were both high school seniors. Wanda's daughter, Rebecca, started picking Brack up every morning for school, so they too became friends.

Wanda and I attended Bible study together and met many young wives we otherwise would not have met. We have remained great friends even after retirement and to this day keep in touch. One of the young wives was Cheryle Hill. When the Hills left Panama she was pregnant, having medical difficulties and dealing with a husband who hadn't a clue about moving. Wanda and I went over and helped her prepare the house for the move. We had certainly had our share of practice. Cheryle quickly became another army daughter.

We hadn't been there long when a flyer was circulated in our neighborhood asking for suggestions to improve our neighborhood. A community meeting was scheduled, so I went. The Bay of Panama edged most of the community, and it was polluted beyond comprehension. Not only did some of Panama City's older sewer systems dump into the bay, but also ships waiting to traverse the canal were not forbidden to dump in the ocean just beyond the bay entrance. Everything from styrofoam products to hypodermic needles could be seen floating in the bay, eventually washing ashore. Our beach was a trash heap when the wind was from the east. I suggested we might make some sticks with nail heads and encourage a Boy or Girl Scout troop to take the cleanup as a project. The post engineers could collect the bags of trash, and a leader would be there to protect the kids from needles and other harmful items. After logging in my suggestion, I forgot about it.

About two months later, someone knocked on our back door. He was standing at the door with a bundle of sticks with nails in them. He announced that he was delivering the sticks I had requested. It took a few minutes to remember why he would be bringing me sticks. So much for the beach cleanup project. No doubt much conjecture had occurred among the Engineer Department over my reasons for needing nail-embedded sticks.

I used some for tomato stakes and did pick up some of the trash myself. They worked great for both activities. Moral of the story: be careful what you "suggest" as the commander's wife.

Brackett and some friends were driving on to the Bridge of the Americas when a chiva bus came speeding along and clipped the back side of the Explorer. It spun the car around throwing Brack's head out the open window so forcefully he lost his hat. The other boys were slightly injured because thankfully all were wearing a seat belt. Brackett, of course, got the ticket. We hired a lawyer who was fluent in both languages. The bus driver swore the boys pulled out in front of him as he was going the speed limit. We had taken pictures of the Explorer, and they proved he was lying. The court system in Panama was often corrupt and filled with paper stampers. We went through several layers of bureaucracy finally appearing before a judge. Because of our pictures, Brack was cleared, and the bus driver fined. USAA was wonderful in getting our car repaired.

Another time, Brackett, his girlfriend, and her brother were walking down a usually fairly safe street after a concert when they were attacked by knife-wielding hoodlums and all their money stolen. His girlfriend was sent to the hospital, and the boys were bruised. They were very lucky but never went downtown again. We put a stop on Brack's ID card as it too was stolen, and he was issued another. The ID card was probably more valuable to a Panamanian than the money.

One day Corey was busy, so I went off post to pick up George's uniforms at the cleaners. George had the security team. I had me.

The cleaners were off a side road, around a curve tucked in a stand of trees. On one side of the road a high chain link fence rose from the waist-high grass partially hiding a high rise ghetto apartment building. The other side of the road was a stand of trees. The shanty town area was known as "Hollywood."

I picked up the laundry, hopped in the Explorer, failing to lock the doors as was my habit.

As the Explorer rounded the curve, a man stepped into the middle of the road, raising a pistol pointed at me. The first thing I did was hit the lock button, the second to put up my hand to, I suppose, stop the bullet. My mind was racing, but what I wasn't going to do was stop or get out. Muttering, "You or me, buddy," I stomped on the gas. He literally leapt from the road disappointing me because he wasn't at least clipped. There were no gunshots fired, so his gun may have been empty. Another man ran out in the road behind me.

Around the next bend, of all things, a military police car was stopped at the light in front of me. Flashing my lights and honking, one MP got out, coming back to check. I retold my experience. He asked for my name as he jotted down notes. He didn't react, so I dismissed it and drove on home.

By the time the car pulled into our garage, George was on the phone demanding if I was okay. The MP figured out whose wife I was, and the alarm went out. It was just another day in Panama and, of course, the armed men were long gone.

Crime was so prevalent in Panama because the people are so desperately poor.

The middle class that worked on the canal was very small in numbers compared to the masses of poor. The extreme rich are also in the minority. Many of the rich do share their wealth such as the elder Mr. Motta of the Free Zone, but most do not seem to.

I had only once before had any help in the house, but in Panama it was possible to hire someone to clean, cook, iron, and handle all household chores for very little money.

After asking around, I was given the name of a darling little lady named Ruthie. She came for an interview, and I just loved her at first sight. She came three days a week for twelve dollars which was top dollar compared to the neighbors I knew about. Many of the maids stayed all day and often stole items daily.

Ruthie left her house that she shared with her two daughters at 5:00 a.m. She cleaned upstairs, since Corey had the public rooms, did the laundry, ironed, and then ate the lunch Corey and I prepared before catching her bus back home around one. She never took a thing and was just a delight. Her long black hair hung to her waist, and she had the sweetest face.

Occasionally, the gardener who came once a week would have lunch with us as well. He was a Kuna Indian who was a genius with plants.

Our days were very full with meetings, activities, and occasionally fun.

Tara's wedding plans were progressing. Her CIA friend, Kim, planned to give them the wedding cake as her gift. We called a master wood crafter we knew of on the Big Island of Hawaii and commissioned a koa wood trunk as our gift to them. He inlaid the flat top with a cross. It was sent to them, and they loved it. We had thought the flat top could be covered with glass and used as a coffee table.

She had picked out dresses for her bridesmaids, Kim and Cheryl. I made a long white flower girl dress for little Mesepa, Tia's six-year-old niece, and found white tights leaving the shoes up to her mother. I made a purse to go with it complete with lace and pull strings. Mesepa was a true tomboy who wore shorts and T-shirts running everywhere with her boy cousins. There was much concern whether she would even consider wearing a dress. We would soon find out.

The table in our formal dining room seated twenty-seven. There were no tablecloths for that table, so I went to a local fabric shop and bought fabric in white and pink which gave me two options. I cut the tablecloths and had enough to make napkins with the rest. To buy them would have cost a fortune, and the homemade ones looked great.

The door to the kitchen had a peep hole for Corey to keep an eye on the dinner proceedings.

For big events when heads of Latin American armies and their entourages were coming for dinner, we would borrow either the kitchen staff from quarters one in Quarry Heights or the distinguished visitor's quarters (DVQ). Corey was in turn commandeered by them. I usually made the dinner rolls, and Corey always made the pies, if we were serving pies because no one made better ones. Protocol handled the place cards, seating arrangements, invitations, and were there to help keep the evening running smoothly. George's senior aide was always in the wings.

One of our first dinners, I had planned a hot soup as a first course. We all sat down, and the soup was served; George asked a blessing, and before the first spoon was lifted our guest of honor rose to give a toast and an extended speech. Needless to say, the soup was cold, and the rest of the meal put back to keep warm. We learned a lesson. After that, we always had a cold soup, and Corey kept watch though his peephole for my signal to take up the soup and bring the next course.

After all dinners, George brought in the kitchen crew to introduce and thank them in front of the guests for their efforts.

After dinner coffee and or liqueur was usually served in the living room prior to taking our guest to the patio where Panamanian dancers gave a short performance.

When the last guest had departed, and the kitchen cleaned, we sat down with Corey and discussed the event. We listed what was good, what wasn't, and how to improve. If any of the others were still there, they too were included. Opened wine was offered, and leftovers were doled out. We received a stipend for these events, but it never covered the cost.

These events made me ever grateful to my gracious home economics mother and my home economics degree.

Shopping in Panama was an adventure to say the least. The best shopping area was El Central, a very long pedestrian street lined on both sides with shops of every description. There were a few large department stores but many smaller shops in between.

Thanks to Sam's advice, I wore old shorts, a loose, faded very old shirt with plenty of buttoned pockets and running shoes when shopping on El Central. The car was parked either at the United States Army's Gorgas Hospital where the parking lot was fenced or one paid someone to watch the car in the lot across the street. The parking lots had several young men who guarded cars for a small fee.

El Central was about two blocks away, so it's an easy walk. Each pocket of my shirt had money in it, so I'd never lose it all by way of a pick pocket.

I truly enjoyed shopping there as the prices were reasonable and many items unique.

An MP's wife, I'll call her Pam and him Tom went shopping there one day only to have her purse snatched. She ran the thief down and hit him over the head with a pan she had just gotten. The crowd roared their approval as she retrieved her bag and continued shopping. The next day in the MP station there was a sign Tom-O Pam 1!

George's security team was driving downtown in the hard SUV with the senior aide transporting a very important document when they were caught by a stoplight.

Several men surrounded the SUV with pistols drawn. The darkened windows of the SUV slowly cracked open for the barrels of the automatic weapons to point out. The would-be thieves fled, leaving a story to be retold many times.

CSM Irtenkauf's wife, Vicky, and I planned the Army Family Action Plan Conference since they hadn't had one for some time.

It was two days long, but good issues came from it, and we felt we had at least gotten the USARSO issues back to DC.

Occasionally the Wives' Club or some other group would organize a trip to the free zone. The last time I had visited the free zone in Colon was in 1968, so it had changed dramatically.

Colon was the world's second largest free zone where buyers from major companies came to place huge orders for everything from jewelry to fine china. Military wives could get permission to bring a bus into the zone for a day of shopping but had a zone guard ride back on the return trip getting off halfway back to Panama City. This was to preclude any of us reselling our purchases.

One of the best deals there was linens. Place mats, napkins, sheets, etc., came in packages of twelve, so often we could split a dozen if we didn't need twelve embroidered tablecloths, for example.

Most shops were very gracious to us, Yanks, as we purchased our dozen this and dozen that. A few were not, and some even refused us entrance, which was fine as long as we knew up front. It is my understanding that John Q Public can no longer shop there, so we were fortunate, indeed, to be there when we could.

Every few months, our house would be swept with dogs and detection devises to determine if electronic bugs had been planted. On one occasion the alarms sounded, and the MPs were searching everywhere for the bug. It turned out to be the garage door opener in the desk drawer.

Brack took some college courses by correspondence and applied to colleges in the United States.

As that first summer approached, so did the wedding. Because we were in Panama, the decision was made to have the wedding in American Samoa so all of Tia's family could be there. Brackett and I would fly to Arkansas, visit the moms, then fly to Honolulu where we would meet up with Cheryl. From there Tara, Tia, Kim, Cheryl, Brackett, and I would catch the first of two weekly flights to Samoa. George would come a few days later catching the Thursday Samoa flight.

Leaving Honolulu, we were loaded with our luggage, the securely packed frozen wedding cake and frosting, the wedding clothes for everyone, wedding paper goods, gifts for the family, and all the wedding bouquets Tara and Kim had fashioned from silk flowers.

We fit right in on the plane with Samoans bringing back, along with their luggage, ice chests filled with food and cardboard boxes laced with heavy twine, affectionately called Pacific Islander luggage. A festive picnic aura permeated the plane. Samoans are not petite people, so we looked like sickly distant relatives at best.

Arriving at the airport, we were met by Tia's brother and a sister. We all piled in their pickup truck, and off we went to the house.

The airport was packed, and we were told it was local custom to often check out the activity at the airport for lack of anything else to do.

George had told me to rent a car to not burden the family, so off we went to the only rental agency in Pago Pago. It was in the parking lot of the only hotel. When told what we needed, we were escorted to the parking lot where two old trucks baked in the sun. "You can have your choice," the rental owner told us. "You can have the one with bald tires or the one with serious engine trouble." We chose the one with bald tires.

Tia introduced us to his mother and the rest of the family who lived nearby.

After unpacking the wedding paraphernalia, we were shown our sleeping quarters. Mesepa's original house had blown away in a hurricane, so this new one was positioned directly behind the concrete foundation of the old one leaving a ready-made patio and basketball court.

Samoa is a lush tropical island laced with lava formations, rich soil, and breathtaking scenery.

The Amuimuia family had spent much money and effort in the preceding year preparing for our visit and the wedding. We were overwhelmed at the amount of effort they had put forth. Beds had been built, an indoor shower and toilet installed (although a perfectly good one was outside in an outbuilding), and a screened dining area had been built.

Cheryl and Brackett were to stay with Tia's sister and her husband in another village. The husband had Brack answer the phone so he wouldn't have to talk to the callers. After a couple of days, they begged to come to Mesepa's house and sleep on the floor mats with the little ones.

George and I had a very comfortable room as did Tara and Kim. Mesepa had the third bedroom where we were delighted to see the Hawaiian quilt we had all made.

Tia stayed with his brothers in the men's house on the hill. It was a roofed structure open on all sides for air circulation. The boys had fashioned a pool table from wood and, I think, used army blankets for the bed and pockets. It worked like a charm, and we all spent time up there playing.

Tia had six brothers and two sisters and all were coming. Most of the nieces and nephews were there most days and slept on mats on the living room floor.

The family held a welcome for us on our first night, led by Mesepa. Since her husband died, she was definitely the matriarch of that family. We doled out the gifts we had brought and gave Mesepa money for the wedding since they were bearing most of the expense.

Every night most families in Samoa have vespers with scripture reading, prayers, and singing. I've never heard more gorgeous voices. I really do think all Samoans have that gift. Tia's father had been a Methodist minister which is highly esteemed there. His older brother, Fáavae, was also a minister but at the time he lived in Western Samoa.

We were fed a huge dinner and enjoyed the first seating since there were so many of us.

The next morning, we were still full from the huge dinner of the night before but were called to an even bigger breakfast. My favorite item was cinnamon rolls soaked in coconut milk. I'm sure there wasn't a calorie in them.

Tara and Tia, with the three of us tagging along, went to get the prerequisite marriage license. It took me back to small town Arkansas as they went from place to place, answered embarrassing questions, had papers stamped repeatedly, and mostly waited in hallways.

We saw several very tall lovely Samoan women, we thought, but Tia told us they were men in drag called Mahus. He could mimic one so well we were all in tears we laughed so hard. They seemed very accepted in society there, and several worked in the hospital and official offices where we waited.

We toured the island in their truck with all but Fáavae and me in the bed sitting on mats. The family was appalled I too would want to ride in the bed of the truck. We drove to the beautiful seaside village of Vaitia where Tia was born and lived as a child. We passed cricket teams playing in their lavalava's barefoot, lush mountains rising from the crystal blue waters of the Pacific, and then through Pago Pago amid the aroma of the Starkist tuna factory, past shops and the Governor's Mansion.

We went swimming one beautiful afternoon. Cheryl was shocked to learn she had to wear a T-shirt over her bikini so she wouldn't embarrass Tia's family. Modestly is highly valued there, but general tourist are given more leeway. We were considered family.

Tia's sisters spent hours making large flowers from crepe paper for the wedding.

Tia's mom had to be taken to the hospital for treatment for a foot infection. Her diabetes kept her prone to such things. We visited her and were somewhat surprised at the hospital. The beds were separated by sheets on wires so the air could circulate among all. Fortunately, she was released before the wedding.

Mesepa had organized her family well for the wedding. She had a meeting in the women's house which was constructed much like the men's, where she doled out responsibilities and did a verbal roll call of each family member's portion of items needed for the wedding. Wesley brought beef from Western Samoa, and fine mats were gathered in a large stack. Each one had been lovingly woven and served as a sort of monetary unit. Two of Tia's brothers were required to provide for the reception a certain number of buckets of corned beef from New Zealand.

I had suggested we bring hams, but Tia was quick to waylay that plan by explaining that first the custom agents would confiscate it, and the guests, who were the soon-to-be recipients of the gifts, would truly prefer corned beef. Okay.

By the third day, we were all looking at our watches asking, "Isn't it time to eat?" We were not only spoiled but getting used to a laden table of delicious food.

George's plane arrived late Thursday night, and he was treated to a formal welcome and told a meal awaited him outside in the dining pavilion. He stated he wasn't a bit hungry. We all glared at him, and I squeezed his arm and reminded him the meal had been prepared just for him, and I just knew he could eat a little something. He is not known for being slow on the uptake so immediately agreed that he probably would enjoy something to eat after all. For two more days, preparations continued.

Brack and Cheryl watched Sefulu's husband shoot two hogs. The carcasses were transported to Mesepa's house where they were placed on corrugated steel, doused with gasoline, and set fire to burn off the hair. The boys used machetes to scrape the hair and char from the skin then washed them. The hogs were butchered saving important organs to cook and give as gifts.

An umu was set up in the backyard cook shed. Lava rocks were heated with wood coals as a base and the pigs, wrapped in banana leaves, were lowered onto the hot rocks with some bread fruit placed around them. It was then covered with more rocks and banana leaves. They would slow cook for hours.

George and I bought every potato and bottle of champagne on the island. We cooked the potatoes for my famous potato salad. It was the biggest pan I had ever made. Pita, Tia's chef brother, cooked chickens for a day and night.

Kim, Tara's pastiche chef friend from CIA, began putting the enormous wedding cake together.

A cousin took Brack to get palm fronds to make baskets. Brack's wasn't as neatly done, but you could tell it was a basket.

Meanwhile, we went to the church to rehearse for the wedding.

We were stunned when Tia sat down at the organ and began to beautifully play hymns. None of us except Tara knew he played.

The minister was fresh from the seminary on Western Samoa spoke with a British accent. He explained the ceremony's literal ups and downs until Tara turned to her daddy and said, "Dad, I don't want to get up and down so much in that dress." George told the minister, "She will stand through that part." The minister said, "Okay."

The sisters had decorated the church with colorful crepe flowers and balloons. We kept reminding ourselves it was another place with customs different from ours.

We all helped decorate the huge canopy erected over the old house foundation. We tied overlapping palm fronds to decorate the support poles and put up folding tables and chairs in a large U shape.

One of Tia's brothers came from Hawaii with a girlfriend he forgot to mention he was bringing. It put a bit of stress into a stressful situation. On the wedding day as Tara was trying to get ready, Chandra was primping in the bathroom for an inordinate amount of time, and we thought she would never get out. She finally emerged, making the rest of us rush to get ready to give Tara plenty of time.

Little Mesepa loved her dress, much to our relief, and she looked adorable. I think she liked the purse best.

Everyone wears white to church in Samoa, so we were all in white except Kim and Cheryl who wore dark purple bridesmaid dresses. George was in his uniform and even the preacher wore a formal lavalava under a white tux coat.

We rushed to get Tara to the church on time only to realize she didn't have her veil. George hustled back to the house to retrieve it, thankfully not getting pulled over for speeding.

She was a gorgeous bride, and the service was very moving. It was mostly in Samoan, albeit very much like a US Methodist ceremony. The overall setting was awe-inspiring: something out of the movies or Hollywood. Tara had taken Samoan two years in college, but the family didn't know that, so many things were said, thinking she didn't understand. Usually, it was just amusing.

George walked her down the aisle where Tia waited with his brothers.

Brackett was filming with our video camera, and every time a balloon would work itself loose, rise to the ceiling to get caught in the fan blades, his camera followed it to its demise.

After the wedding, they told us they thought we used balloons at weddings. We answered, "No, we assumed it was a local custom."

Tia's older sister, Sefulu, was a strong-willed person who rather took over much of the planning that Mesepa hadn't previously told how she wanted it done. It was a small problem.

The wedding cake had been finished at 1:00 a.m. with all four of us, Kim, Tara, Cheryl, and me helping. It would be placed on the center table in the U-shaped guest tables.

Immediately following the ceremony, we all went next door to the preacher's house where refreshment had been set out. The choir entertained with songs, Tara and Tia sat on raised chairs, and we all danced to Samoan music. A sweet elderly lady gave me a kukui nut necklace that I still have. They served fruit cocktail and juice for refreshments. Small children did a special fertility dance for the bride and groom.

After about an hour, we left for Mesepa's house and the reception.

All of the invited guest sat at the tables and listened to the talking chief give the family history in an ancient language only talking chiefs usually spoke and understand. It took about forty-five minutes. A blessing was given. After that, food was served. A group of young women served each diner with a foil-covered tuna packing box filled with food. It was enough to feed our family for two days. Roast pig from the umu, chicken, bread fruit, my potato salad, rice, and on and on. As we ate, the official giving of gifts called a Sua began. The room of donations from the family members had been doled out for this purpose. Originally, a traditional coconut with a dollar in it was given to each important guest, but today a can of coke works even better.

Several girls would parade the gifts on outstretched arms to the recipient. The minister received the second cooked hog, bolts of fabric, five-gallon buckets of corned beef, and fine mats to name a few. The other ministers there received all the above, but the hog. Other VIPs received bolts of fabric or large buckets of corned beef or both. It appeared it was very lucrative to be a minister there.

The beautiful three-section towering wedding cake was hacked to smithereens in seconds as the girls cut huge hunks to place in front of specific diners. The lonely little cake boxes we had stacked by the cake looked sad. One of the girls finally went to the slashers and reminded them of the boxes. "Oh, yeah!" We watched in southern horror as the icing caked knife cut smaller chunks, slapped each chunk into the little box, and the knife blade cleaned off on the box edge. The top was smashed shut, and each guest looked perplexed when presented with this sticky gift. The Samoans don't do small cake boxes, we deduced.

The champagne disappeared like magic, and the dancing to a local band began. Tara and Tia danced and then everyone else.

One of Tia's cousins had obviously been given the duty of entertaining Brackett but when he asked Brack to dance that was a bit much. Brack claimed he had "stuff" he had to do and fled.

After most of the guests left, Tara and Tia opened gifts people had left.

It occurred to me that the guests had received a lot more than they gave. Weddings were darned expensive. We found out later that funerals are even more expensive since you have to buy gifts for everyone who comes. To me, there is something so wrong in requiring the grief-stricken to buy gifts for supposedly grieving friends who come to a funeral.

As we packed up to return, leaving Tara and Tia to spend a few more days there, we each left a set of clothing to signify we would return one day.

Back in Panama, sometime after the wedding, Cheryl came to visit for a week with the highlight being the day we took her and Brackett to the Gatun locks on the Panama Canal. We toured the facility, and they both got to turn the simple lever that opened and closed the locks. We loved having her, but the visit was way too short!

Brackett had been accepted by two universities: the University of Texas, San Antonio, and Washington State. He and I took a side trip to

Seattle and a quick visit to "WASU" in Pullman. We rented a car and toured the campus of Washington State University. It truly was in the middle of nowhere, but I told him the Snake River and skiing were nearby. That couldn't compete with the corn fields and flat vistas. He decided on the University of Texas, San Antonio, as his only alternative.

I made a trip back to the States in the fall with Brackett to enroll him in the University of Texas in San Antonio and get him settled in his dorm.

For some reason, he had decided his rather longest hair would look cool in corn rolls. There is a very good reason Caucasian people don't wear that hairstyle. The straight slippery hair just doesn't like to be braided like that. His friend in Panama fixed it for him for the trip. Oh, yeah! We had learned not to overreact about hair, sure the phase would be short-lived which it was.

We located a bike shop, and he selected a bicycle to get to and from class. He registered and signed up for classes before I left. I felt bereft as I flew back to Panama. The house would seem so empty upon my return.

Back in Panama, life continued at a fast pace.

Trips to Argentina, Brazil, and Guatemala followed each other in rapid succession. Family support activities, our command group (we named "JUST CAWS,") Officer's Wives Club, NCO Wives' Club, and daily activities filled out the already crowded calendar.

The Joulwans left for Europe, and General Barry McCaffrey with wife, Jill, took command. There were dinners and parties to farewell the Joulwans and then more to welcome the McCaffreys. We had not seen Barry since retrieving him from the airport on his medevac return from Vietnam when George was an aide for his dad. Jill was an absolute joy. She was great fun and was loaded with common sense.

After they had been there a while, she and I would dress in old clothes, take a lawn chair, bathing suit, towel, toiletries, and a bit of money to board the boat to Taboga Island. There was a single golf cart on the island for transportation because the landmass was so small—everyone walked. We'd walk to the hotel, pay a few dollars to use the beach, change clothes, and settle down to a day of baking, reading, gathering beach glass for Jill's collection, and enjoying a leisurely lunch at the outdoor café attached to the hotel. There were no phones, so we got a true break from the world and expectations. Because we both loved to sun, we called ourselves the BGs. That didn't stand for Brigadier General but Bronze Goddesses. It's all in your mind!

We made our getaway several times then suggested to the OWC we have our board meeting over there one month just for fun. It was a big success with few absentees.

Friends from Arkansas, Jim and Pat McClelland and John and Kathy Roberts, came for a visit. We were so excited to see them and had planned their visit in detail. Jim and Pat were good friends with President and Mrs. Clinton, so we included in the plans an office call with Panamanian president Endara.

Upon their arrival, the security team whisked them through security, and we drove the long way home to show them Panama City.

We had an interesting visit with the president. It was scheduled for ten minutes but lasted forty-five minutes.

We took a camera with us, but after the visit we forgot to turn it off, and we had footage of our feet walking downstairs along paths and down hallways swinging back and forth all the time. Exciting stuff!

We planned to spend one night in the San Blas Islands with the Kuna Indians. George and I had been there twice for a formal visit. On one island, we had been welcomed by the head man and given a tour of the village. They were very proud of their clinic that a US general had sent engineers to build. A wizened elderly woman, bent with age, tugged on George's uniform sleeve. The interpreter said she was insisting he go view the birthing room. The entire entourage tagged along as she pulled him along by his sleeve. The birthing room had one bed on one side and a metal delivery table on the other. The table had a twelve-inch hole eaten through the metal where countless babies had entered the world. The bed was taken by a young mother whose baby was premature but surviving. Our elderly guide begged for a new delivery table.

It was a complicated request as the Panamanian government gave very little to the Kunas, requiring gifts go through the government in Panama City.

When we returned, George tried all avenues to get them a new or better-used one.

Another stop on the tour was the local school. As a teacher, I was immensely interested in the condition of the one-room school. I vowed to get them supplies as they had absolutely *nothing*. Before we left Panama, the cayukas sent an emissary to pick up the huge boxes we filled with leftover school supplies from the American school. Each of the schools in the archipelago received enough supplies to keep them for several years.

This trip would be only for pleasure. Half the security team preceded us to the island. The rest flew with us in a small plane. George had to sit in the copilot seat. As we flew through dense cloud cover and when we began blindly descending, Jim became really worried. The planes instrument panel was primitive (no GPS), and we had to fly over the mountainous spine of Panama to get to the archipelago. We assured Jim the pilot had done this thousands of times, but he didn't breathe easy until we broke out of the clouds on the ocean side of the mountains.

The pilot landed the plane on a tiny airstrip that ended in the ocean. He made an about-turn on the grass and parked. We unfolded from the plane, grabbed our bags, and waited for our transportation to the "resort." The girls needed a bathroom break, so I took them to the facilities waiting to get their reaction. We walked out a long pier to an outhouse perched over the ocean. The usual one hole was there, but nothing under it but the sea. Children were swimming nearby but appeared healthy enough considering. The girl's reaction was just as we anticipated.

The resort was on another island one got to by cayuka, a hollowed-out boat with a small motor. The swimming pool was a concrete enclosure where seawater could come and go with the tide with the bottom teeming with lobsters. The lobster dance at 10:00 p.m. was a big draw. For some reason, they circled the pool every evening as if trained. No one swam in the pool while we were there.

The rooms were Spartan, the saltwater shower paired with a tub of rainwater to rinse, and again the real toilet flushed directly into the blue waters below.

Lobster is a staple which we had for breakfast, lunch, and dinner. We ate at a long picnic table under an awning, and although we could see into the dirt floor kitchen, we tried not to look too closely.

The security team had set up satellite communications before we arrived so George could monitor the army business.

We took another cayuka ride out to another small island to snorkel around a shipwreck. While we were there, we bought several molas from the local women who lived in tents there.

When we flew home on the second day, some of us didn't feel well. We were to fly to Contadora Island the next day for another overnight. By morning, all of us were literally green from food poisoning except George and Pat McClelland. They must have had stomachs of iron. The entire security team was green as well.

We made it to our rooms on Contadora Island which were much better equipped than the San Blas accommodations.

I don't remember much of it since we spent most of the first day in bed. George and Pat toured the island while all the rest of us tried not to die. By evening, we crawled out of bed and went to dinner. In the lobby, the security team was trying to look efficient without moving. George and Pat had been at the bar in the center of the swimming pool while the rest of us thought soup might be a safe choice for dinner. It took two weeks for some of them to feel better, but by then they were all back in Arkansas.

We absolutely loved having them as they brought with their long-standing friendship a bit of home.

Meanwhile, Cheryl's husband, Todd, who had only had one short-lived job on a tree farm, tried to practice his karate on her one night. The result was a restraining order, locks and checking account changed, and divorce papers signed.

The last few months we were in Panama, Fidel Castro began the second huge boat lift from Cuba to the United States. He cleared his prisons and jails as well as normal Cubans who wished to leave Cuba for whatever reason. The US Navy intercepted the flotilla. Instead of a formal designation as refugees, had they gotten to US soil, they were classified as "persons seeking asylum"—a major difference under international laws and protocols. Overnight in Panama, large-fenced compounds or camps were constructed with tents in rows to accommodate ten thousand Cubans.

The military wives collected thousands of pounds of clothing for them.

Toiletries kits were put together, and volunteers filled the command center. As each busload arrived, a group of wives would be there to greet them.

Sam had a full-time job, so although George had given her husband the job of the daily running of the camp itself, since George was to be out of country on business, I assumed she would be pleased if I helped out in the volunteering department. As it turned out, she was livid that I had supposedly undermined her authority. I apologized and explained, but she was seriously offended.

The criminals who were on the boats soon had agitation at a fever pitch in the camps and a major riot ensued. George returned, took over, and struck back in the middle of the night, rounding up the troublemakers and separating them from the masses. He was appalled it had gotten so out of hand. The easygoing days were over for the camps.

When George got orders, it was difficult to drag him down to earth. He was selected to command the 82nd Abn Division which was a dream he had had his entire career. I too was excited but for other reasons.

It would put us back in the USA where all of our children lived and into a setting on a post I knew like the back of my hand. Through all the commands George received, I had learned hard lessons. I had watched, choosing ones to emulate like Kathy Boylan and Jill McCaffery as well as those to never be like. I won't name them, but rest assured they are out there.

We had a lovely farewell, made a final trip to the free zone to have lunch with Mr. Motta and do a bit more shopping, and prepared the house for yet another move.

Our old friends, MG Lawson Magruder and his wife, Gloria, were to follow us and be the last occupants of the great house before Panama took it back. They wanted the pool table, so thankfully it was left behind as the quarters at Fort Bragg weren't big enough for it.

George ran in a relay for the army as a last event insisting the security team stand down. At the end of his run, he glanced back to see Sergeant Vasquez riding a bicycle a few yards behind him. He refused to let "the Boss" take such a risk. He was a wonderful man, and I appreciated him more than he will ever know.

The Christmas ornament from them is hung each year with great memories.

Our farewell was heart wrenching for me. Deana Sawdy, Freida Huddleston, CSM Irtenkauf's wife, Vickie, and all the army wives who kept their home fires burning even in a foreign country would always have a spot in my heart.

That move was one of the easiest since the entire security team plus the aides were with every mover every second. Nothing had a chance to be pocketed so was safely packed up and shipped.

20 | Fort Bragg, North Carolina
"The Final Hooah"

THE CHANGE OF command was most impressive, and we were overjoyed to greet old friends as well as looking forward to new ones.

I was rather nervous because although I had attended hundreds of change of commands, it was usually a knee-jerk reaction to stand when the head lady stands, sit when she sits, and clap when she claps. Rather like watching the hostess to know which fork to use first. This time everyone was watching me. I prayed I would do everything at the right time.

When we arrived, Bert Tackaberry was the Assistant Division Commander for Operations (ADC-O). His wife, Donna, was a lovely lady. It was difficult to tell them farewell so soon after our arrival.

The Assistant Division Commander for Support (ADC-S) was Steve Rippe. Shortly after we arrived, he married Susan LaSalla, who was a producer of NBC News in DC. Both ladies were fabulous. Both couples left soon after our arrival. Replacing them were Ed and Jan Smith and P. T. and Jan Miklochex. The "Jans" would be great friends and right arms for most of our tour.

The chief of staff John Marsella's wife, Jane, was rather cold and haughty. He had a reputation for being horrid to those beneath him in rank but appeared great to those above. *This should be interesting*, I thought.

The brigade command teams were in a class by themselves. Each couple was extremely capable with the wives being an A-one group. They all had experience, were savvy, and loved to have fun together.

First Brigade was John and Kathy Abizaid followed by Dave and Holly Petraeus.

The Abizaids were a great couple but weren't there long. Holly and Dave came in to replace them, so we had another change of command ceremony. With each of the battalion and brigade changes, we went to the ceremony. They were all similar and in the summer hot as blazes! Dave was brilliant and Holly very serious. We enjoyed them both.

Second Brigade was Tom and Susan Turner followed by John and Katy Scroggins. Tom was selected by George to come to division headquarters to be the chief of staff, and Susan was my right-hand lady as I had been for Edna Johnson. She was wonderful! Katy and John were great additions to the division. Both brought a wealth of experience and good common sense.

Third Brigade was John Schmader followed by Clyde and Vicky Newman. The Schmaders were a great command team, and we were so sad to see them leave. When the Newmans arrived, we realized they were from Berryville, Arkansas, which is a small town next to the tiny North West Arkansas town of Green Forest where my mother grew up. They were both heavily into fitness.

DivArty was Larry and Jane Gottardi followed by Ned and Ann Spohn. Discom was lead by Lannie Pankey followed quickly by Bob and Anne Dail.

Lloyd Austin was the G-3 and the aviation brigade commander was Ted Larew. His wife, Anne, was very intelligent and charming. They had two wonderful little boys who were always up to something.

Steve England was the Division Command sergeant major. His wife, Renee, worked full time but participated when she could. Their daughters, Heather and Amanda, were beautiful girls.

Every move we made was to me an opportunity to get to know new people and renew old acquaintances. I always went in preparing to like everyone, understanding that people come from different backgrounds and had different personalities. Most made the army better for their differences. I had a difficult time with Jane Marsella who seemed bent on making everything difficult. Accounting for money from the command group wives was not forthcoming nor was any information. The command group was so wonderful it was like having a very comfortable pair of shoes on with a thorn stuck between your toes. All the wives were getting exasperated with her secretiveness and unwillingness to share the smallest item of information meant for us all. I got the feeling she had feathered herself a little fiefdom and was loath to give it up. I tried to get to know her better to understand her, but that was never possible.

Fortunately for us but probably unfortunately for the army, someone thought her husband should get a star and be a general. Everyone who knew them was aghast. The Marsellas wanted a promotion ceremony at division headquarters, so it was arranged. We all went, or course, and were speechless when we noticed she and her mother both were sporting large one-star earrings. We were horrified. Usually, generals' wives go out of their way never to be perceived wearing their husband's rank and would never have even considered such a blatant display. It was just tacky. Thereafter, if any of the ADCs got promoted, I made them enormous cardboard earrings covered in glitter. At an OWC fashion show that December, we decided we all must have the models ball gown that was covered in stars then doubled over with laughter knowing we would *never* wear such a dress.

Marsella went off to Charm school with other new generals with all our hopes they would learn something. George asked Steve Gardner to come up and be the interim chief of staff. I was thrilled as Cat and I had been fast friends for ages. Before leaving, Marsella hadn't cleaned out his office and insisted he would do it when he got back. George had it packed up to be ready for him as he was not willing to have his chief of staff in the hallway while the pompous one was away hopefully getting charming.

We had to scrap the finances and start fresh from scratch after they left because no one could figure out the financial mess.

The Jans, Cat (later Susan Turner), and I took turns visiting with all the new wives in the 82nd as they came through orientation. To most of them, a general's wife meant far less than the first sergeant's wife with whom they had much more interaction. The sergeant was definitely the one the men talked about.

I again would periodically take a load of laundry to the local Laundromat, pretend to read a paperback book while it washed and dried, listening carefully to the conversations of the young army wives. It was amazing what I heard. Many misconceptions but also lots of true distress and problems. I would return home with clean clothes and an earful for my hero. He usually checked into the complaints and most often fixed the problem. I never asked him to, but it was a useful method to hear what the young ones truly think and find out problems no one is going to share with the general. I thought of myself as the back door for George to hear of family issues.

Family support was alive and well at this point, but all spouses didn't participate. If they had, our job would have been easier, and they would have been happier.

Meanwhile, Cheryl had met a young man from Boone who taught her to rock climb. He was a short young red-headed freckle-faced man who seemed okay. He told us he had a degree in recreation and had worked for years on oil tankers in charge of their computer systems. It sounded better than Todd and as always we tried to make our children's choices feel welcome.

We found out years later his "degree" was a two-year associate's degree from the tiny college Lees-McRae in Banner Elk, North Carolina. Furthermore, we were all very puzzled, especially Cheryl, that he had little to no computer knowledge. It was later revealed that he had been a bosun on those ships which meant he swabbed decks and was a gopher. The mountains he claimed to have scaled were ones I could easily have climbed. He also had a nasty habit of saying truly unkind and often untrue things behind one's back. We tried not to leave a room as the knives would be in your back if you did.

Cheryl had moved into his house with him. It sat on a hillside near the Blue Ridge Parkway.

He did teach her the basics of art framing which he crafted in his basement. Cheryl encouraged him to open a frame shop in the area, which he eventually did. They took the art framer's certification test which she passed easily but even with her tutoring took him four more tries to pass. She encouraged him to enlarge the shop to include an art gallery. He finally agreed, and she spent weeks multilayering the floor with a faux finish, redoing the walls and arranging it as a truly interesting gallery. It took off and became very successful.

Tim throughout this time would often act strangely. It appeared he couldn't handle stress and at one point disappeared from the shop. When Cheryl went to find him, to see what was wrong, he was found curled on his bed in a fetal position and had cut big chunks out of his hair.

Our outspoken, strong daughter was slowly changing into a quiet young woman who walked on eggshells not to disturb what was becoming a volatile persona. His reactions were so bizarre a normal person would never have even thought of them. It was terrifying for her, but we were unaware of it all except her personality change.

When Cheryl became pregnant, they seemed thrilled. They had not married, and we never suggested they should, even with this new development. It would be our first grandchild, for that we were delighted.

They drove down to Fayetteville, and we went baby-bed shopping. We found a beautiful bed at that shop that threw the sheets at us years before, and I even mentioned the event to the new owner as a reminder that in a military town you can definitely get return customers. They loaded it up and headed back to Boone.

We had a feeling Tim was bipolar or had some mental problem, and supposedly his family doctor had prescribed some sort of medication which he took sporadically. When he took it, life evened out for them, but when he didn't life for Cheryl was a roller coaster.

Tara meanwhile graduated from the University of Hawaii with an almost perfect 4.0 grade point. George and I flew back to Hawaii for the momentous event.

In her second year she had applied to major in education to teach. She worked forty hours a week as a chef, attended the University of Hawaii full-time, but had one afternoon a week free which she spent volunteering for an elementary class on Fort Shafter. She did that school volunteering for a year until it became too much.

The Japanese instructor who interviewed her asked the name of the teacher for whom she had volunteered. Tara couldn't remember her name. The instructor said, obviously, it meant little to her since she couldn't remember her name so turned her down for the education department. We were stunned but should not really have been surprised since Hawaii had one of the worst school systems in America. We told her it was not meant to be, so make a choice. She decided on history which was to be her new major.

The ceremony was outside on the University of Hawaii's Manoa campus with mu-mu's and flower leis everywhere. We all had leis for Tara after the ceremony, took them out to eat to celebrate, and returned to Bragg.

Brackett, meanwhile, had been caught with marijuana in the dorm so was evicted. I helped him find an apartment he would share with another boy. Every time we called, we got the same, "Everything was fine. Could you send money?" He had a bank account we put money in at the beginning of every month. When his grades arrived and we realized he hadn't even been going to classes, I drove down to pack him up and bring his fun-loving body home.

Cheryle Hill, my "army daughter" who was at Fort Hood a few hours away, drove over with her baby daughter, Grace, to help me clean up the disaster of an apartment.

She was a trooper. The boys helped too, of course, but how hard is it to pick up after yourself? How a bathtub can get that dirty without someone refusing to get in it is a mystery. Pure comet on a scrub brush got most of the mold and bathtub ring. I kept thinking, *This isn't real, it's a commercial!* Cheryle helped all that day then drove back home.

Two days later, after scrubbing every surface and cleaning the carpet, meeting old friends, Chaplain Mike and Amy Tarvin, for a great Mexican dinner, and loading up the SUV we planned to head to Fort Bragg before daylight. It would be a very long day's drive back to North Carolina.

We left San Antonio February 4, Brackett's birthday, in a driving rain storm which turned to sleet within ten miles. Our healthy clip turned into a crawl as the roads got icier and icier. By the time we reached Dallas to turn east, it was stop and go. The trip east got slower and slower and by four o'clock, we learned our southern option, I-10, had closed. At one point that afternoon a semi had jackknifed, closing all lanes. We sat there for hours not moving an inch. We both had to go to the bathroom in the worst way.

We had watched people leaving their cars, sliding across the road to the trees so decided to do the same, one at a time. Brack went first, slid across the interstate and into the trees. I could still see him, but with his back to the road he was decent.

I decided to go over the rise as no tree was big enough to hide me in a squat. The icy road was maneuvered, so I climbed the tree-studded hill to the top only to come face-to-face with a bull on the other side of the barbed wire.

Plan two went into action as I was about to pee my pants and the cold icy air didn't help. Back down the hill, across the interstate, cross the Median across the interstate west, into the trees on the other side, I slid. Behind a clump of thick bushes, I finally found relief, noticing I wasn't the first one there. Stepping carefully out of the thicket and back to the SUV, we decided even if we were dying of thirst, we wouldn't drink anything else till we got moving again.

Finally, the long line of cars began to inch forward.

At the next exit with facilities, we left to try to find a motel. We stopped at the first one we came to and was told they were full. We obviously looked really pitiful because she said, "We do have one left, but it has no phone." "We'll take it!" we chorused.

I called George on the house phone to tell him of our dilemma, and he said he had really been worried but counseled us to stay put and be careful.

We had dinner in the restaurant and at my whispered request the waitress brought Brackett a cupcake with a lit candle. It was no doubt one of the most bizarre birthdays he had ever spent.

The restaurant was full of truckers as the interstate had closed just ahead of us, so we had exited just in time. At breakfast we asked around and were told the interstate would reopen as soon as they could clear it. It was still sleeting and spitting snow. Brackett told me we really should stay put at least another day, but I chose to creep on home hoping it would get better as we got further east.

We were averaging ten miles per hour and occasionally going sidewise down the highway, but the 4x4 would catch hold, and we'd head east again. The conditions did get better as we went east, but few people were on the roads. Most had more sense than I did.

Brack and I talked, sang, reminisced, listened to the radio, and talked some more.

The hours slid by as we slid down the road. By the time we reached Atlanta, the roads were clearing, so we picked up speed. We rolled into Fayetteville late that night very grateful to have made it.

The ice storm didn't abate until a couple days later so had we hunkered down that second night, we would have been there at least another two days.

Brack decided to move to Wilmington and get a job. He worked at a pizza place driving the truck we bought him. He roomed with Mike, an old junior high school buddy.

He had been there a month or two when Hurricane Bertha headed to Wilmington, so we called Brack to come home and his reply was, "It's too late, we're staying here to ride it out." "Just be careful and call when it's past," we begged. Bertha roared ashore, the eye coming over Wilmington where the boys were enjoying a hurricane party, and headed right for Fort Bragg.

The post looked like a war zone. A huge pecan tree in the front yard tumbled over hitting two pines on its way to Brackett's room. The boughs hugged the roof encircling his windows. The pines kept the full force of the pecan from smashing into the house. We lost two more huge trees including a priceless seventy-year-old magnolia, which unceremoniously slammed into a neighbors new Ford Explorer.

The roads were littered with fallen trees, branches, and debris. The Explorer of the next-door neighbor across the street was a special edition NASCAR model originally titled to (on paper) a famous driver. Nature had no respect for it or its dash plaque which named the famous "original" owner.

George commandeered the 82nd troops to help the engineers clear roads and housing areas.

Brackett and Mike were fine with only flooding at their apartment complex. Even their car and truck were unscathed. Had he been home, he would have probably been in more danger.

One weekend when Brackett was coming home, he received a speeding ticket and a DUI. He had to go to court and after two trips to Wilmington he paid it off, but lost his driver's license. We repossessed his truck when he lost his job and couldn't pay for it. We gave it to Cheryl whose used car was on its last leg.

All three of our children were so different, but Brackett seemed to be a magnet for never-do-wells, plus he seemed to have no ambition. We pondered what we could have done differently in his upbringing. I do believe we all do the very best we can for our children, and we love them with all our hearts, no matter how often they screw up. Brackett seemed to be going for the screw-up prize.

George went for a run one afternoon, noticing our collie Windy was following him. He sent her back, awaiting till she turned around to head home then continued his run. She never made it home. When George returned, we realized she was nowhere to be found. We searched all over the neighborhood. We notified the vets in the area and the animal shelters. We posted a reward in the Fayetteville paper. At one point, we received a call about a collie seen roaming with other dogs near a shopping center. We rushed over there, our hopes high, only to discover the collie wasn't Windy. About that time, we began hearing of a group of people who picked up dogs from yards and anywhere they weren't in view of the public to sell to research labs. It broke our hearts that this might be what happened to our Windy. We never found her.

John and Kathy Abizaid lived next door, and we were stunned when some jealous person turned John into the army inspector general for accepting a farewell gift that supposedly cost more than the limit of three hundred dollars. It did not happen, but the allegation put John in an awkward position requiring a formal investigation by the army inspector general. He was, of course, exonerated; but it must have been frustrating knowing he was being considered for promotion to brigadier general. Kathy was a great army wife who persevered through all the angst like a trooper. She never lost faith all would be well.

A similar situation occurred to another great army family, John and Katie Scroggins. John was on the one-star list and a similar allegation kept him from being promoted. The shameful delays caused by a congressional staffer with a personal axe to grind drug on so long it caused John to give up and retire. It was a great loss to the army.

George was so paranoid about farewell gifts he bought his own when he left division command and continued to do so until he retired.

The 18th Abn corps commander was over the 10th Mountain Division, 101st, and the 82nd. He was stationed at Fort Bragg where the headquarters of the corps was housed.

When we arrived, Hugh Shelton was the commander. His wife Carolyn was a beautiful blonde who knew the 82nd inside and out.

I went with Carolyn to a "Mary Kay makeover day" that the president of the OWC had arranged. We were all to be made beautiful with the makeup women and then have our pictures made for the OWC board which would be prominently displayed at the Officers' Club. Neither Carolyn nor I had ever used that makeup, but we wanted to be gracious since the girls had gone to so much trouble.

When we arrived, we were whisked on to the makeup stools. So much makeup was slathered on us, not the tiniest flaw could be found. We had the pictures made joining the lineup of flawless skinned board members. On the way home, all we talked about was how anxious we were to get home and scrub our faces. For the first time in my life, my face broke out in reaction to the heavy handed makeup application. The pictures turned out great, but while we were there, we looked much like what a stripper convention might resemble.

In November of 1995, George had been invited to be the guest speaker at the Old State House Museum Foundation in Little Rock, Arkansas. He had accepted, and we were in Little Rock for the dinner later that night when we received a chilling call from Fort Bragg.

A sniper had lain in wait in a copse of trees as three battalions and the Second Brigade staff formed for a traditional four-miles-in-thirty-six-minutes formation run. As the units peeled off and John Scroggins led his men up the hill out of the lower field, the sniper began shooting. The S-2 was killed, and Guy Lafaro was badly injured.

George kept in touch minute by minute, gave the speech, then we canceled all other plans flying back to Fort Bragg.

Penny Lafaro was by Guy's side as we all prayed for his recovery. As usual, the units stepped in; Katy Scroggins was certainly a veteran army wife knowing what to do. I checked on Penny occasionally myself as she had been with us before and was dear to me but got daily and sometimes hourly updates from George, Katy, or I checked it myself.

As in the bigger society, mentally ill people are around, often undetected for years. Such was the case here.

We joined the Sheltons at the memorial ceremony for the young man killed. The 82nd community was still in shock.

Guy did recover in large part by Penny's devoted care, much to our relief.

We were all sad when the Sheltons left for a new assignment. Their replacement arrived from Fort Campbell, and we really knew nothing about them. They knew little of Fort Bragg.

Deaths occur far more often than any commander would like. No deaths would be a perfect number, but in the army that is not reality.

After years of dealing with grieving families, a tried and true process had been developed in the 82nd. After the initial notification of the family, a survivor assistant officer was assigned and depending on the victim's unit, the company, battalion, or brigade commander and spouse would take over. A personal visit to the home would be made, food taken, special needs seen to, and anything else to ease the trauma of the family. The division commander would visit a spouse, but until the memorial service the unit who knew them best was in control.

Soon after the new corps commander arrived, a death occurred in the division. It was in one of the companies, so the company commander and his wife took over and had everything under control. The new corps commander and his wife showed up at the bereaved home. The bereaved had no idea who these people were and when the corps commander told them the memorial service would have to be delayed so he could attend, the fallen soldier's father himself, a retired army sergeant, told him, "No, it would not be delayed as they had people coming in from all over, plane tickets, burial, etc., could not be changed for the general's convenience." When we found out, we were appalled! George was out of town for that ceremony, so I went with the Jans and their husbands. The family was in a back room of the chapel before the service, so we went back to offer our personal condolences and for me to relay George's sorrow at not being present.

Several people were lined up to do the same, so we got in line with the others. The new corps commander and wife came in and came up to us. We were about four from the front at this point with several behind us. The corps commander placed his hand on my arm and literally pushed me back as he said they should go first. We were all too stunned to do anything but stumble back. They both turned to share that they had been out to the house to visit with the bereaved family but hadn't seen us there. I almost asked if they planned to fly to Fort Campbell and New York for every death. We were all so stunned and angry it was all we could do to keep our faces placid and mumble, "How nice" and get through the line to share our sorrow with the family. We fled to the ladies' room just staring at each other in disbelief. They just had a really hard time adjusting from division command to corps command. When they finally realized how many funerals and bereaved families there were in a corps of fighting units, they rarely came to another service, but for me the damage was done. I could only hope he did not mean his action the way it was taken.

One night, I was called by the corps commander and asked if I would go on a jump with his wife. I told him I didn't think it was legal but would check with JAG. I of course would love to do that as I had been an airborne wife many years. Local business men and women were often taken up to share with the local civilian community what their military neighbors do. Wives of soldiers were not in that category. He told me it would be fine, but I felt if anything was ever said it would be me that would be hung out to dry. Delaying my answer, the next day I checked with JAG and was told not only no but absolutely *no!* My resulting negative response was not taken well by the corps commander, and I think his wife went on the flight anyway.

After these two experiences, I never really trusted him, and as always I have found there are usually very good reasons people react as they do. As I got to know her, I did indeed understand her better. He did a decent job as a corps commander according to the men, so I suppose that is the most important issue.

Jan Smith's husband, Ed, and Jan Miklochek's husband, P. T., were promoted to two stars so departed for new posts. I just didn't know how much we would miss them.

Steve and Cat Gardner had been reassigned with Tom and Susan Turner taking their place as chief of staff. They were yet again a wonderful couple.

As usual we did birthday parties for each other on our birthdays. Ann Dail's was a blue birthday with everything blue including the cake as that was her favorite color. Ann LaRue had two darling boys so hers was harder to work around their activities, but we gave her and Jan Smith a twin birthday as they shared the date. Holly Petreus had played on the TV show *Jeopardy* once and lost, but she swore she knew every answer of the group on next. *We* believed her! Her birthday had a French theme. Katy's was at Fun Land so she could be a kid again. Jan Mikolashek's was a tacky party since she was anything but tacky. Vicki Newman had a jock party and Renae England (CSM Steve's wife) enjoyed a pool party in our back yard. The others were just as creative and all of them fun.

For the OWC, Anne Spohn put together the best cookbook I've ever used. I was so afraid they would have trouble getting recipes, I sent in lots. So many, in fact, some of the girls called it my cookbook. It was rather embarrassing, but the intent was honorable.

The Assistant Division Commander for Operation's (ADC-O's) wife, Pam Vines, was a sweetheart of a lady I had known in past assignments, but the Assistant Commander of Support (ADC-S) was a new couple, Joyce and Kip Ward. When I called Joyce and asked if they both would like me to pick them up for their first function, Joyce said, "No." She had called the ADC-O's wife and they were going together. I didn't care but the cold shoulder became frozen in the months to come. I couldn't decide if the ADC-O's wife was as uncooperative as the ADC-S's wife or if she was being coerced. I found out later it was coercion, but by the time the ADC-O's wife figured out she was being manipulated, it was too late. No one trusted either of them for anything as they seemed to constantly try to undermine everything we did. The birthdays continued without their participation. Susan and I tried everything we could think of to get them to be part of the group, but nothing worked. Where the ADC-O's wife didn't go, the ADC-S's wife didn't either. It was so sad to have this division among the wives. Finally, we went on about our lives, trying not to worry about them but always hoping they would come around. No one was required to do anything, so to do nothing was certainly their prerogative, but we did miss having the entire group together.

We had a big event on post at Christmastime where units had various jobs. The 82nd had always done the Santa's workshop where children could shop with parents' prepurchased tickets. A child would go into the plywood "store," select items with the help of an elf, have the item wrapped and labeled, then leave by another door carrying their wrapped present.

Gathering the items to sell was always a huge job as was pricing. We begged most of the items but bought some if we needed more.

The previous year with the Jans, we had had a great time, and the store was a huge success. They had compiled an amazing amount of items.

The new ADC's wives were in charge of the items. They got so few we had to rush out and buy more at the last minute. Joyce complained nonstop and tried to blame it all on the other wives. As we say in Arkansas, she was a piece of work! The group survived them, but I was happy to leave those two behind when we departed.

Thankfully, Corey and family were still with us. Corey went to jump school at Fort Benning to be able to jump with George.

Jim Mingus was George's senior aide and was one of those young men you know are going to do well. We took him into our hearts as we did Corey as "army sons."

Just before we started the countdown for our departure, we heard from John Pickler, the corps chief of staff. He told us of his new boat from a marvelous boat company, *Bryant* Boats in Sweetwater, Tennessee.

George and I went over to see it. John, his wife, Karen, George, and I climbed in to sit in the boat in John's backyard. It was wonderful. We are big water skiing fans. Daddy's boat had been sold at auction, so we had not had one for several years.

We called Jim Bryant and arranged to have one built and delivered to Arkansas the first chance we had to get back to take possession.

One and two-star promotions are determined by selection boards, but three and four-star ranks are appointments at the recommendation of the army chief of staff with confirmation by the US Senate.

George was selected for a third star and subsequently assigned to command the army's First Corps at Fort Lewis, Washington. We were thrilled, but I was especially delighted to be going somewhere new.

The change of command was on a cold winter day. It was to be a parachute jump at Sicily drop zone. Sadly for George, high winds cancelled the jump. Our household goods had been packed, loaded, and headed, this time, to the west. We were staying in the post guesthouse until after the change of command.

Farewells were always poignant. Mine was wonderful, filled with hugs and tears. John Scroggins had made a beautiful box housing under glass the unit crests of each of the division's regiments. It was on a wrought iron stand. It also featured a hinged lid one could close over the display. It was a lovely farewell gift I treasured. Susan Mountcastle, a fabulous artist and my friend from Germany, Durham, North Carolina, and West Point, had been asked to paint our quarters. It was gorgeous, and both items are wonderful memories of the 82nd Abn Division. The 82nd Airborne Chorus that had entertained us all so wonderfully all those years gave us a final performance.

George, meanwhile, bought his own gift, an enlarged James Dietz painting of the 82nd in action at the Nijmegen Bridge in World War II.

Knowing his determination to buy his own gift, the staff borrowed a Harley Davidson, put a huge bow on it, and presented it as a serious gift. To their shock, George, having recognized it as one he had borrowed once, thanked them and rode off through the Officers' Club. He returned with a big grin and a roar of pipes as they all enjoyed the joke. Although a few admitted heart palpitations that he might think he could keep it.

The change of command, despite the cancelled arrival by parachute, was awesome but cold. The troops formed on a jump zone just over a rise. As the ceremony began, the troops advanced. First we could see the tips of the standard bearer's flag staffs, then the flags, then the tops of the leader's heads. It was like a movie set with wave after wave of troops coming closer and closer. It gave us all chills.

George was promoted to three-star lieutenant general and presented awards.

My brother, Voland, and wife, Penny, came from Virginia Beach;

George's mother, Aunt Francis, and Uncle Jeff from Arkansas, as well as, Mrs. Montgomery, George's third-grade teacher from Dardanelle, Arkansas. Cheryl attended as did Brackett who brought a friend at whom we tried not to stare. Brack's friend had his shirt unbuttoned halfway down his chest, long hair, and was strange. We all deduced he was high on something.

After the change of command, we went back to the guesthouse for a final meal together before everyone left.

The next morning early, we were off to the west coast.

We drove the Ford Explorer and pulled the Nissan Maxima we bought from Fayetteville Nissan dealer and great 82nd supporter, Peter Stewart.

As we went farther west, the weather got worse. We only had a few days to get to Fort Lewis before the change of command. Corey, Gwen, and family had left earlier with George's uniforms. We suggested they not take the Northern route (I-90) in winter but understood they had family in Chicago.

At one point in the midst of a Utah blizzard complete with driving snow plus half a foot of accumulation, we looked to our left to see the Nissan spinning out beside us. George was not saying nice words as he tried to get in front of it and ease us off the road. The U-Haul hitch was no match for ice. We got everything working again and took off.

As we got into the last mountain range in Oregon, we were stopped on top of the last mountain. A semi had jackknifed, blocking both lanes of the interstate. We were parked behind and beside semis. One trucker got out to investigate. He stepped on the ice-covered highway and was literally blown across the lane by the wind gusts. We were stranded there for several hours until the state police cleared and sanded the road.

We continued with little trouble but at a slower pace as the snow was so thick it was hard to see.

Vonda and Corey Smallwood in Hawaii

Tara and Tia's Wedding in Samoa

Brackett Soccer Player

Vonda with US Army South wives

Vonda and Wanda Holt in Panama

Jill McCaffrey and Vonda at Panama International Bazaar

Vonda and OWC President Deana Sawdey in Panama

82nd Commad Wives: Vicki Newman, Holy Petreus, Susan Turner, Renae England, Jan Smith, Jan Miklochek, Ann Dail, Ann Spohn, Ann Larew, Katie Scroggins, and Vonda

82nd Abn Chorus bidding Vonda farewell.

LTG Keane promoting George to three star.
Vonda pinning on the stars.

21 | Fort Lewis, Washington
"Final Army Adventure"

WE PULLED INTO Fort Lewis the day before the change of command.

We were housed in a small guesthouse near quarters one while our future home was readied for occupancy. The quaint white cottage had a covered front porch that in nicer weather would have begged for a rocker and hanging plants. The snow and ice we had driven through to get to Washington State was now a cold rain. The lush greenness of the area made the weather bearable.

We had a bedroom, bath, tiny kitchen, and living area. It was perfect for a transition.

The next day was the change of command. It was cold and raining but most concerning; Corey and his family had taken the northern route getting stranded in Montana. They were safely harbored in a church which was a relief, but he had taken most of George's uniforms planning to arrive before us. George and his senior aide, Ralph (Rob) Baker, another army "son" scrounged a complete throw-together uniform, taping on some of the insignia just praying the rain didn't cause a major melt off.

The change of command was the coldest I've ever experienced. Tents had been erected on the edge of the parade field in front of quarters one. I had worn the green wool German hunting cape George had given me in 1975 and still shook all through the ceremony. When the rain-filled canopy reached overfull, it dumped a deluge of freezing water down my right side. This should have been an omen of things to come.

As a good army wife, I smilingly shook off the water and trooped off to the reception where it was much warmer. Everyone was so helpful and kind we felt welcomed immediately.

The day after the change of command dawned chilly and cloudy but not raining. George and I suited up for an early run.

We both rechecked the map of post, and I even wrote my route on a slip of paper. We took off, enjoying the much modulated weather.

Somewhere en route after running about forty minutes, the rain began, and I realized I was lost. Continuing to run, searching for street signs on my map or anything familiar, I finally saw the Army Community Service (ACS) sign on a building ahead. Ah, the answer place! I dripped in, no doubt looking like a cold drowned rat!

At the desk, two young women were discussing a third absent person. The topic moved on to men, totally ignoring me. I said, "Excuse me." But they continued to ignore. So I looked around, and everyone was busy visiting with each other. Finally, to the two gossips I said, "Excuse me. I just need directions. I seem to be lost." With great exasperation, one turned and said, "Oh, all right. Where are you going?" I didn't know the name of the cottage but described it. They hadn't a clue. So I asked for the parade field, and they knew where that was. They told me to turn right, and I'd run into it then quickly returned to their conversation. I exited the building, turned right as instructed, and realized after another ten minutes she obviously thought the parade field was the air field. Totally soaked and freezing, I stopped the next soldier who gave me the general direction I should run. I took off and finally saw something familiar. When I reached the cottage, George had begun to worry. My run had lasted over an hour, and all of me was freezing.

He ran me a hot bath which I sat in for twenty minutes waiting for the ice crystals to thaw. After that, I took a post map with me, not daring to ask ACS again.

We moved into the lovely huge quarters with its three fireplaces, ten bedrooms and six baths. Again a large formal Duncan Fife dining room suite took up the formal dining room, so we put ours on the large front porch.

A furniture outlet was discovered where we bought several single beds that we hauled up to the third floor for the bedrooms there. It had obviously been designed for servant quarters as it had one bath, two small bedrooms, and one large dorm-type room. A fire escape went from a larger end bedroom to the ground. Fortunately it was semihidden in a wonderful large circle of fir trees, forming a protective inner glade for all kinds of possible uses.

A huge attic hid behind a door from the back stairway. We filled it with Christmas decorations, all those drapes that never fit another set of windows, out of season clothes, and the usual boxes of mementos, military papers, and manuals.

We had furniture for most parts of the house which was most helpful! There were several quartermaster pieces we used to fill in.

The front porch that spanned the first floor was mirrored on the second. Two-thirds of it was outside our bedroom and the bedroom we used as an office. The other one-third was outside another bedroom.

A few days after we got settled, I was given a courtesy visit with all the family support areas on post. One of those was a visit to ACS. What fun! After hearing their spiel, I mentioned my visit on our third day at Fort Lewis which I had not only been ignored but given incorrect information. As a farewell gift three years later, ACS gave me a map with a star over the guesthouse and you are here at ACS. It was laminated to keep it dry in the rain. I loved it! Without a sense of humor, some days are really hard to get through.

The family support building was a gem in the army family support's crown. It is an incredible building used for family events. It resembled a huge family-style home with kitchen, dining area, large central room with cozy fireplace, meeting rooms, computer room, and even a child-friendly room. I spent many hours there for various activities.

Part of being the wife of the commanding general (CG) included a long list of boards one sat on usually in an advisory position. When presented with the list, I decided to share the wealth and as I had always done. I asked the other command team wives what they wanted to do, for example, the board or boards on which they would like to sit. It was a perfect opportunity for everyone to share the "board" experience. Otherwise, that's all I would ever do is go from meeting to meeting. It seemed that way anyway!

The thrift shop was an interesting experience. As I said before, it was fun to work there, but the thought of going wasn't my favorite thing. At one of the first meetings, the thrift shop board declared they had lost money. We delved into the finances, discovering the overhead was way too high. Some paid workers got an automatic raise every year no matter what. The cleaning lady who had been there for years was getting more money than the manager! The merchandise was so packed it was hard to find anything and the place was looking very rundown.

We decided to close it for a month to restructure, move to a larger place, paint, and generally clean it up. We wrote job descriptions, hired a new manager, scaled down the staff, and got to work.

Murals were painted at the entrance; clothes long unsold no longer consigned were donated to a rag company; the finances were straightened out; dressing rooms were built; and it was all done with volunteer labor.

George and I had everyone who helped over for a BBQ as a thank you.

With all the events we had hosted over the years, that was the only time we found an item missing. Of all things a chess piece disappeared as well as one of George's knives from an eclectic collection. Each knife had great meaning so that one was missing was noticed immediately. If the thief had asked, I would have given them the entire chess set but not the knife.

On every post, there is drama, and Fort Lewis was no exception. Personality clashes abounded as well as some turf wars. It was much like a small town where those who have been there longest have much invested. Permanent staff was the worst. Often, it would have been so helpful to just fire those who sat at their desks doing as little as possible, but yell the loudest if anyone wants to improve or change. I learned several basic truths: one is to learn the lay of the land before even suggesting changes, two is to ask opinions from all involved, then compromise with their suggestions, and three, don't fix it if it ain't broken. There were many things not broken and many very capable people making military life the very best they could. The difficulties were handled one by one.

The commander's wife before me had vetoed the Women's Conference so a Women's Conference committee asked for a meeting with me our first week. Since we had enjoyed so many fabulous Women's Conferences in years past at other post, I was all for it! They were thrilled and got going for the following spring. Judi Bramlett had started the first one in Hawaii with Cat Gardner as one of her helpers. The Women's Conferences offered the classes taught by volunteers on every subject that might interest army wives. A nominal fee was charged to cover lunch and goodie bags with scholarships and child care offered at most posts. It was a huge positive event! The hospital commander's wife, Lynne Brown, and I teamed up to offer a class on "Party, Party, Party" with party ideas on the cheap. Lynne also taught a class on home decorating.

By the second month at Lewis, I had yet to see the sun. I grabbed George by his shirt collar when he said he "had" to go to Hawaii on business and begged him to take me too. I could stay with Tara and lie in the sun like a pale turtle. He gently, but firmly unhanded himself and said, "Sorry." I understood perfectly why people spent so much money on those lightbulbs that duplicate the entire light spectrum of the sun.

Tara called me several days later to share that when George's plane landed, it began raining and hadn't stopped during his visit. I felt so much better. It would have been more than my southern blood could have handled to get to Hawaii and rain.

While he was gone, the sun actually came out one day, and I almost wrecked the car when Mount Rainier suddenly appeared in all its majesty just like the postcards. I had begun to think someone painted those cards, and the mountain really wasn't there.

Quarters one sat in the middle of a semicircle of large stately quarters built in the early 1900s.

Supposedly a fabulous view of Mount Rainier was at the end of the parade field in front of the house, but like I said it was two months before I saw it. Even then, some unthinking group had erected an enormous statue, dedicated to a World War I unit, directly in front of the house at the end of the parade field. If it had been put at the other end, it would have been perfect. After every storm, earthquake, and lighting, I would check to see if nature hadn't given us a gift and moved it. There was always hope. As far as I know, every occupant of those quarters felt the same way.

The backyard was large with a private green area of vines, trees, and wild plants. Years before someone had planted roses, but they had been seriously ignored. I fertilized, mulched, and pruned; so the first summer they were lovely.

Every summer we hosted a huge reception and BBQ on the back lawn for a VIP list of guests from governor (who never came), diplomats (who did), to all those who were friends of the army. Three hundred plus guest were invited. Protocol erected tents with tables and chairs. The O' Club cooked on grills in the circle of firs by the house. We had entertainment and homemade ice cream for dessert.

A real southern BBQ.

The first year, Mother was visiting, so she and I held a painting marathon in the garage painting plain flower pots and saucers red, white, and blue.

We cut a star shape on potatoes and used them as stamps around the pot rims.

We had red, white, and blue flowers in jelly glass inserts.

The second year, we inverted the pots, topping them with the saucer holding candles.

That was the summer it rained but even though umbrellas were offered, locals were so used to the rain it bothered them not a whit. Only tourists used umbrellas!

One thing the weather does in the Pacific northwest is allow flowers of one sort or another to bloom year round. The weather is very damp to wet, but the temperature is moderate. The forest on and around post would have been the perfect setting for *Hansel and Gretel*. The depths were dark and gloomy with the occasional fir tree branches sweeping the ground.

Every post and surrounding area have a certain feeling. I could understand most, but I never could understand the Olympia to Seattle Area.

There wasn't a single thing but a general feeling while there. The locals were not rude but either were they open and friendly. The only way to describe it was a bit of reticent pioneer spirit. Most seemed to keep to themselves, sharing little. Having spent my youth and most of our military life in the south where open warmth to all strangers and common graciousness were drilled into us from birth, this was a new experience.

We had a delightful dinner one evening with the secretary of state. I felt his wife, who was raised in Washington, was bored spitless, and frustrated at having spent her evening entertaining these military people. He took us on a tour of their lovely grounds, but she demurred. It was indicative of other events we attended in Washington.

The military presence was the third largest employer for Washington State. We invited the governor several times to our home, but he never came. On one, momentous day, we, with the top navy and air force husband and wife command teams, were invited to the Capitol rotunda to honor Metal of Honor recipients. We were arranged in a semicircle on a raised area with the governor and honorees. None of the military commanders were recognized during the ceremony, although everyone else on the platform was welcomed by name. It was as if we were invisible.

One female legislator came up to us as we were leaving and asked, "Who are you, people? You were never introduced." Guess what? We noticed that! We, of course, would never have said that, but we did think it.

In a new place, it is always interesting to get to know your neighbors. Often, the longer you are a military wife, the more often you find yourself with old friends. After thirty-one years, this was especially true at Fort Lewis.

Several of our neighbors we had not met, so it was always fun to add to the list of new friends or acquaintances.

It has always been the army way to take food to a new family moving in, and this time was no exception! We had many delicious dishes appear at our door and shared our contributions with new neighbors when they moved into the neighborhood.

Standing in our front door to our far left lived General George Brown and his wife, Lynne. George was commander of Madigan Army Medical Center, and it was flourishing under his command.

On the other side of us was an army aviator who was the deputy corps commander. Shortly after we arrived, Dan and Maureen McNeill took that house and Dan the deputy's job. We had been with the McNeills several times before at Bragg, so it was old-home week when they arrived.

When we knew they were coming, I shared with the Officers' Wives' Club board, for whom Maureen would be senior advisor, not to underestimate her or make the mistake that her high energy meant she was ditzy. She was very astute, clever, and full of common sense. She did everything quickly, including conversation, which made her often appear a space cadet. She was anything but! We were thrilled they were at Fort Lewis.

In the next house lived other old friends, the Smiths. Zany, who was the corps chief of staff, and his wife, Brenda, had also been with us before.

Brenda was called the epitome of army mama by countless young wives. She was all heart, willing to do anything for anyone.

Hondo Campbell, George's chief of staff, and his new bride, Diane, were next. Diane was from Texas, could execute a mean two step, and had the requisite big hair.

Diane worked full time in a key position for Sprint Telecommunications in Seattle so drove out the back gate very early every morning for the very long drive to work. Daily en route she pulled rollers out of her hair, tossing them into the backseat. Her makeup also went on in the car.

One of her first days at Lewis, the gate guard saw the two-star sticker on her windshield and called her Mrs. McNeill. Since she didn't have on her makeup and her hair in rollers, she smiled sweetly saying, "Y'all have a good day." She was an absolute delight. Most women who marry generals don't get all the lessons most wives learn along the way to their husband's higher rank, but Diane learned fast. If she didn't know, she never pretended she did, but asked. We all adored her.

There were several people who were there such a short time; we didn't get a chance to really get to know them.

Diane Edwards's husband was the deputy Fifth Army commander but unfortunately, they weren't there very long. I liked her very much and would have liked to get to know her better. She and Maureen had been friends since they both lived in Korea. They really enjoyed being together again.

The command team consisted of the following:

First Infantry Brigade was led by Jay Dodd. His wife, Tolley, was very active. Shortly after we arrived, they were replaced with Steve and Cathy Gardner, our dear friends from assignments past.

Second Infantry Division's Armor Brigade was led by native Washingtonian Pete Chiarelli. His wife, Beth, also from Washington, was a terrific army wife. She was very personable, cute as could be, and had a soothing quality about her that was most helpful when things became tense, which they often did.

Before we left, they were followed by Mark and Sue Hertling. She was tiny and a ball of energy.

The Fastabends were head of the Engineer Brigade. Mary was a hard worker who also taught school.

The G-1 was Colonel Glenn Beard whose wife, Lois, commanded the Military Police Brigade. They were both outstanding.

The G-2 was John Custer whose wife, Audry, was a really neat gal.

The G-3 was our old friend from Fort Bragg, Tim Scully. His wife, Joann, was never still. She was very involved in all aspects of army life.

The G-4 was Michor Genteman. Lee, his wife, was an awesome lady. She seemed to have boundless energy and full of clever ideas. She was an expert in child development and family dynamics. When she offered her classes at the Women's Conference; they were always filled first. They were both in home territory so were a wealth of knowledge about the area.

Special Operations was led by Col. Dave McMillian. His wife, Bridgett, was another fabulous army wife. No matter what needed to be done, Bridgett could do it and still smile.

There were a few other units attached to us, but we didn't see them very often.

The command team, in Yakima, Washington, over the mountains at the training area did come over on occasion, and we went over there as often as we could. They felt very isolated sometimes, so we tried to include them in most activities. The clouds seemed to stop over the mountains meaning Yakima was in a dry, high desert. The sun was a big draw for me!

Just like civilian life, there are all kinds of people in the military, but we seemed to have fewer of the mentally ill or truly evil types. I always went into a post planning to like everyone, no matter what their foibles and rarely met someone I just didn't like. There were those few exceptions, but usually a "bless their heart" would suffice.

Once a month the newcomers to Fort Lewis were gathered in an auditorium. The troops were encouraged to bring their spouses.

George and the CSM welcomed them first then I did, followed by all the agencies on post. During my spiel, I always mentioned the family support groups the spouses could and should join, the beauty of the area, and always welcomed them to our home which really belonged to the army. I told them, if the door is open, we're home so come on by. I had always wondered what the big houses looked like inside, and this was their opportunity to find out about one. We would give them a ground floor tour and always had sweet tea. During our three years there, two single young troops came by, had sweet tea, and got the tour. We heard from them occasionally after that, and they both did well.

In the summer, if we were lucky, we had a few weeks to a couple of months of sunshine. The dreary weather molded my soul, so those days of sunshine were glorious! If I could squeeze a few hours out of a day, I'd low crawl out the third floor window, lay a towel on the porch roof, and lie in my bathing suit to soak up some rays. I never got tan, but it did kill some of the soul mold.

On our second Fourth of July, however, I wore a ski jacket and carried an umbrella to the fireworks at the post stadium.

George and I loved to ski and discovered Crystal Mountain a couple of hours away.

We had a trip planned for Thanksgiving weekend.

Lynne Brown and I went to shop for Christmas trees. We tied them both to the top of the Explorer. We dropped hers off, and as I drove into our circa 1920 tiny garage, I forgot to put the hatch down and broke the rear window.

I called a glass replacement place the insurance company recommended, and they took it and replaced it that evening.

I was so proud to have handled it so quickly by myself so we could ski with the window fixed.

George was furious! Eight hundred bucks after the deductible.

He swore we could have replaced it at a junkyard simply taping it until then, or many glass shops came to our house for free and charged nothing other than the amount above the deductible.

Oh, well! Learn something every day. It took him a long time to forget it.

On one trip to Arkansas for leave, we had the Bryant boat delivered to my parents' Arkansas lake house on Greer's Ferry Lake. Jim Bryant was coming nearby, so he brought it from Sweetwater, Tennessee, himself. It was gorgeous! Arkansas Razorback red and white, twenty-three feet, with enough power in the 4x4 CID V-8 to pop George out of the water on a slalom.

We almost couldn't make the hill to the lake house with the Ford Explorer, so we drove to Little Rock and traded for a red Ford F-150, had a bed cover made for it to protect luggage and anything else we might carry from the Washington rain. It had enough power to pull the boat and anything else we might need uphill.

We arrived back in Washington with a new red truck and boat. We stored the boat in a MWR-heated storage bay on post.

There was a small lake near post where we put in on the rare beautiful weekends.

On one especially lovely weekend, we decided to take it farther. We found a beautiful little lake in the Olympic Range on the Washington map so stocked up with lunch, Sunday's paper, and stuck out for an all-day getaway.

We launched the boat with no trouble and were amazed no other boats were there. We hadn't run it all out so raced it from one end of the lake to the other twice. It got up to sixty-five miles per hour, so we felt it had gotten a good warm-up. We cruised around the far edge of the lake, noting all the kayaks and canoes, finally spending a few hours anchored at one end, having lunch and reading the paper in a lazy stupor we so badly needed. As the day drifted away, we reluctantly prepared to pull the boat out. The truck had trouble getting enough traction to pull the boat over the irregular launch area. Several people had been standing around watching us and finally came over to help. Four of us stood on the back bumper to get enough traction to get the boat out. We thanked them all profusely.

One of the men said, "You know, motor boats aren't allowed on this lake. It's owned by an Indian tribe." All we had noticed that day slid into focus! We were so embarrassed we immediately asked for forgiveness. Nowhere were there signs, but I guess everyone around there just knew.

The water in Washington State is so cold the usual potty relief of slipping quietly into the water, swimming around a bit, then when relieved casually climbing out was a no go. The first time I tried to quietly slide into the water, my gasp was heard across the lake, and my legs immediately turned blue. Jim Bryant had so graciously given us a small chemical porta potty to slip into the under console storage compartment. It is amazing how one can become a contortionist when the need arises. I spent many blessed moments with my flashlight under the console. Getting your bathing suit down was easy, but repositioning it in a three-by-four-foot space was far more difficult.

The weekly schedule was packed with meetings of family support groups, HQ coffees, thrift shop, Bible study, Protestant women, teaching Army Family Team Building, and going to meetings with George when invited and on and on.

On one occasion George, as first corp commander, was invited to California for Bob Hope's birthday celebration. The air force and navy commanders were also invited.

The other wives were there, but the army would not okay my travel although my name was also on the invitation.

It reminded me of the bachelor commander who had an army paid hostess for his required parties. When the new guy came in with a wife, the paid position was eliminated.

She demanded the same pay as she was expected to do the same work.

The army truly does get two for the price of one. I loved helping in many ways on post, especially for the young families, but it meant not working outside for a salary.

There also is no such thing as overtime. For all the years George was in the army, it was a twenty-four-seven job, even on vacation.

Corey was a huge blessing as was his wife, Gwen. She was a great asset in Army Family Team Building, teaching and often running the office.

Corey kept George's uniforms ready to go, accompanied him when needed, and kept the public areas of the house spotless. We joked that he was death on vacuums because we had gone through so many. The Kirby I bought used in Hawaii was repaired repeatedly but continued to work like a charm.

Corey still made great pies, and I still loved to bake bread, so for formal dinners we continued to plan the meal together. He would make the dessert, and I would take care of the bread.

He had a pseudo office downstairs in the basement where he kept the house records and planned events. He even had his own bathroom down there. There had been two bedrooms for staff, but we used them for storage.

It was a tremendous help to know the public area was always clean for the frequent visitors. We treasured him and felt like he, Gwen, and the children were part of the family.

We were most anxious for him to get the formal training he needed to advance in the army, so he did manage to get in a couple of courses in DC.

The men were often gone for training or other events, so on one occasion I invited the command spouses to the house for a sleepover.

We had a blast. Every one of the bedrooms was taken with several staking-out spaces on couches in front of fireplaces. Colonel Pat Egan, the post commander, came by early for wine and snacks but hurriedly left before bedtime. I think some stayed up talking most of the night, but I remember turning into a pumpkin about 1:00 a.m. Many personal stories were shared, so everyone left the next morning feeling closer to each other.

Cheryl came for our first Christmas with ten-month-old Laurel Glenn, our first grandchild. I had been in North Carolina for her birth but missed them being so far away. Cheryl, Laurel, and husband, Tim, flew into Seattle.

We put them on the third floor for privacy and during the day turned a couch to the wall in the entrance for a quick fix crib. We borrowed one for her nighttime upstairs with her parents. She was so adorable. Cheryl loved visiting the various art galleries in Seattle. Tim didn't seem to like anything, so we left him to his own devices when he refused to go with us on ventures.

We took them skiing one day on Crystal Mountain, but Tim complained the entire time.

They had just been to Europe to take the European framer qualifying course. Cheryl passed easily but just as with the US test, Tim struggled.

The math seemed to be a real problem for him. He finally went to the national headquarters in Maryland to take the US test the fourth time and passed.

He did pass the European course. He had wanted Cheryl to do his French mat which she refused to do. They were both glad he passed the first time. Had he not passed, her life would have been even more miserable.

General George Brown, an internist, retired from the army and as commander of Madigan Army Medical Center. A BG Hill came in to replace him. Hill was an administrator, not a doctor, so he had really odd ideas about running a hospital.

Part of his job was to oversee Tricare in the area. He seemed to be more comfortable traveling and doing that than running the hospital.
His wife was also in the military. They told us he was about to retire when his name came up on the BG list, so she retired instead.

Casey Jones was the deputy hospital commander. Casey, one of the country's finest hand surgeons, is married to an incredible woman, Elizabeth. They have eight children, all who have excelled. Casey made beautiful furniture in his spare time and held things together at the hospital.

The hospital chief of staff was Colonel Cahill who was married to a real go-getter, Mary Jo. They were an awesome team. Mary Jo and Elizabeth Jones and Lynn Brown could always be counted on to help with any post-wide event. That was not always the case with a hospital staff.

We were blessed with several army friends who retired in the area and still attended some events such as Fourth of July and change of commands.

Ed and Pam Trobaugh, the past 82nd command team, retired in Steilacoom near John and Joan Shalikashvili, the past chairman of the

Joint Chief of Staff. Harley and Pat Davis, lived on Whidbey Island; Tom and Dottie Cole from West Point days retired in Olympia, plus Greg and Carol Ann Tillit from Germany lived in Puyallup. It is indeed a small world.

General Dennis Reimer was army chief of staff and would visit on occasion to check on things. Mary Jo Reimer was most interested in family support activities, for which Fort Lewis was justifiably proud. She also was instrumental in getting states to at least think about standardizing requirements for army kids. As I previously mentioned, our children went to multiple high schools and most required state history to graduate. Mary Jo suggested US history might be a credit in lieu of state history and subject requirements standardized. She worked tirelessly, but some political rocks are hard to move.

Some of the outstanding army wives I remember from Lewis were Linda Goller, Cass Harrington, Lee Miller, Jean Miller, Nancy Ham, Lyn Holloway, Margie Hansen, Jo Ann Scully, and the list goes on, too many to name.

Tara was deep into police work in Hawaii and loving every second of it. She had been on the *Bike Detail*, had a bit part in *Blue Hawaii*, been in *Vice* posing as a prostitute, and was into drug enforcement. Tia was a sergeant in the Federal Prison System managing the warehouse laundry and commissary on Oahu.

Cheryl was pregnant with Olyn but working hard at the gallery. She and Tim had quietly married, but Tim was becoming increasingly frightening as his bizarre behavior seemed to be escalating. Our vivacious daughter was becoming withdrawn, quiet, and unsure what was wrong with him.

Brackett, always a concern in our hearts, was barely making it in Austin, Texas. He was working part time, and it sounded like he had again connected with some less-than-stellar friends. He asked if he could come to Washington State and go back to college. We said, "Yes, absolutely!" He packed his few belongings in his old car and headed across Texas on I-10. He made it halfway before running out of money. We gave the motel operator our credit card number for him to be able to spend the night, have the free breakfast, and fill his car up for the last leg.

When he arrived, we gave him the second-floor bedroom with the sun porch attached. He settled in and began college classes on post. He was doing very well, and we had a sense of a positive turning point for him.

Corey was off to DC to take another course. To fill in we had a charming capable young man, Andy McCaughey, to be his temporary replacement. Andy and Chie were a delightful couple, and we felt so fortunate to have him.

George and I were asked to serve on the panel for the new BG's Charm course. We flew to Fort Leavenworth, Kansas, in a small army plane for the overnight. We did our duty on the panels, George was finishing up his part, and I was packing up ready to check out of post guest quarters. I had just had a catch-up conversation with an old army friend, Coleen Mundstock, who lived in Leavenworth.

George and Rob Baker walked in with ashen faces. I asked what was wrong, and George told me our worst nightmare was happening. Our son, Brack, had been rushed to Madigan in a coma, and it was not looking good. We raced for the plane as George filled me in on what he knew.

Evidently, Andy had arrived at the house that morning to find the back door open, pizza boxes, and coke cans opened in the kitchen. He cleaned up, putting dishes in the dishwasher, and expecting Brack to come downstairs to leave for class. When time for class came and went, Andy later said, he felt like God was pushing him up the stairs. He knocked on Brack's door and heard what sounded to him like a moan. He opened the door and found Brack in bed on his right side unresponsive.

Andy called 911, and the EMTs arrived moments later, rushing our son to the ER.

He had overdosed on what appeared to be almost pure black tar heroin. He was on total life support and slipping away by the hour.

As we flew over first one state then another, George and I prayed our only son would live until we arrived. We called Madigan Hospital over every town we could see lit from our aerial view. It was the only time we could get a signal to call. The news became more and more dire as we raced through the night to his bedside.

When the plane landed, a car was waiting to rush us to the hospital. We literally ran to the ICU where our son was strapped to multiple life-support systems. He was indeed comatose, but we stroked his face, telling him we were there and how much we loved him.

The only solace I felt during those awful hours was in George's arms. He had always been my strength in times of crisis. We called the girls but shunned their plans to come immediately. In all honesty, I did not know if I could handle being Mom and certainly not gracious to another soul. We told the girls we would let them know when they could come and promised to call daily. I moved into the ER in an empty room with a bed. George planned to move his communications into the hospital across the hall from the ER in an empty room.

George Brown heard about the crisis and was at Brack's bedside when we arrived. The hugs from George Brown and Casey Jones were most welcome. We didn't' see nor hear from BG Hill, but one brief moment several days later.

Back at the house, Rob Baker manned the phone as the CID combed the house for clues.

A plastic bag with syringes was found near the bed so was taken for fingerprints.

Andy had washed the glasses so had eliminated fingerprints on those.

The phone rang, and Rob answered. A man asked to speak to Brackett.

Rob told him Brack couldn't come to the phone right then but could he take a message.

The caller said he was just checking to see if Brackett was okay and gave a number.

The CID traced the call and posing as Brack's cousins went to the house of a young man on parole from Texas who knew Brack. They thought he may have seen the big house and thought to get Brack hooked.

The man and his girlfriend were taken into custody given a lie detector test which they failed.

We were totally immersed in Brackett's survival so didn't give the guy nor his girlfriend a second thought.

When I called my best friend and prayer partner from Panama, Wanda Holt, to ask for prayers she told me as an emergency room nurse anesthetist she had never seen anyone be able to take the syringe out of the arm with an overdose. The one found in Brack's room was in a baggie.

Madigan is a teaching hospital so full of interns and residents. The resident with Brack in the ICU was, from of all places, George's hometown of Russellville, Arkansas. God does care for us in amazing ways. Eric Shry was with Brack the entire time he was in the ICU rotation.

It seemed that according to the doctor's research, no one had survived such an overdose as Brack so there was no protocol.

We had mini meetings with physicians of all specialties, brain, muscle, eyes, etc. They, at one point, took Brack to University of Washington where the MRI was new and more defined in its scope. Brack came back looking terrified. I wished I had been allowed to go with them. The MRI showed the brain demyelinating with the white areas growing.

At these meetings, we asked that they pull out all the stops, keep good notes, and try *anything* they thought might help.

Brackett had lain on his right side for so long the muscles tissue was dying. He was taken to surgery to remove the debris of dead muscle tissue. His arm was cut to relieve pressure of swelling and debris. His hip and right leg was also debried. His arm incisions were left open for over two weeks to ensure more debris removal was not needed. The sciatic nerve from his thigh down was affected.

After a few days, he was slowly taken off life support, and each was a victory as he breathed on his own. He was still in a coma or permanent vegetative state (PVS).

We called the girls to come. We sent airline tickets, so Cheryl and baby Olyn could come from North Carolina and Tara from Honolulu. The incredible staff at Madigan set up a hospital baby crib in the room where George's office had been. He moved back to his office but was in ICU at lunch and after work.

The girls went to the house, got on the Internet, and pulled everything they could find for comas and PVS. They made Brack a huge mobile with bright colors, pictures of his favorite sports, family, and events, and hung it over his bed.

We took the research and pulled everything we thought would help.

All the doctors felt there was no hope of recovery. His prognosis was a permanent vegetative state. I told them we believed in miracles, but if we only got a vegetative state, we would make the best of it. They all looked at me with pity.

Brack would break into huge sweats where even his belly button would fill with sweat. His sheets would be soaked.

His mouth would get very dry, so we used pink foam brushes to wet his mouth. He was put on an automatic mattress that inflated at different fullness and rolled every few minutes to prevent bed sores.

George spent football night giving him blow-by-blow football action from the tiny TV hanging over his bed. Brack couldn't see, but we hoped he heard.

I read books to him and talked about anything that came to mind, hopefully reminding him of long lost memories.

We decided to put the girls' research to use because what could we lose?

One afternoon I found myself totally alone with Brack. I put my hand on his head and prayed with all my heart. "Lord, I know you have a plan for each of us, but we have free will so often mess it up. If it would work out for your overall plan, we would love to have our son back. If it doesn't fit your plan, we will accept that and do the best we can with your help. In Jesus's name, amen."

Since the girls had found success had occurred for coma victims when the senses were challenged, we launched our challenge strategy.

I shared our idea with Beth Miklos–Essinberg, the hand rehabilitation specialist who had been working with Brack's hands after surgery. She jumped on the idea returning the next day with a stash of spices she and her small children had selected to put on his tongue.

We used sandpaper, feathers, satin, cotton, etc., on his skin to stimulate tactile memories.

Beth's spices on his tongue hopefully triggered taste bud memories.

He hated opera and country western but loved jazz and oldies but goodies. We played all four on a cassette with earphones for fifteen-minute intervals.

Charles and Jaynie Jones owned a flower shop in Steilacoom, outside the Fort Lewis gate. They offered me their demo pack of Nikken Magnetic products. I had never heard of Nikken nor Magnetics for health. By this time, if a robin had offered me a magic worm, I would have taken it and thanked him. I firmly believe God sends us tools, and if we are too stupid to use them, then we deserve to fail. The magnetic roller was used near his head and on his surgery areas. The pillow was under his head, the magnetic mattress later sneaked under him. The far infrared blanket was often over him.

We put different smells under his nose and talked about them. I had used Estee Lauder Private Collection for years so that went on a cotton ball as did George's Laugerfield, popcorn, deodorant, flowers, and many other smells, including ammonia capsules.

We constantly bombarded him with stimuli.

Just before the girls left, an army reservist was doing his weekend duty as an ICU nurse. He was so awful; we never left Brack alone with him. He kept suggesting he take one thing or another off Brack, and we literally had to demand he back off. It was scary.

When the girls were with Brack, George and I dropped in on a prescheduled Top Ten gathering. George very clearly stated what had happened, and I thanked each for their prayers and for taking over in all areas where I could no longer. The outpouring of love and concern warmed us both.

We got daily cards from several of the wives. One especially touched my heart as she had lost a brother to a drug overdose. All of them thanked us for being so open about Brack. Almost everyone had been touched by drugs in some way.

The girls both returned to their families with our heartfelt thanks and deep love for each of them. Little Olyn had gotten spoiled by Grandma and Auntie Tara between times with Brackett. Someone was with Brack always.

George had called General Reimer, army chief of staff, to offer his resignation since Brack had OD'd in Quarters. General Reimer told him to worry about Brack first, but we all knew the Fourth Star and commanding the US SOUTHCOM was not now going to be. Mary Jo Reimer sent me a pair of pillowcases to embroider as I sat in vigil. It was a touching gift that I greatly appreciated.

My old buddy, Cat Gardner, who had been through multiple surgeries with Kristy, their beautiful daughter, understood exactly how I felt. She'd sneak into the hospital daily with chai tea or a thermos of hot tea. She was a lifeline. We had asked that everyone leave us alone unless we asked for help. Sometimes, people come because it's "the general's" son, wife, etc., not because of a true sense of caring. Others come out of caring but take precious moments from the vigil. So Cat would sneak in for a quick hug, cup of tea, then off again. I doubt anyone outside the ICU knew she was there for us. She is one of those special friends that are more treasured than gold.

After two weeks, one evening Casey and Elizabeth Jones asked us to come to the hospital conference room. We walked in the door to find the conference table set with four place mats, china, wine, and the delectable smell of one of Elizabeth's famous soups bubbling in a Crock-Pot, complete with homemade bread. The effort and kindness of that evening is a wonderful memory. It was the sort of kindness that cemented our friendship with the Jones and Brown families. We still had only that one brief glimpse of the Hills.

Brackett meanwhile was being bombarded with tests of all sorts, meetings with all specialist were occurring, and I would run home every few days to shower, change clothes, and check on things.

On Halloween night, we asked Andy to play host at quarters one since we had lots of candy and the cast of thousands usually came by. He went all out! He used my carved pumpkin, cutting out the bottom, put it on his head, and sat slumped on the front porch bench. As kids came up, the pumpkin man came alive to dole out candy. We think he terrified more than he amused, but he had a blast and even without us, quarters one did its share.

Housing was building a ramp up the back steps to handle the wheelchair when we brought Brack home, but it was slow going.

After weeks in ICU, Brack was sent to a step-down unit.

The doctors had determined a main line near his clavicle that would cut down on the hundreds of pricks he was enduring. A nurse skilled in that was asked to insert it. She did a great job, so all seemed well.

The next day, George and I were in Brack's room when a resident came in, looked at his chart, and took out the main line. All of us in the room were staring at him in shock!

George was in his face in a count of one yelling at him. What did he think he was doing? Could he not read that it was put in the day before? Who was his superior? Never came near our son again, etc. The head of the team came in quickly, was told what had happened, and we requested the young doctor be taken off the team and not allowed near Brack. It was done. We saw him once later, and he turned and fled. The line was put in again. It just reinforced what we had learned. We could not leave him alone even in as great a hospital as Madigan. We met with the social worker to discuss options for Brack.

We asked the Good Samaritan Hospital in Puyallup, Washington, to come see Brack to determine if they would take him for some rehabilitation. The lady who conducted the visit saw something in Brack's face when George talked to him that made her accept him.

We thought they were going to help Brack, but they thought they were going to teach us to care for him at home. Little did we know the rehabilitation was more to prepare us to handle a PVS child than for Brackett.

Dr. Judish was Brack's rehab doctor, and at the first visit we shared our belief in miracles but acceptance of whatever. I received another arm's pat and told all mothers feel that way even though there was no hope. He gently reminded us that less than two percent of patients who are PVS longer than three weeks ever awaken. Even then "awakening" means they only respond to loud noises by moving their eyes or offering an occasional grunt or groan.

The therapy at Good Samaritan was amazing! I arrived every morning around 9:00 a.m. to find Brackett already in therapy.

During physical therapy, he had two therapists and an aide stand him at a standing table for ten minutes or so. Then he was lain on an exercise table where he was stretched and his extremities were exercised for him. He had water therapy, occupational therapy, hand therapy, speech therapy, and recreational therapy, all while comatose.

Brack got a roommate that first week who had suffered a heart attack due to drug use. One day I heard him call his mother on the phone, cuss at her, and vow when he got out he would go right back to the drugs that almost killed him. We asked that he be moved to another room as soon as possible, and he was.

Every day I left the house about 8:00 a.m. to arrive in Puyallup by 9:00 a.m. George would come after work arriving between six and seven. We would grab dinner in the cafeteria and stay with Brack till about 10:00 p.m. when he was down for the night.

After the first week, Dr. Judish announced that we had learned to transfer him from point A to point B, clean the stomach feeding tube, and keep him sanitary and all relevant needs of a comatose patient; so he would be discharged. I told him the quarters were not ready for Brack. We needed at least another week, and we still believed in miracles. Another pity pat was delivered, and he was off on rounds.

The second week was more of the same except Brack got a new roommate. Glen was a very tall promising basketball star from a Seattle high school. He and his white girlfriend had gone to a party with her high school crowd. Several boys had taken exception to his presence, and one hit him in the head with a beer mug. Several days later, he suffered a brain aneurism and lapsed into a coma. His beautiful mother had been a model in New York, and Glen and his sister inherited her good looks. Glen's girlfriend was just lovely, as well. His mom, Hazel, and stepdad, Donald Cameron, and a multitude of friends were there often. One coach came and brought a device that had soothing sounds like ocean waves. After our research that was the very last thing we wanted, something to lull our son deeper into a coma.

A week before Christmas, BG Hill arrived with an entourage. The nurses told me he had called to alert them of his imminent arrival. It was the first and last time we saw him. BG(R) Brown and Colonel Jones had been by several times and never preannounced their arrival.

Mike Tarvin, our Chaplain friend from Fort Bragg, was the head corps chaplain at Fort Lewis. We were delighted to be with them again. He and Amy were there for us throughout our ordeal. I don't know how many prayer lists Brack was on, but there were a lot!

A week before Christmas, Brackett's speech therapist, Hope, was sitting in Brackett's room facing him in his wheelchair. She said, "Say baa,

Brackett." He said in a whisper, "Baa." We both sat straighter, and she said, "Say it again, Brack, say baa." He said, "Baa." Hope and I were crying and laughing and hugging Brack and each other. He had awakened!

The floor was alive with nurses coming by to see the miracle of Brackett. Dr. Judish came up, disbelieving. He asked Brack where he was, and he of course didn't know but when told, he whispered, "Good Samaritan Hospital." And he didn't forget.

When he went downstairs for physical therapy, the girls had him on an exercise table where they were stretching his legs. One said, "Count to ten, Brack, and I'll stop." Never thinking he could do it. He whispered really fast, "One, two, three, four, five, six, seven, eight, nine, ten." The entire room went still and quiet, then erupted in cheers.

I called George and the girls to share our joy. George came in to a son who knew him and could hold a whispered, if short, conversation.

On New Year's Eve, Dr. Brown and Dr. Jones with wives, Lynne and Elizabeth, came by with snacks and champagne to celebrate the New Year and the miracle.

George Brown leaned over his bed and said, "You know, Brack, your dad and I worked on your car. And he isn't as good a mechanic as I am, so your car is fine now!" Brack laughed. It was another first.

Brenda Smith came up once a week to keep me up to date on post happenings and let me think I still had a handle on post family matters. She was a huge blessing.

Two of his nurses from Madigan came to visit just before Christmas and brought him a Christmas ornament. It was a nurse holding a giant spoon. It is on our tree every year.

The gift shop downstairs had a cute six-inch white bear with a blue toboggan hat and scarf. It seemed a neat gift for Brack to put by his bed. When I gave it to him, I had to lean close to hear what he said. "The bear sucks," he whispered. I laughed and called it Sucky Bear. He still has it.

Cat gave him a pillow that state "I believe in angels." He still has that too.

Brackett was in Good Samaritan Hospital as an inpatient for five months. During that time, his eyesight went from 400/100 to 20/20. His coordination improved daily. He first moved his fingers, toes, hands, feet, legs, arms, etc. He went through five different wheelchairs, including an electric one he used to almost take out some of the staff and me.

A recreation therapist went into his room about month two, counseling Brack to accept that he would always be in a wheelchair and never drive. He told her to get out of his room. He told her emphatically he intended to walk out of Good Samaritan. I asked Dr. Judish to assign him another therapist which he did. The new recreation therapist took several of the patients out to eat at a local restaurant, horseback riding, van trips, etc. Brack only did the dinners as he chose not to try the others.

Brack was practicing walking with a walker with his right foot in a brace to keep the foot from flopping. It was very tiring, but he kept a great attitude and determination to succeed.

One Saturday, George and I decided to take a break since our boy was doing so well and go ski at Crystal Mountain. We would come back by the hospital that afternoon to visit and have dinner with Brack. It was the first day, I hadn't spent with him. We had a great day skiing. When we went back by Good Samaritan, Brack had tears in his eyes and said, "Mom, I can't do this without you! Please don't leave again." So I didn't.

When Glen's parents were gone, Brack would say, "Give Glen my pillow and music." I would do that, and you could tell Glen was reacting. We had shared our research with his family, but they weren't interested or probably scared to try. When Glen would listen to opera, he would stiffen, and like Brack, he loved jazz. It broke our hearts that this fine young man wasn't being given every chance to come back. Every parent does what they think is best for their children, so we didn't want to judge but did wonder if the therapies we used would have worked for Glen.

Cat Gardner agreed to be me for a few days when I went to Arkansas to check on my mother. She spent the days with Brack, and I think he enjoyed the change. You find one or two true great friends in this army life, and Cat is one of mine. A true treasure.

For several weekends we were able to bring Brack to the house to see how he would do, and it was a joy to have him there.

Brack did indeed walk out of Good Samaritan if only with a walker. Outside the door, he fell into his wheelchair, but he did what he said he would do.

We drove back to Good Samaritan several days a week for months as well as hand therapy at Madigan with Beth.

When we got Brack home, he would get up the stairs on his bottom, one rung at a time and down the same way.

We took him to pick out a recliner so he could be comfortable. He chose one that was very large and had a TV remote and phone in the arm. If we went out, he could sit in his chair, watch TV, and call if he needed us. It was perfect for him and gave us peace of mind.

George's public affairs officer was another army officer who became friends. She was Melanie Reeder, whose husband, Bill, had been a POW in Vietnam. Melanie had served with George in Panama, and they had a beautiful home with horse stables. She came and got me one afternoon, and we rode for several hours. It had been years since I had ridden and was a true gift. The peace of that ride and warmth of their friendship stayed with me for days. How do you adequately thank someone for that?

Retirement was looming. We would both miss the army life but mostly the people!

I held a huge garage sale where I sold all those curtains that never fit any windows anywhere else, the extra beds, the formal dining room set to a chaplain, gave Corey a bed and the camping gear, and did a major clean out. We arranged to store most of the furniture for a year since the Arkansas lake house I had inherited was full of mother's furniture. We planned to ship our bedroom furniture and a few other things.

We had taken the Bryant boat back to Arkansas the previous summer so only had the truck and car to drive back.

I received a wonderful picture of our quarters at my farewell, as well as small thoughtful gifts from ACS, FSG, and other groups.

George, as usual, bought his farewell gift. We had ordered a set of Adirondack-like wooden lawn furniture made at the post prison. For our farewell, since we had already paid for it, they burned a First Corp crest into the wood.

Every commanding general had a tree planted in their memory. George had selected a hardy variety of Bradford pear, so we had a planting ceremony.

Tara and Tia came for the farewell and change of command. We had sent Cheryl a plane ticket, but Tim had destroyed it. We got it reinstated, but he threatened her with the business and children if she came. By this time she was walking on eggshells for fear of setting him off. She had also learned his maternal uncles were in prison. One was serving time for murdering his wife and another for attempted murder. Not the heritage one would wish for, so she was scared.

Cheryl did not come and was sorely missed. The farewell was wonderful, full of memories, funny stories, and thirty-four years paraded on screen. It was awesome!

The change of command was extremely well done and not as cold and wet as the one before. I did not know the incoming but had heard lovely things about them and certainly wished them well. They too had a handicapped child, so all of our adaptations were a bonus for them.

After the change of command, CSM Johnny Austin, put us in a van, drove a few blocks, then asked us to get out. We were at the end of our street which was lined with First Corp NCOs standing at attention. George and I walked hand in hand down the long corridor of troops giving the commanding general a final salute.

Tears were coursing down my face and glistening in George's eyes as we began the next phase of our life together.

82nd Division Change of Command. Penny and Captain,
Jim Yoland Jones with George and Vonda

George, the late General Shalikashvili, his wife Joan, and Vonda

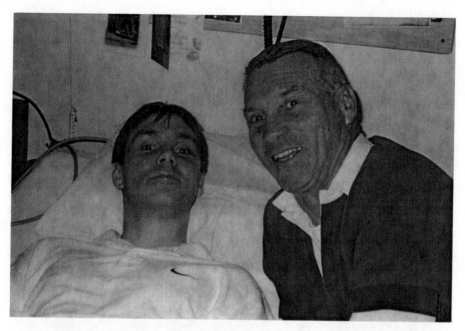

George and Brack

Brackett and Vonda on a weekend visit

Brack and Rob Baker, George's Aide de Camp

Brackett in water therapy at Good Samaritan

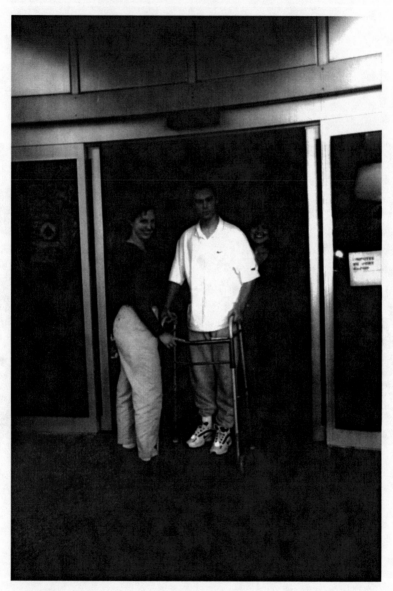

Brackett walking out of Good Samaritan Hospital. Another miracle!

Cat Gardner and Vonda at Fort Lewis

Traditional Farewell Roses

The final walk between I CORPS NCOs

Final army hug

BIOGRAPHY

VONDA J. CROCKER is a native Arkansan, graduate of University of Arkansas, and wife of Lieutenant General (R) George A. Crocker. They have three children and four grandchildren.

Vonda was a pioneer in army family programs; earned three black belts in karate; taught school; coached track; was an army trained facilitator, Girl Scout leader, ski instructor, crafter, and Army Family Team Building instructor; and for thirty-four years kept the home fires burning.